CASEBOOKS ON MODERN DRAMATISTS
VOL. 14

# JOHN ARDEN AND MARGARETTA D'ARCY

GARLAND REFERENCE LIBRARY
OF THE HUMANITIES
VOL. 1355

# CASEBOOKS ON MODERN DRAMATISTS

KIMBALL KING
*General Editor*

# JOHN ARDEN AND MARGARETTA D'ARCY

## A Casebook

*edited by*

Jonathan Wike

**GARLAND PUBLISHING, Inc.**
*New York & London / 1995*

Copyright © 1995 Jonathan Wike
All rights reserved

**Library of Congress Cataloging-in-Publication Data**

John Arden and Margaretta D'Arcy : a casebook /
edited by Jonathan Wike.
    p.    cm.  — (Garland reference library of the
humanities ; vol. 1355 ; Casebooks on modern
dramatists ; vol. 14)
    Includes bibliographical references and index.
    ISBN 0–8240–6993–5 (alk. paper)
    1. Arden, John—Criticism and interpretation.
2. D'Arcy, Margaretta—Criticism and interpretation.    3. English drama—20th century—History
and criticism.    I. Wike, Jonathan, 1956–    .
II. Series : Garland reference library of the humanities ; vol. 1355.    III. Series : Garland reference
library of the humanities. Casebooks on modern
dramatists ; vol. 14.
PR6051.R3Z76   1995
822'.91409—dc20                                    94–9804
                                                         CIP

Printed on acid-free, 250-year-life paper
Manufactured in the United States of America

# CONTENTS

# GENERAL EDITOR'S NOTE

John Arden and Margaretta D'Arcy have worked together for more than three decades, producing plays, novels and essays, both jointly and under their individual names. Nevertheless, as this collection reveals, even their separately published works bear each other's influence as critic, editor, or source of inspiration. Jonathan Wike has assembled a series of articles on a remarkable theater couple who are known as much for their political beliefs and disdain for changing fashions of dramatic presentation as for their landmark plays in modern drama, such as *Sargeant Musgrave's Dance, The Island of the Mighty, Pearl* and *The Non-Stop Connolly Show*, to name only a few.

This volume will offer evidence of an enduring collaboration of major artists and will update scholarship on important and recently neglected literature. Jonathan Wike, who has published articles on poet and novelist Thomas Hardy in *Nineteenth-Century Literature* and *The Thomas Hardy Journal* has turned his attention to a complete reevaluation of Arden and D'Arcy in an attempt to rectify critical neglect and misunderstanding of two highly significant playwrights.

Kimball King

# INTRODUCTION

Students of modern drama know the work of John Arden and Margaretta D'Arcy chiefly through one play, *Serjeant Musgrave's Dance*, written by Arden over thirty years ago. This work has become a runaway academic success, but the preponderance of attention it has received—well into the eighties new studies of Arden were about as likely to deal with *Musgrave* as with any other play—may have been more hindrance than help to a proper recognition of Arden and D'Arcy's great and varied achievement. Working together and separately the two playwrights have removed their work from nearly every category the Musgrave play has fallen into. Though it contains some unusual elements, *Musgrave* can still be handled as a standard English company stage play with apparent liberal sentiments, but these labels hardly apply to their later work. They consider themselves more Irish than English, and the liberalism originally ascribed to Arden, however the debate over Musgrave's message is finally settled, has given way to a continually redefined socialist stance. Various factors have led to their withdrawal from mainstream stage writing; much of their most recent work has been for radio. And they have done more together than apart; significantly, the latest collection of their plays is the first to enshrine their collaboration, *Arden/D'Arcy, D'Arcy/Arden, Plays: One*.

   I point these things out to explain the need for more study of their work at this time. It would be difficult to imagine two writers of Arden and D'Arcy's stature who have been more at odds with their critics over the years, whose works have produced such varied responses, ranging from admiration to exasperation, from delight to annoyance. For their part, critics have been frustrated with the playwrights for not continuing in the *Musgrave* style or some other suitable fashion. On the other side, Arden and D'Arcy have sought to increase the directness and force of theatre with an impatience that suggests that in many ways academic or even critical reactions to their plays are almost irrelevant; if one takes them at their word, a job well done means actual social change, not critical approval. The result of this standoff has been that while a large body of scholarship exists, too much of it looks too far back and responds only to some of the writers' purposes. One could easily get the idea that John Arden simply wrote some interesting plays in the late fifties and early sixties and then left the scene to pursue a whim. Arden scholarship, even early on, can have a peculiar valedictory note; though the point of no return may vary, those who write about him seem often to lose sight of him as he wanders into the territory of inexplicable behavior. This dismissal may not be intended by any critic, but when one considers the whole career of Arden and D'Arcy, the effect is disappointing, for their works have an obvious provisional quality and are so clearly part of a continuing search for forms and techniques.

Their search continues to this day, and it is hoped that the issues raised in these essays will lead to new interest in their work. Readers will find that in many respects these pieces reflect the whole range of Arden and D'Arcy scholarship as it already stands, but the emphasis will also be seen to have shifted to the less appreciated and more recent dimensions of their output, to writing done after the troublesome period of *The Hero Rises Up* and *The Island of the Mighty*. Later plays that have received little attention outside of reviews or have been dismissed by belated champions of *Serjeant Musgrave* are now given their rightful place alongside Arden and D'Arcy's more discussed works; these include *The Non-Stop Connolly Show*, *Pearl*, and *Whose Is the Kingdom?*

This collection has been directed with one main purpose, to encourage readers of Arden and D'Arcy's plays and other writings to reevaluate them as important contemporary playwrights and to provoke further study of their work. D'Arcy and Arden have been engaged in a very ambitious project, one that defies quick description. Their critique of dramatic tradition, their synthesis of politics, history, art, and myth, and their social commitment demand conscientious reaction. One vital aspect of this project is its collaborative nature, something the playwrights have insisted on but that has nevertheless been largely neglected up to now. Groundbreaking essays by Tish Dace and Claudia

Harris expose this neglect, and several of the other pieces suggest how profitable a clearer understanding of D'Arcy's role in their collaboration will be for future readings of their work.

Although only three of his plays were produced at the Royal Court Theatre (counting from the list in *Arden/D'Arcy, Plays: One*), John Arden's name will always be associated with that stage. His stage writing career began there in 1957 with the production of *The Waters of Babylon*. As Jeffrey Roberts observes in "John Arden's *The Waters of Babylon*: A Maverick on the 'New Wave'", reaction to Arden's deliberate deviation, not only from the conventions of West End theatre but even from those of his own "neo-naturalist" contemporaries, was already characterized by impatience. It was with this play, however, that Arden began to provide an alternative "anti-illusionistic," Brechtian direction in British drama. In an engaging reading of the play, Roberts locates the qualities that proved to be Arden's strengths as a dramatist and the questions that would continue to preoccupy him: "the unresolvable conflict between private and public interest and the destructive consequences of the struggle between the forces of human anarchy and the powers of external social order in a variety of uniquely stylized dramatic situations."

The conflict between order and anarchy would become an important informing principle in Arden's plays from the late fifties on; his and D'Arcy's work has consistently forced the audience to expand its conception of theatre beyond the confines of the traditional stage. In "Pragmatic Anarchy: The Early Experimental Plays of John Arden, 1958 to 1963," Marianne Stenbaek looks at three early efforts, *When Is a Door Not a Door?*, *The Business of Good Government*, and the *Kirbymoorside '63* festival of entertainment, the last two produced with D'Arcy. A counterforce to society's desire for "good order," Arden's controlled or "pragmatic" anarchy serves as an antidote to contemporary political apathy, an alternative to theatrical conventionality, and a relief from cultural stagnation.

Whatever its importance in the Arden and D'Arcy canon, *Serjeant Musgrave's Dance* has achieved considerable prominence in the canon of post-war drama. It has become one of those plays that, like John Osborne's *Look Back in Anger*, take on an eminence that can obscure their actual merit. In "Why Read Arden?" Douglas Bruster looks at *Musgrave* in a very broad cultural context and finds various shortcomings in this play, and in others of its time, as a result of stylistic and even generic choices which now seem either dated or inappropriate. Bruster's critique is sometimes caustic, but *Musgrave* warrants such a trial—on the one hand, its reception has always been problematic; on the other, no work should be enshrined without skeptical re-examination.

As a team, Arden and D'Arcy have always sought to take theatre beyond its conventional boundaries, often by writing plays for production by non-professional groups. As much as any other play, *Ars Longa, Vita Brevis*, written for Yorkshire Girl Guides, marks their move away from established theatre. In "An Undeviating Path: Margaretta D'Arcy and John Arden," Claudia Harris shows how the dramatic patterns of social action presented in this play have given shape to the writings and activities of the playwrights ever since, including the protests that led to D'Arcy's imprisonment at Armagh and her account of it, *Tell Them Everything*.

After *Musgrave*, the most celebrated, and studied, of Arden's early stage plays is highlighted in Susan Bennett's "Brecht—Britain—Bakhtin: The Bridge of *Armstrong's Last Goodnight*." Bennett nicely isolates the moment *Armstrong* occupies in Arden's career and in the accommodation of Brechtian approaches in British theatre. "*Armstrong's Last Goodnight*," Bennett observes, ". . . can be read as an important threshold text. It stands between a British resistance to Brechtian practice in the fifties and sixties and a mainstage and academic canonization in the seventies and eighties of the German playwright's work."

A major stylistic feature of Arden and D'Arcy's writing has been their distinctive employment of verse in drama, not simply in imitation of Brechtian practice but as part of their long-time effort to re-connect drama with its ancient popular sources. In "The Person of a Poet: John Arden and Modern Verse Drama," Kayla McKinney Wiggins places Arden's early plays in an English tradition of verse drama, comparing his efforts at verse revival to those of T.S. Eliot and Christopher Fry. She then turns to the very important play *The Island of the Mighty,* an Arden and D'Arcy collaboration, and in an extensive study identifies one of the central concerns of this and most of Arden's and D'Arcy's works, an "investigation of the theme of the poet in society."

While *The Island of the Mighty* develops Arden and D'Arcy's concerns with poetry, myth, and imaginative history to the fullest, their other major collaborative effort of the seventies is a remarkably ambitious exploration of socialist history. *The Non-Stop Connolly Show,* first performed in Dublin on the fifty-ninth anniversary of the Easter 1916 Rising, has evoked reactions ranging from dismay to recognition as a major dramatic work on the history of socialism. In "James Connolly: A Fit Story for the Playwright of *Serjeant Musgrave's Dance,*" one of two essays on the Connolly plays in this collection, Tramble Turner shows how problems in the reception of this cycle are related to earlier problems with *Musgrave:* "by reconsidering aspects of how the cycle brings to life the contradictions and paradoxes in Connolly's career and by assessing the merits, via stage performances, of the music-hall elements of the cycle, critical assessment of this epic may undergo a shift similar to that which has occurred in the case of *Serjeant Musgrave's Dance.*" In focusing on continuities between this D'Arcy-Arden series and an important Arden play, Turner shows how critical understanding has lagged conspicuously behind the playwrights; *Connolly* has often been rejected in the same spirit with which critics once rejected *Musgrave,* but *Musgrave* is now held up as a model of how Arden should write a play.

The second article on the *Connolly* cycle concentrates on inherent problems of audience reaction to dramatic technique and shows the need to evaluate the play as the collaborative effort of two writers whose perception of theatrical purpose has been transformed appreciably in the past thirty years. In *"The Non-Stop Connolly Show:* The Role of a Non-Traditional Audience in a New Theatre Tradition," Catherine Graham attributes critical and academic slighting of D'Arcy and Arden's *Connolly* cycle to "the methodological difficulties involved in the study of popular political drama." Arguing that "an appreciation [of the

Connolly plays] must be based on the understanding that dramaturgies can be founded on sets of presuppositions other than those that govern conventional bourgeois drama," Graham draws on "Possible Worlds" theory to prescribe an aesthetic incorporating "trade-union discourse, Celtic artistic traditions, popular culture, and Catholic religious ritual" in an essay that redefines critical discourse as the play in turn defines its audience. What may seem willfulness to some may be steadfastness to others; while Arden may appear more and more an anomaly in the late fifties, post-*Anger* drama is difficult to imagine without his and D'Arcy's work and example.

As much as anything he and D'Arcy have written, Arden's radio play *Pearl* presents their ideas on political and historical drama in a way that is at the same time based in the playwrights' own experience and in those of English and Irish audiences, and playwrights, present and past. Though written by Arden alone, it is still the product of his collaboration with D'Arcy, as Mary Karen Dahl makes clear in "John Arden's *Pearl*: Historical Imaginings." In showing how through the title character the play "structures correspondences between historical and contemporary problems and possibilities" in a "dramatized tale of artistic misjudgment and disappointment" that "links past errors with the present and opens a discussion about how artists and citizens can break with the past," Dahl brings out the many resonances in a play that is central to the Arden and D'Arcy canon.

It would be difficult to imagine two playwrights more aware of dramatic tradition than Arden and D'Arcy; indeed, their work can be seen as a dialogue with past dramatists, with an unusual amount of exposition of this coming from Arden in various essays and interviews. Particularly important are his readings of sixteenth- and seventeenth-century English dramatists, whose importance for Arden and D'Arcy as models Michael Cohen discusses in "Exemplary Drama: Arden's Shifting Perspectives on Sixteenth and Seventeenth Century Predecessors." Arden's early admiration for Jonson and Shakespeare by no means disappeared, according to Cohen's survey, but as time went on earlier figures, such as the very complex John Bale, took on equal importance for him. Treating especially the radio play *Pearl* and the novel *Books of Bale*, Cohen shows how Arden's approaches to his "sixteenth- and seventeenth-century peers" serve as an index to the evolution of his and D'Arcy's ideas about playwrights and audiences.

The most impressive product of D'Arcy and Arden's shift of emphasis to radio drama is the nine-part series *Whose Is the Kingdom*? This chronicle of the events that shaped early Christianity exhibits as much as any other project the strengths of the D'Arcy-Arden collaboration, as Donald Sandley explains in "Defining Orthodoxy: Power and Perspective in *Whose Is the Kingdom*?" According to Sandley, this play, which now fully incorporates religion into the playwrights' study of individual and social responsibility, "is a watershed in the collaborative careers of Arden and D'Arcy in that it blends the styles more effectively and presents a more unified voice than previous co-authored works."

That very collaboration is the issue Tish Dace takes up in "Who Wrote 'John Arden's' Plays?" Although Arden and D'Arcy have written plays together since *The Happy Haven* (1960), critics and scholars alike have barely acknowledged D'Arcy's contribution or have treated it as a negative influence that has kept Arden out of the kind of predictable career other playwrights of his generation have pursued. This oversight has been unfair, to D'Arcy, of course, and to Arden, and to scholars, who are unfortunately most prone to perpetuate the most basic assumptions in the "secondary material" about the authors they study. In a chapter which should alter forever perceptions about the legitimacy of the D'Arcy-Arden collaboration, Dace documents this oversight through the major "Arden" criticism and suggests the various reasons, including plain sexism, which account for it. Readers are encouraged, by the way, to consult Dace's chronology of plays by Arden and D'Arcy as well as the one included in the new collection of their shorter co-authored plays: *Arden/D'Arcy Plays: One* (London: Methuen, 1991, vii-viii).

The final essay in this volume, by the editor, is called "Empire and the Goddess: The Fiction of John Arden." Although it does not deal with co-authored works or even with plays, this piece is still very much concerned with the Arden-D'Arcy collaboration and with their ideas on theatre. It also raises questions about Arden' changing conceptions of history in a discussion of his three major works of fiction, *Silence Among the Weapons*, *Books of Bale*, and *Cogs Tyrannic*.

# John Arden and
# Margaretta D'Arcy

# JOHN ARDEN'S
# *THE WATERS OF BABYLON*:
# A MAVERICK ON THE "NEW WAVE"

## Jeffrey L. Roberts

The explosion of the British "new wave" theatre in the late fifties is most commonly associated with such works by neo-naturalist playwrights as John Osborne's *Look Back in Anger*, Shelagh Delaney's *A Taste of Honey*, Arnold Wesker's *The Kitchen*, and Brendan Behan's *The Hostage*. Radically different from the then-current West End theatrical fare, these plays dealt with contemporary social problems, especially those pertinent to the lower classes. And, like Oscar Wilde, G. B. Shaw, and John Galsworthy before them, who had used the theatre as a vehicle of social and political criticism of late-Victorian and Edwardian life, these new dramatists were treating problems of their own era such as class and race discrimination, alienated youth, capital punishment, and the corruption and insensitivity of the postwar Establishment.

This new theatre movement was encouraged by the improved climate for playwriting with the founding of the English Stage Society at the Royal Court Theatre in 1955 with its avowed intention of fostering talented yet unperformed dramatists (Taylor 33). It was this company which introduced Osborne to the London audiences and enabled him to achieve his first success with *Look Back in Anger*, which was followed by several other new plays by unknown dramatists, among them Ann Jellicoe, N. F. Simpson, Harold Pinter, and John Arden.

Since the majority of these new playwrights, including Wesker and especially Osborne, chose more often the conventional styles traditionally associated with social realism, dating back to Shaw and Ibsen, the stylistic disparity between the West End and the Royal Court was not enormously significant. After all, for over a century, the major playwrights of the English-speaking drama had cultivated and satisfied the urge of the audience to identify itself vicariously with the stage characters and their circumstances; as a result, most of the anti-realist forms—expressionism, epic theatre, absurdism—were still met by West End audiences with a qualified reception. No great effort was made to re-educate the English theatre-going public to the anti-illusionistic techniques of contemporary continental dramatists or to offer them anything else but the well-made plays to which they had become accustomed since the late nineteenth century. In fact, on the whole, the most successful of these playwrights were those who confined themselves to constructing entirely realistic stage situations and creating characters who were lifelike and believable.

The early works of Harold Pinter and John Arden were two notable exceptions. In the case of Pinter there was an obvious tendency toward the oblique and austere style of the European absurdists, Beckett and Ionesco, while the plays of John Arden bore striking similarities to the fiercely anti-illusionistic epic theatre of Bertolt Brecht. Against the background of the new naturalistic theatre of social realism, their plays seemed both foreign and puzzling to British audiences compared to those of Osborne and Wesker which were received with warmth and enthusiasm.

Though the works of Pinter have a decidedly realistic surface since the author recreates the precise nuances of everyday speech and places his characters in the most ordinary settings, upon closer examination, one finds that his plays convey a confusing ambiguity because the characters are either unwilling or unable to communicate with one another and because the exact nature of the conflict with which they are concerned is often only vaguely defined. What would appear, then, to be a conventional representational drama on the surface is actually a study of the metaphysical absurdity in which these realistically conceived characters find themselves.

John Arden's work seemed even stranger and more inaccessible to modern audiences but mainly because of its presentational style. His desire to reach beyond the metropolitan center and take his message to the working classes of English towns and villages prompted him to draw upon elements of native English drama such as song and dance and the tradition of English balladry reminiscent of medieval morality and mystery plays. This fondness for non-realistic forms also extended to the use of masks and abstract sets. In fact, from the outset of his career, Arden was always artistically more comfortable with non-realistic forms, exhibiting a total distrust of the theatre of illusion, and constantly experimenting with unfamiliar and unorthodox techniques. In one of his most precise statements concerning the purpose and obligation of the dramatist, he says: "It seems to me that this tradition is the one that will always in the end reach to the heart of the people, even if the people are not entirely aware of what it is that causes their response" ("True Tale" 24). Unfortunately, however, these techniques often rendered his plays even more limited in appeal and at times alienated the very audience he hoped to reach. During his most commercially successful period between 1958 and 1965, he often found himself confronted with apathetic audiences and a less than enthusiastic critical reception.

When asked why the majority of theatre reviewers seemed unable at first to respond to his plays, Arden once suggested that the problem might be his reluctance to restrict himself to one particular style, but he defended his eclectic method by saying: "I like to think that for each subject I have handled I have tried to find an *appropriate* style: the theatre should not be a place where one worries about brand images" ("Revolution" 51).

One finds the same ambivalence regarding Arden's moral and political philosophy, especially in those works composed before 1965. Though the major themes of most of Arden's plays concern the life of man within a political or social system of one form or another, he has a perplexing tendency to withhold judgment of that order or of the behavior of that individual who struggles to survive within it. As Albert Hunt suggests, Arden is "less concerned with leading our minds step by step, and he's less concerned because he's much more aware of the irrationality of human experience. . . . In his plays, the most right-*minded* people come to disaster because they can't cope with the complexities and accidents that cut across rigid ideas" (Hunt and Reeves 35).

What does emerge from these plays is a vivid impression of the tragic consequences which result when the private self comes in opposition to public order. It is not that Arden sanctions the particular viewpoint of an individual as opposed to that of a governing body or vice versa but that he recognizes that the life of modern man within a contemporary social order is by necessity inexorably complicated by a conflict of interest. That is, man is aware of the necessity to live within the law of the land and to respect its ethnic values, but at the same time, he is torn by forces inherent in his very nature that war against his complete submission to externally imposed restrictions. There is, in fact, as Arden sees man, an irrational tendency towards disorder and anarchy regardless of the sophisticated level of civility and organization his society has achieved. As Hunt suggests, "It's Arden's great strength that he's able to come to terms with these irrationalities, not by surrendering to them, nor by trying in vain to dominate them, but by *using* them. His plays explore the very fine balance between being willing to adapt yourself to a situation when it's tolerable, and refusing to adapt yourself when it's intolerable" (Hunt and Reeves 35).

It is this highly complex situation which Arden attempts to dramatize in his major plays composed between 1957 and 1965 beginning with *The Waters of Babylon*, which was first produced on the London stage in 1957. We are all entangled in political problems, in the broadest sense of the word, whether we mean to be or not. Because Arden is so sensitive to the dilemmas of the individual who must cope with the demands of everyday existence and because he is aware of the maze-like fabric of modern society, he realizes that there are no simple answers to the problems which he examines in his plays.

This is not to say, however, that the theatre of Arden is simply a bland presentation of conflicts or arguments, the resolutions to which carry no meaningful implications whatever. The point is that he is so intent upon presenting both sides of an argument and giving each a fair hearing, that an audience accustomed to having judgments made for them is often left hopelessly confused when cast adrift on their own. To complicate matters even further, Arden's style of presentation is designed not to convince us of the truth of what we are witnessing but to remind us constantly that we are watching a play, an artificial situation frequently interrupted by music, song, poetry, dancing, and soliloquies by various characters. Arden presents us with a set of facts and hypotheses; it is our responsibility to ferret out the significance of the events and the implications of their outcome. As Albert Hunt observes, "the theatre of illusion is a theatre of persuasion. Arden's theatre, like Shakespeare's—like Brecht's—is a theatre of skepticism and questioning" (28). But, instead of being willing to look for possible justifications for the action of an antagonist, as a jury might consider the motivations of a defendant, and thereby achieve a broader and more meaningful view of the complexities of human nature, many audiences and critics become impatient and frustrated in their efforts to place the blame where it is due or to pass sentence on the guilty party.

Recognizing the limits of the theatre when it comes to preaching social dogmas, Arden initially restricted himself from anything approaching authorial comment or judgment much less a clearly articulated political argument. Beginning with *The Waters of Babylon*, virtually all of the full-length plays written for the legitimate theatre reveal a striking consistency in his efforts to demonstrate the unresolvable conflict between private and public interest and the destructive consequences of the struggle between the forces of human anarchy and the powers of external social order in a variety of uniquely stylized dramatic situations.

In *The Waters of Babylon*, Arden explores the consequences of both political extremism and isolationism, illustrating the dilemma of modern man who is forced to come to terms with the complexities of contemporary society. The central character of this play, Sigismanfred Krankiewicz, has learned from his past experiences that in order to survive he must avoid at all costs any type of political entanglement or party identification whatsoever. A confirmed anarchist, who has long since passed the activist stage, he has withdrawn completely into himself. His determination to remain aloof proves futile, as he is swept into the conflict between two political extremists and destroyed.

Krank, as he is called, is a middle-aged Polish national who attempts to carry on a dual existence as a respectable architect's assistant and slumlord of an overcrowded bawdy house inhabited by pimps and prostitutes of various nationalities. He is able to keep his legitimate professional life separate from his more questionable private life until he finds himself suddenly indebted to a fellow Pole, Paul, who threatens to involve him in a bomb plot against two Soviet dignitaries. To prevent this "indefatigable patriot" from using his place to manufacture the bomb, Krank must come up with five hundred pounds in payment of an old debt which Paul inherited. With the help of a devious old ex-alderman, Krank succeeds in setting up a municipal lottery from which he plans to embezzle the funds. In the meantime, Henry Ginger, a right-wing extremist, discovers the assassination plot and mistakenly suspects Krank is in league with Paul. On the evening of the drawing, not only does Krank's scheme to rig the lottery fail as the result of the drunken alderman's bungling, but he and Paul are openly accused of criminal collusion in front of the entire audience. In a mad rage, Paul draws a revolver, fires at Ginger, but hits and mortally wounds Krank instead.

This play is much more than the account of political intrigue and the destruction of a hapless alien, for Arden has literally riddled his text with jarring ambiguities that constantly cloud the issues and thwart conventional distinctions between good and bad, vice and virtue. He persists in showing us both sides of the coin, so that we find ourselves condoning and condemning the actions of the wily Krank at the same time. Though we censure him for exploiting the ignorant and poverty-stricken aliens whom he attracts to his boarding house, they themselves don't seem to mind. On the contrary, they regard him as a friend and protector in the hostile anonymity of metropolitan London. We may resent Krank's hypocrisy in leeching his livelihood from a society which he finds disgusting and refuses to acknowledge, yet there is something admirable in his determination to remain independent and self-reliant.

Thus, at the center of this novice work, Arden has placed an extremely disturbing and complex character who deserves yet defies our judgment. Moreover, Krank's death fails to resolve the central question that the play raises: can one indeed remain politically uncommitted or uninvolved without suffering the consequences? Krank, after all, is shot and killed not because of his non-partisan philosophy but because he happened to get in the way of an extremist's bullet intended for another radical. To add to this confusion, no real victors emerge in this play: the revolutionaries Paul and Ginger are chased off the stage by policemen, leaving the others singing of their blindness, oblivious to the significance of the events they have witnessed.

What is apparent in all of this confusion is the extent of destruction that may occur when the forces of anarchy, represented by idealists like Paul, confront the forces of order, represented by right-wing radicals like Ginger. Ironically, it is Krank, who sought to avoid involvement in this conflict, who is destroyed.

Paul and Ginger actually form the two poles between which Arden has placed a colorful gallery of minor but somewhat more clearly defined characters with Krank in the middle. Though all of these characters are actually outside the Paul-Ginger conflict, it is interesting to note that each, to a greater or lesser degree, shows a fundamental yearning toward order tempered by a tendency toward disorder. In other words, the irrational forces of passion are balanced in some of these characters by their rational desires for a proper place in the order of society.

Bathsheba, the whore from Barbados, is baffled by Krank's Dolorous Song which strangely alludes to three of the most infamous concentration camps of Nazi Germany. She is fascinated by the by the far-sounding names of Belsen, Buchenwald and Auschwitz, without understanding the hideous connotations which those names hold for Krank. She has easily adapted to the city life of London because her needs are simple and her emotions basic. Though she is vaguely aware that Joe Caligula, a fellow West Indian, is devoted to defending the "Right of the Coloured People of this Country," her main interest is to lure him into her bedroom. Caligula himself strives desperately to live up to his self-styled image as the liberator of the black race. He has established himself as an eminently respectable leader among his people and has learned to deal patiently with the racists. In a ritualistic love dance at the end of Act II, Bathsheba mesmerizes and then seduces him by an occult-like spell. Arden shows us that this ostensibly rigid facade of a man devoted solely to restoring order and justice for his people is vulnerable when he succumbs momentarily to her primitive charms.

Krank's right-hand man, Connor Cassidy, may have had an avid interest in the I.R.A. movement in his youth, but now that is all in the past, and he is no longer an activist for anything. He despises the hypocritical chauvinism of Ginger and even assists Paul in ripping down the placards of the moderate Alexander Loap, M.P. Cassidy simply does not have the energy to sustain his enthusiasm long enough to champion a political cause. Nothing but the most mundane issues interest him—he will pimp for Krank and wash lavatory floors to make his bare living, but anything more idealistic overtaxes him. When he discovers that his sister Teresa, who was at "one time the most virginal white darling in all the world" (68), has been corrupted and misled by Krank, he strikes out against both of them in a furious rage but is soon cowed and finally resorts to whiskey. Cassidy has given up; he has no more fight left: "Oh God, what a world—it's nothing but misery—fornication, shame, and misery: and never a drop of whisky in between" (73).

Teresa, on the other hand, takes the world for what it is and capitalizes on the vice which so depresses her brother in his more sober moments. Since severing her ties with Krank, she has been operating quite successfully on her own, having attracted the favors of Loap, who has promised to build her a house in gratitude for her services. By no means does she measure up to her brother's sainted images of her, but she does know the meaning and power of sex, and she is honest about her relationship with Loap. She openly admits to Barbara Baulkfast, Krank's boss and owner of the architectural firm, that she is "the harlot of Mr Loap" (33). Identity is not the problem for Teresa that it is for Krank.

Even Butterthwaite must also be counted in the number of foreigners surrounding Krank insofar as he has been "out of touch" with London and politics for a long time. He tells Krank, in fact, "I'm like a foreigner myself in this city" (26), and he dotes on his past political reputation in the north where he was known as the "Napoleon of Local Government." Butterthwaite is, to be sure, a politician by nature, but he is also a pathetic has-been, simply going through the motions now. He succeeds in setting up the lottery, but at the most crucial moment when the drawing is to be rigged, he lapses into a drunken stupor and raves about the glories of his past, stumbles, and inadvertently gives the signal prematurely. His sincere intention to help Krank is easily subverted by his urge to play the politician and resurrect his past image. Butterthwaite cannot connive, for he lacks cleverness; he is entranced by the glamour and outward trappings of politics, just as Caligula is driven primarily by his passionate nature and not by a humanitarian mission.

Alexander Loap is the London foil to Butterthwaite in that he is just as ineffectual. His motto is temperance and moderation; as a result, he does not act. Loap is only a facade of rhetoric and pretension, but unlike Butterthwaite, he succeeds in staying in office. Butterthwaite would be corrupt if he could follow through with his schemes; Loap is incredibly self-righteous and self-consciously upstanding but, nevertheless, just as ineffectual. Both are clearly drawn parodies of politicians.

What binds this array of characters together is their divided loyalties. They may identify with a cause superficially and temporarily, but each is always ready to compromise his convictions for the sake of his own comfort. Teresa declares she is the harlot of Mr. Loap, who, in turn, is always aware of his political identity and the importance of preserving his public image. Henry Ginger confides to the audience that he will track down the "Subversive Threat, / And he'll rescue England yet" (58). Krank, on the other hand, is constantly at pains to elude any identification whatsoever. By disclaiming allegiance to any cause, he remains free of responsibility and thus free from guilt or recrimination. He will not be governed by any imposed set of social norms and is determined to be responsible only to himself. When Paul tries to coax him to join his plot to assassinate the Russian dignitaries by reminding him of the Polish fatherland, Krank declares: "I am no longer a citizen of anywhere" (37), and as he makes one of his daily transformations from slumlord to respectable architect's assistant, he announces to the audience in soliloquy:

> My employment, as you observe, is now immaculate, professional, appropriate to this body sparkling new from its matutinal rebirth, you see, I am a man of no one condition having no more no country, no place, time, action, no social soul. I am easy and able to choose whatever alien figure I shall cut, where and wherever I am, in London: not any place in London but all places of London, for all of it and none of it is mine. (29)

Krank obviously revels in living his double life as brother-keeper by night and architect by day. In so doing, he is proving to himself that he can remain uninvolved by adopting these elusive habits which he tells Paul "protect me from women, from creditors, from my tenants, from my own old convictions" (39); as long as he can sustain the masquerade, he avoids identifying himself. In short, Krank has vowed to destroy his identity completely in the belief that he will be able to prevent all outside efforts from dominating him. Thus, true to his two namesakes, Sigismundo, the Italian tyrant, and Byron's Manfred, who defied the laws of God's greater creation, Sigismanfred Krankiewicz maintains sole dominion over himself and utterly rejects the laws of man which his bitter experience has taught him serve no end.

Krank has not only shielded himself with a respectable disguise, but he has also insulated himself from contamination by the English society he so detests by gathering around him other aliens to share his self-exile. He has, in effect, created a literal island within the city limits of the English Babylon. His boarding house is a kind of refuge for foreigners where they may band together under his protection and tutelage. In Act II, Bathsheba describes to Cassidy the three young women she picked up at the train station: "Two today from Trinidad and there was one from Jamaica . . . not what I'd call flying fish or torpedoes. No sir, just kind of sad and quiet gentle sea-weed laid out dark on a hard cold beach" (42).

These refugees find themselves abandoned on the "shores" of London which Arden presents as the seat of idle luxury and corruption, the modern counterpart to the Babylonian city of exile described in Biblical accounts. Having established himself as leader of these exiles, Krank tells Butterthwaite before Paul intrudes with his threat, that he intends "to acquire a second house, to convert it to similar lodgings" (27). Krank, we presume, is bent upon setting up an empire—a colony of aliens—within the Babylonian universe, thus ensuring his alienation forever as the undisputed head of the self-supporting, self-perpetuating, independent state of his own making.

Krank's intentions are clear from the beginning of the play, as is his philosophy of life, which he explains in a more or less straightforward manner. The troubling question is why has Krank resorted to such extreme measures to cut himself off from his past, and what drives him to conceal his identity? The clues to these questions lie in the songs and verses which the playwright has embedded throughout the text, a technique which Arden will use more often and to even greater advantage in the plays to come as a means to reveal his characters' innermost thoughts and motivations. This device, often cited as a source of fragmentation and confusion in Arden's plays, is often the key to the meaning of the action as it is in *The Waters of Babylon*.

Quite subtly, fragments of Krank's past are revealed in song and verse during moments of heightened emotional intensity, giving us a glimpse of his innermost fears. When during the first few minutes of the play Bathsheba asks Krank to sing his Dolorous Song, he at first hesitates, then comments that what he is about to sing is the true story of his life, and in singing, he remembers what he had hoped to forget. In a brief three-stanza ballad Krank curiously alludes to three Nazi concentration camps: Belsen, Buchenwald, and Auschwitz. He says he saw in each camp a dear one who urged him to "go by" (21-2) first his mother, then his brother, and finally his sweetheart. The song ends as abruptly as it began, and we hear no more allusions to these volatile place names from Krank's past until the end of Act I. After Paul gives Krank his ultimatum,

Krank is suddenly overcome with fear and slips into his past again, muttering: "Bombs, violence, conspiracy, all of it again, pale faces, sweaty fingers, jigging on my heart, hooded fanatic eyes like letterboxes watching me. I was alone, and confident, and uninvolved. Now look at me" (40).

Then, before the curtain closes, Krank sings another strange three-stanza ballad, a nightmarish tale recounting his gunning down children in a row who then arise to seek terrible vengeance on him and his lover:

> They drove down the doors,
> And set fire to my roof,
> And they pulled away the pillars of the wall;
> I stood in the street
> With the rain upon my feet;
> While my house so majestical
> Did fall —
> Oh did fall. (40-1)

Just exactly what connection this dream-like tale has with the events in his past is not at all clear at this point in the play. But Arden, through song and verse, cleverly suggests there is a source for Krank's guilt and fear of retribution which motivates his extreme behavior. It is not until the end of the play when Henry forces Krank to admit the truth that we discover he was actually a Nazi perpetrator of atrocities in Buchenwald rather than a prisoner as everyone had thought. Even then, Krank still insists that identity is relative, explaining:

> That was the time of the world
> That I know to myself I have no year, town, or
>                                        family, . . .
> In Buchenwald was I prisoner, was I convenient soldier
> So many thousands of people all lost in that cold field.
> Who knows what I was? (80-1)

Caught between two political revolutionaries, Paul and Ginger, he lashes out at their idealism and points to the futility of their anger and patriotism:

> This is the lunacy,
> This was the cause, the carrying through

Of all the insensate war
This is the rage and purposed madness of your lives,
That *I*, Krank, do not know. I will not know it.
Because, if I know it, from that tight day forward,
I am a man of time, place, society, and accident:
Which is what I must not be (81).

Here Krank reveals the depth and seriousness of the identity crisis which has plagued him since the war, and now it is clear to us why he has resorted to such extreme measures to isolate himself from society. His vision of the world is informed by past experiences hideous beyond imagination. To him, there are no causes left worth dying for.

The world is breaking up as far as Krank is concerned. It is "running mad in every direction. / It is quicksilver, shattered, here, here, here, here, / All over the floor." He tells Paul to "chase it," but he himself chooses to follow only such "fragments" as he can easily catch (81). In other words, Krank is satisfied drifting from one identity to another, and as long as he can maintain his exile in Babylon, he is safe from recrimination, blame, and guilt.

But regardless of his desperate efforts to remain uninvolved and nameless, he is suddenly caught in the crossfire between Paul and Ginger and mortally wounded. His masquerade over, in his dying words he exclaims to Barbara, Loap, and his fellow exiles:

I'm going to declare my identity at last.
Place and time, and purposes,
Are now to be chosen for me.
I cannot any longer do without knowing them . . . (96)

Unable or unwilling to see the corruption around them, none of these survivors seems to grasp the meaning of Krank's struggle or the lessons he tried to convey, and Arden leaves us with a final tableau with Butterthwaite, Cassidy, Teresa, Bathsheba, Caligula, Barbara, and Loap singing together a grotesque roundelay:

We're all down in t'cellar-hoyle
Wi't' muck-slaghts on t'windows.

We've used all us coyle up
And we've nowt left but cinders. (97)

Evidently, those who are oblivious to the treachery and selfishness of their leaders can afford to ignore the impassioned pleas of rebels and loyalists like Paul and Ginger. Those like Krank, on the other hand, who might have achieved wisdom from their life's experiences, either become immobilized by their cynicism and withdraw from society or are destroyed.

*The Waters of Babylon* was first produced by the Royal Court theatre workshop in October of 1957. It was only one of a series of Sunday night performances without decor and received little critical attention. Kenneth Tynan found the general theme "obscured by over-illustration," calling the play a "no-man's-land" without "signposts" (1957 review quoted in Page 13). Ten years later, the Washington, D.C. Theatre Club's full professional staging provoked a favorable and perceptive response from one critic who praised the play for its "variety, imagination and poeticism," adding that "It is characteristic of Arden's talent to depict a private life in a public arena with such richness" (Pasolli 574).

In his subsequent professional plays, *Live Like Pigs* (1958), *The Happy Haven* (1960), and *The Workhouse Donkey* (1963), he draws upon contemporary social problems or political issues for the context; while, at other times, he has chosen to place his characters in historical settings: *Serjeant Musgrave's Dance* (1959), *Armstrong's Last Goodnight* (1964), and *Left-Handed Liberty* (1965). Two plays from the latter group, *Armstrong* and *Left-Handed Liberty*, are undoubtedly among his most artistically successful works. The central characters stand out more brightly in their rich primary colors and possess an earthy vitality which seems missing in most of the more commonplace modern figures of the former group. Also, Arden's presentational techniques appear to be more suited to period drama: the ballads and verse passages ring truer to us in the company of ribald Scottish clansmen or eleventh-century prelates than from the mouths of twentieth-century tenement dwellers or ne'er-do-well foreigners in post-war London.

In retrospect, *The Waters of Babylon* is of key significance since Arden establishes his philosophical dialectic and introduces the fundamental elements of his unique anti-illusionistic style. It should therefore be considered a seminal work and a most useful and appropriate point of departure for the study of the considerable body of works he and his wife, Margaretta D'Arcy, have composed for the legitimate and community theatre to date.

## Works Cited

Arden, John. *Three Plays: The Waters of Babylon, Live Like Pigs, The Happy Haven*. New York: Grove Press, 1961.

———. "Telling a True Tale." *Encore* 7.3 (May-June 1960): 22–6.

———. "Who's for a Revolution?: Two Interviews with John Arden." by Walter Wager and Simon Trussler. Ed. Kelly Morris. *The Drama Review*, 11 (Winter 1966): 41–53.

Hunt, Albert. *Arden: A Study of His Plays*. London: Eyre Methuen, 1974.

Hunt, Albert, and Geoffrey Reeves. "Arden: Professionals and Amateurs." *Encore* 12.5 (Sept.–Oct. 1965): 27–36.

Page, Malcolm. *Arden on File*. London: Methuen, 1985.

Pasolli, Robert. Rev. of *The Waters of Babylon*. *The Nation*, 1 May 1967, 573–4.

Taylor, John Russell. *The Angry Theatre: New British Drama*. New York: Hill and Wang, 1962.

# PRAGMATIC ANARCHY: THE EARLY EXPERIMENTAL PLAYS OF JOHN ARDEN, 1958 TO 1963

## Marianne A. Stenbaek

John Arden's early plays have to be looked at in the general context of the traditions of British Drama until the early post-war years and the Angry Young Man movement that was a reaction to that tradition. Although it is, of course, impossible to collapse several centuries of world and theatrical history into a few paragraphs, one can say that British theatre, with such notable exceptions as Bernard Shaw, had become a polite upper-middle- or upper-class theatre, essentially produced to amuse in a light-hearted manner or edify the audience. The comedies of Terence Rattigan and Noel Coward amused in a brilliantly worldly and light manner as the piece's heroine, usually the chatelaine of a delightful country house, arranged flowers next to the French doors erected on the proscenium stage. The usual alternative to these plays were the classics, Shakespeare, Webster, and so on. Only Irish writers, generally speaking, such as Sean O'Casey and Shaw, dared speak openly of revolution against the status quo and the despairing life of the working class. In spite of Continental experimentation, by such playwrights as Brecht, Ghelderode, and Artaud, almost all commercial British theatre followed the successful, fourth-wall, proscenium-arch style.

Socialism and a greater attention to the working-class had made inroads throughout the twentieth century in England, but the country was still ruled and run by the Establishment until after W.W.II. The war had shown the folly of many of the old ways and had destroyed traditions; it had also made it possible for working-class people as well as women to advance "through the ranks," first in the military and then in a broader context. The stage was set, so to speak. In the decade 1945-1955, England underwent unprecedented social, cultural, and political changes: the Empire over which the sun never set was lost, the

Labour Party increased its power, a cultural revolution took place in the education system by the addition of "red brick" universities which offered education to less elitist students than those attending Oxbridge, and women gained a higher profile. The "arts," including theatre, were no longer the sole proprietorship of the political Establishment. A strong reaction was underway in the novel (e.g., Kingsley Amis), popular culture (e.g., the Beatles), and the theatre (e.g., John Osborne, Arnold Wesker); the practitioners were often people of working-class origin who dealt with working-class concerns and whose characters spoke in the vernacular. They also attempted to find new forms more relevant to their own context.

It was against this background that John Arden emerged. He was an outsider; he came from Yorkshire, not London; he was a man of the people, though not really working class, a man of socialist tendencies, and maybe above all a pragmatist with his feet planted firmly in the life of Yorkshire, specially trained in architecture rather than in literature. He was what one might call a pragmatic anarchist given more to reality than to the "sublime" in the tradition of Bernard Shaw.

At this time Arden was also a prolific writer, writing one to two plays a year, including such important and enduring works as *Sergeant Musgrave's Dance* (1959) and *Armstrong's Last Goodnight* (1964). In the early sixties, John Arden started to work with the Irish playwright Margaretta D'Arcy, who had a profound influence on his plays; in fact several were co-written. They later married. As a result of her influence, Arden's plays became more socially oriented, more socialist, and more experimental. In the peak period 1967-1968, he wrote and staged eight experimental plays or happenings, plays which offer an intriguing view of Arden's authorship and the forces that shaped it. At the time, in the late fifties and mid-sixties, this kind of experimentation often baffled audiences and even turned audiences and critics against him because they did not know what to expect; as soon as they thought that they had deciphered what Arden was all about, he startled them by going off on a new track. This, after all, seemed quite un-British to some; experimentation is all right for foreigners, but it appears to be mere pretentiousness or foolishness if done by an Englishman, as one critic has said.

*When Is a Door Not a Door?*, the first of his minor experimental plays, was written as an acting exercise: "the experiment here was to provide parts in a play of specific length for a specified list of young men and women" (Preface 11). It was first produced at the Embassy Theatre, Swiss Cottage by the Central School of Drama on June 2, 1958. Though he enjoyed writing the play because of the technical problems it presented, he later found it quite unsatisfactory, conceding that "after all, the essence of an experiment is that it must imply a strong chance of failure" (Preface 9).

Arden has always put a great emphasis on telling a simple story which may open up several levels of meanings. *When Is a Door Not a Door?* depicts a Monday morning in a factory when two workmen arrive to fix the door in the Managing Director's secretary's office. Apparently quite a simple story, it comments in a subtle way on the contemporary situation in England and, though a minor play, offers some insight into the kind of subtle political satire that Arden writes as well as his concern with social issues. At a time when most British playwrights were busy attacking the Establishment, Arden is knocking both the Establishment and the working class. Of course, it may be argued that the working class is what it is because of the Establishment, but Arden doesn't seem to argue this; his viewpoint is quite different from Osborne's and Wesker's.

His main target is the apathy which infects England. The first workman states this theme early in the play:

> FIRST WORKMAN. (*disgusted*) That's what I mean, then . . . You stand there: and you ask me what's Russia got to do with it. If it wasn't for your apathy, you'd know. (158)

As the First Workman planes the door, he continues expounding his theories:

> It's a botched job and that's *all* it is. You see what I'm telling you, you see what I'm telling you, there's no passion these days, there's no what I call a lust, it's a

> botch all round, six ways on the compass. Look at
> Hitler . . . He's a soldier. He's seen life. And more than
> that. He's suffered. He was a corporal, see. Then they
> put him in prison. I mean, he knows the force of
> strength, doesn't he? I mean, like, you're Hitler: I'm
> Chamberlain. So I come along with the old umbrella
> up, *crawling*: "Oh play the game, old boy, play the
> game." Well what do you do! (165-6)

Apathy and the gratuitous violence in society are Arden's target.
Apathy has often been declared the main enemy of progress in
England; so far Arden says pretty much the same about apathy
that many others have said. But Arden is often deceptive; his
train of thought seems to lead straight on, but then a subtle
ironic discourse takes place as is also true in better-known plays
like *Serjeant Musgrave's Dance*.

The First Workman's last words are:

> You see, what I tell you. That's a nice girl, but she's
> like the rest of 'em in a place like this. They're
> walking dummies. They've no passion, they've no
> heart on the job at all. Offices or the assembly-lines,
> it's the same thing everywhere. All rush—no
> urgency . . . Don't let 'em catch you smoking here,
> mate . . . Apathy all over.
>
> SECOND WORKMAN. The bigger the firm—the less
> the initiative.
>
> FIRST WORKMAN. No passion. Nothing. Ah, it
> needs a craftsman to feel an honest rage about the
> world. I mean, take Krushchev. He's been a collier,
> hasn't he? He's worked in the pits, he's seen life: he's
> suffered. We-ell . . . (173)

What then makes this an ironic discourse? Arden doesn't have
one character come out with a punch line that ridicules the First
Workman's ideas; this would be too easy and would smack too
much of the usual West-End theatre. Rather he does it visually
and by means of the story itself. Arden has often said that the
clue to his themes lies in watching the development of the story;
he usually also, probably because of his architectural training,
strongly emphasizes his theme by visual means. Arden has a

tremendous feeling for and competence in language, but he always correlates it closely with the physical action and the visual elements; these are of course the two elements that make a play *theatre* and not just a literary exercise. Arden, almost alone among British playwrights in the fifties and sixties, combines literary and theatrical elements in an exciting and complementary manner. Hence it is no wonder that he has a wider appeal among the "common" people than the purely literary playwrights.

How then do these visual and story elements work here? Arden constructs a play within a play: the two workmen paint the door while expounding their views; the factory is turning to chaos all around them; the boss yells at his subordinates; the girls in the Packing Shop strike; the Shop Manageress and the Shop Steward have a very stormy session with the managers; a deputation of strikers arrives in the office; the rest of the factory threatens to strike and paralyze what appears to be a major industry—incidentally, the factory is manufacturing gun parts for use in the Suez crisis, but why worry about that!—and finally the secretary and the tea girl have a fight over a broken teacup. So one can hardly say that there is no passion even though it might be said that England is only capable of small passions over domestic problems. The irony is that the two workmen are the most apathetic of the whole group; Arden has emphasized this aspect in the introductory General Notes:

> The two WORKMEN do not take any notice of the conversation and actions of the others, except where indicated in the text. They may now and then look up, but without any apparent interest or comprehension of the events taking place. (155)

Not only does the play afford Arden an opportunity to criticize England's way of life, but he is able to criticize the British working class, who talk a lot about the problems but who, when a situation arises that they could actually do something about, are even more apathetic and entrenched in their set pattern than other classes of society.

*When Is a Door Not a Door?* may be said to be constructed like a riddle, as the title[1] implies—people and things are not what they appear to be. The supposedly passionate workmen are apathetic. The title implies much the same thing, namely, that what appears to be open mindedness (door = open space) actually may be narrow mindedness (jar = enclosed space). Throughout the play, this point is emphasized by a strong visual element. There is plenty of physical action in the constant running in and out of the office by the actors, which makes the apathy and inattention of the two workmen even more remarkable. The other nine characters actually pass through the door twenty-five times in approximately half an hour.

The play displays Arden's feeling for language, in, for example, the racy double-entendres with which he spices the play:

> FIRST WORKMAN. Right. I'll hold her this time, you screw.
>
> GIRL. (*laughs*).
>
> FIRST WORKMAN. (*to* SECOND GIRL). I'll tell your mother! (167)

Arden never uses sex in a perverted or sensationalist manner; rather he uses it the way the Elizabethans did because it's part of life, one of its anarchical forces, and because it's fun.

The other elements of British life that Arden criticizes are the English preoccupation with "playing the game" at all costs and the influence of "the old school tie" as well as Anthony Eden's handling of the Suez crisis. These same subjects have been attacked, often quite heavy-handedly, by the other Angry Young Men; Arden handles them in a more light-hearted, almost incidental, and thus probably more effective manner as in the following exchange by the workmen:

> FIRST WORKMAN . . . Now take Suez.
>
> SECOND WORKMAN You take it.
>
> FIRST WORKMAN (*beginning to plane the edge of the door*). Well, what happens? He says: it's lah de dah this, and it's lah de dah that, and play the game, Britons, play the game. And what does Nasser do? He walks in, *don't he*? He nicks the old canal. And

wouldn't you? He's a smart man, Nasser, he knows the Old School Tie when he sees it. "You play the game, me boys, and I play dirty." That what *he* says.

SECOND WORKMAN Huh. And what about Eden's free holiday at Bermudas, eh? What about *that*? After all that shambles. Just like, in'it?

FIRST WORKMAN Look, you go back to the yard this afternoon. You tell our boss: "Look here, boss, you said go and see to that doorway, it's jamming. We gone and done the window by mistake: what are we to do?" And what does he say to that? He says: "All right, my lad, don't you worry, my lad, all you done, boy, is make an error of judgement. Anyone could do it. So take yourself a week at Brighton and credit it to the firm." It's likely, in'it? Bleedin' likely. (160-1).

However, it is not just the Establishment and its obsession with "muddling through somehow" that comes in for criticism; the labor unions also have a few shots aimed at them through the caricature of Harry Stobo, the shop steward who bellows "like a radioactive hairbrush" (169), quite reminiscent of Peter Sellers's portrayal of a shop steward in "I'm All Right, Jack."

Since many of the components of *When Is a Door Not a Door?* become important elements of his major plays, it can be argued that it provided Arden with valuable apprentice experience. Stylistically and technically this play may well be the forerunner to such later plays as *The Happy Haven* (1960). Arden had intended it to be given a "completely realistic" (Preface 12) style, although in the "General Notes" he states that the scenery, except for the door, needs only to be sketched into place. The first director, Robert Cartland, decided to ignore Arden's request and instead to give it a *commedia dell'arte* treatment which brought out more of the farcical elements and resulted in a more stylized treatment, each person becoming more a type than an individual. This is the way Arden handles the situations as well as the characters in *The Happy Haven*, though there he goes one step further by adding masks. Arden himself has remarked in the introduction that he feels Robert Cartland's treatment was right and made him see the play from a different point of view (Preface 12).

Arden's next experiment, *The Business of Good Government*, written with Margaretta D'Arcy, was the first of his plays scripted so that it could be acted by children. It was also the first which actively displayed Arden's interest in the possibilities of community and amateur drama, as he explains in the Preface:

> There is a great deal of amateur drama in Britain today, but in far too many cases it does not contribute as fully as it might to the general life around it. The performance of plays is an activity that should come as naturally as preparing a meal, eating it, singing, dancing, kissing or football. It should not be associated with snobbishness, superior education, improved accents, and an enviable knowledge of "what they do in London." Nor should it merely be a means of extinguishing the provincial professional theatre by feeble imitations of its slicker successes. Amateur and professional must respect each other's work—complementing one another, rather than competing. (5)

Arden would like to make drama an integral part of everyone's life as it was in Greek society or Elizabethan times and by means of drama to invigorate and bring new truth and consciousness to the audience. The play was especially written for and first produced in the Church of St. Michael, Brent Knoll village, Somerset, during the Christmas season, 1960. The "actors" were the ordinary parishioners, which created special problems in acting, costumes, language, and setting. However, as Arden and D'Arcy had deliberately wanted to write a play for amateurs, they were therefore prepared to deal with these problems.

In the acting, Arden and D'Arcy and the parishioners "concentrated . . . on bringing out the meaning of their lines until, without entirely realizing it, they created from their own personalities a character, completely natural, belonging both to their own experience and to the world of the play" (5). This also affected the language and speech patterns; for example, the characters spoke more slowly than Arden had envisaged, and the play therefore took almost twice as long as planned. The costumes, too, were improvised as the rehearsals progressed. No specific historical period was aimed for; rather Arden and D'Arcy wanted costumes that fit into the play unobtrusively and complemented the characters' personalities. Most of the costumes consisted of what the participants brought along from home; this had the added advantage that the amateur actors felt less awkward in their costumes. Arden has since used a similar method several times in his plays.

The setting was also made to fit the circumstances, using Brecht's premise "if it works—it works." The setting of the church blended in quite naturally with the theme of the play, but Arden and D'Arcy have constructed the play in such a way that it can be adapted to any auditorium or community hall. Apart from the practical implications of this, it also shows their concern with a fluid environment in the theatre. This is brought out further in the Preface when Arden states that if this play is to be performed on a proscenium stage, "the producer should start by removing the proscenium frame, curtains, and footlights" (7-8). His concern with a non-restrictive and fluid environment would be of major importance in his later works, such as *The Workhouse Donkey* (1963) and might also account to a large extent for his strong interest in the radio and television media. Arden's whole approach to acting, costumes, languages, and setting is indicative of someone who is extremely concerned with the vigor and interest ordinary people can bring to a community undertaking of this kind. Arden has given much of the credit for the evolution of this approach to his wife, Margaretta D'Arcy, who was also the producer of the play at St. Michael's.

Arden is here already seen to be pre-eminently a pragmatic playwright, probably because of his architectural training—architecture is a practical art. His preoccupation with the practical is also mirrored in his themes; though often concerned with metaphysical issues, he always pragmatically asks: "yes, but does it work?—will it work?" Arden is not an abstract playwright like Pinter or Beckett, though there is the occasional superficial similarity. Rather he is a playwright who uses his practical and common sense to study people and issues as they appear in everyday life: that is, never all black or white but often subject to instinct or natural forces and often acting according to ideals which ultimately fail and with a deep understanding of the anarchy of most human existence; again, he is a pragmatic anarchist. Simon Trussler, one of Arden's more perceptive critics, makes the following comment on this important element in his writing:

> John Arden's mistrust of abstract concepts, and a consequent moral ambivalence in his writing, has perhaps been at the root of the incomprehension with which audiences and critics have tended to greet his work. Freedom, like liberty, is easy enough to hypostatise, difficult to translate into meaningful human terms. But a cautious attitude to dogma does not make him, as John Russell Taylor once suggested, an "amoral" dramatist: rather, it makes him a dramatist in search of a *practical* morality. His plays have been episodes in this search: examinations of ideas, people and attitudes, which have deliberately and honestly rejected an easy synthesizing. The attitudes dramatised are seldom absolutely right or absolutely wrong, and although Arden's instinctive preferences may occasionally be discernible, they are unobtrusive and, as he insists, irrelevant. (4)

The title of the play, *The Business of Good Government*, indicates Arden's preoccupation with practical concepts; as Trussler goes on to say:

> all Arden's recent work has been concerned with the very practical business of good government—the relationship, if you like, between principle and expediency. (7)

Arden has examined the relationship between principle, practicality, and expediency in several of his heroes, in Krank, for example, in *The Waters of Babylon* (1957), and more subtly in Musgrave, and it continues to be of major importance in most of his heroes. Herod affords a fascinating opportunity for a study of this relationship, which often results in pragmatic cynicism. This becomes apparent in Herod's first speech, a reply to the Angel's outburst of joy and peace:

> Goodwill, great joy, peace upon earth—I do not
> believe they are altogether possible. But it is the
> business of good government to try and make them
> possible. (*Government* 18)

The focus of the play is on Herod and his political maneuvers
and not, as expected in a nativity play, on the Holy Family. It is
characteristic of many of Arden's plays that the thematic
emphasis is often centered upon someone who would otherwise
appear to be a secondary character. Herod has traditionally been
a villain, but Arden chooses to portray him as a man caught
between Roman and Judaean powers, a man whose every move
is being watched over by a Roman secretary. Herod's choices are
conditioned by the society around him; it is the society more
than the individual which is to blame. Arden very cleverly
allows Herod to be crossexamined as to his motives and uses the
Angel, ironically, as the devil's advocate in order to get across to
the audience the central node of principle, practicality, and
expediency as seen in the following exchange:

> ANGEL. (*deadpan*) The situation should be within
> your control. Are you not the king ?
>
> HEROD. (*petulantly*) I am not trained to understand
> prophecies and superstitions! Those that do under-
> stand them have assured me that it is very unwise to
> ignore their political importance. Here are the King of
> Persia's men, looking for what might well be a
> claimant to the ancient line of Israel. If Persia deter-
> mines to recognize such a claimant, Rome will punish
> *me*. . . . They will send in an army to secure their
> Legitimate Interests. A Roman Governor will be
> appointed in Jerusalem. If I am lucky, I may be per-
> mitted to wash up in his kitchen. . . . (*bitterly*) [M]y
> loyalty to Caesar is continually being doubted. . . . (*He
> speaks now with great sincerity*) The object of my life is
> the integrity of my kingdom. What am I to do? . . .
> [P]ity the King: and pray for his policy. (40)

In Herod's last major speech, Arden and D'Arcy portray
him as a man who almost selflessly is willing to give up his own
honor for the sake of his people:

> The end of my world. The end of peace of life. The
> end of good order. . . . The king must rule his human
> subjects by means of his own humanity. And
> naturally, within his rule must be comprehended such
> difficult extremes of good and of evil as may be found
> from one end to the other of his unfortunate
> kingdom. . . . (*He assumes a rhetorical posture, and*
> *addresses the audience*) Citizens! Patriots! Through the
> years I have been your leader I have kept you free
> from war and provided unexampled prosperity. You
> are richer and happier than ever you have been! Your
> children are receiving opportunities for education and
> advancement that your own fathers could not have
> imagined in their wildest dreams. Dare you see this
> prosperity destroyed in one night? You answer me—
> no. You answer me—King Herod, do you believe to
> be necessary and we your faithful people will follow
> you as always in loyalty and trust! (*To the* ANGEL).
> You understand — I am putting a very particular
> mark against my name in the history books, and I
> know it, and I am not afraid. *It is fitting that the honour*
> *of one man should die for the good of the people* . . . Send
> out an instruction to my officers. They are to put to
> death all the children. . . . (49-50; emphasis added)

Arden has managed to portray the traditional villain in a
favourable light, as Herod is seen to have freely chosen to
become a villain for the good of his people. Arden has thus again
restated his firm principle that there usually is a discrepancy
between appearance and reality, that one has to analyze a person
or a situation from all angles before one passes judgement on it,
and more importantly that what seems an anarchical action is
sometimes needed to create order anew and a new order.

The form is that of the medieval miracle play,[2] which is a
perfect vehicle for Arden's whole approach to drama. It tells a
simple story which appeals to all levels of the community and
uses the community as the resource for actors, costumes, and
setting ( in this play, the village church[3]). The story itself has also
been used often in the medieval miracle plays. The manuscript of
the York cycle of miracle plays (ca. 1430-40) lists the following

play which was put on by the "Orfeveres [goldsmiths], Gold beaters, and Moneymakers":

> The three kings coming from the East, Herod asking them about the child Jesus: the son of Herod, two counsellors and a messenger. Mary with the Child, a star above, and the three kings offering gifts (Pollard xxxii).

The further developments in the story were acted by other guilds, as the practice was to divide the popular stories among several guilds.

Arden, who instinctively seems to have a feeling for tradition, follows that of medieval England by making his play reflect contemporary England rather than the biblical Palestine and, maybe more surprisingly to modern sensibilities, making Herod into a popular "villain." E.W. Parks and R. C. Beatty explain:

> When the villainous Herod began to declaim against the Hebrews, they [the medieval audiences] evinced a noisy approval which the often vain actor enjoyed. This made him declaim still more. He became a ranter, a figure whom audiences finally applauded on sight. (2)

The role of the popular "villain" has its own tradition on the English stage; the medieval Herod found his counterpart in the Renaissance, and Arden continues the tradition with many of his characters, such as Herod, Krank, and Butterthwaite (*Babylon*; *The Workhouse Donkey*, 1963).

*The Business of Good Government* explains the human and philosophical complexities of a hero who in almost all other depictions has been portrayed in a singularly two-dimensional manner; King Herod has traditionally been one of literature's great "bad guys." But Arden portrays the anarchy of life, the lack of clear unequivocal positions, the complexity of decisions, and the ever-shifting terrain of right and wrong. Life is complex, life is anarchical—maybe the only way to stem the chaos and the anarchy is to develop a strong sense of pragmatism. Herod exemplifies this approach to life—he is a man Arden can identify with because he adopts the same approach in his plays. In *The Business of Good Government*, Arden handles the traditional form of the miracle play so intuitively that it seems almost custommade for his ideological and dramaturgical exigencies. In other plays, he handles the traditional ballad form in much the same way.

Arden's next experiment is very reminiscent of the ballad, not by its formalistic but by its conceptual framework. What has come to be known as "Kirbymoorside '63" was a communal composition centred around a "dichter" emanating ideas which were then picked up and evolved by the surrounding group(s). *The Business of Good Government* had already made manifest Arden's and D'Arcy's fundamental interest in the community. "Kirbymoorside '63" was to expand this interest into an ideology resembling the one underlying Wesker's "Centre Fortytwo" and Joan Littlewood's "Fun Palaces." It is significant that Wesker's ideas about "Centre Fortytwo" came to fruition in 1962; it was also in that year that Wesker and his associates had mounted several trade council festivals quite successfully. In short, Wesker's ideology[4] views the theatre as being a resource centre for the community and the community as a resource centre for the theatre. In practical terms, the idea was to have a theatre building, in this case the Round House[5], which should serve not only as a theatre but also as a pub, center for various political activities, local restaurant, debating society, youth club, and so on. In other words, there was a real cultural and political center for the community, but also by the community because its various functions were to be staffed mainly by the locals; the theatre itself was to use both professional and local amateur groups. It is, to some extent, the contemporary equivalent of the medieval market place with its own special spirit and multitudinous functions. Wesker hoped to forge a new artistic reality out of working-class life as well as to show art's responsibility to the people and people's responsibility to art.

In the same year, 1963, Joan Littlewood staged *Oh, What a Lovely War* at the Theatre Workshop and was evolving the ideas for her Fun Palaces, also based on leftist ideologies. The *zeitgeist* of '63 was very much one of community involvement in the theatre based on various leftist political dictums. It is no wonder, therefore, that Arden and D'Arcy's next theatrical experiment assumed a form and substance theoretically very similar to Wesker's, and to some extent to Littlewood's, though for obvious reasons the practical details were different.

What Arden did was to publish a mock Victorian play bill ad in *Encore* proclaiming that for a month spanning August-September 1963, he would stage various theatrical and cultural experiments at his home in Kirbymoorside:

### AN APPEAL BY JOHN ARDEN

Living as he does in Kirbymoorside, a small Yorkshire country town . . . From which the Railway has been removed: in which there is neither theatre nor cinema: nor indeed much industry (save for a small Glider Factory and a Brickworks): near which the principal Sign of our Times is the alarming, unearthly, impossibly beautiful and probably totally unnecessary Early Warning Station on Fylingdales Moor. . . .

And where the population in general, deprived of their old social entertainments such as. . . .

A German Band
A Dancing Bear
An Annual Goose-Fair
The arrival of a daily Train at the Railway Station

(all remembered with grave nostalgia by the older inhabitants)

Resort to no fewer than five distinct sectarian Churches of a Sunday, thereby splitting into exclusive fragments a community already sufficiently fragmented by the Cruelty of the Twentieth Century and the Affluence of the South. . . .

JOHN ARDEN

Has conceived the idea of establishing

A FREE PUBLIC ENTERTAINMENT

in his house.

To take place at intervals between the fifteenth of August and the fifteenth of September.

MR. ARDEN has been indirectly described by MR.
WESKER as a Paralysed Liberal. . . .

If anybody wishes to assist him to overcome this
paralysis, which he is inclined to admit. . . .

MR. ARDEN is resident in London until the tenth of
July at: 9 Kings Avenue, Bromley, Kent (Tel.:
RAVensbourne 1991) and thereafter at Mill Cottage,
Kirby Mills, Kirbymoorside, York.

He would be inordinately grateful for suggestions or
offers of assistance towards the furtherance of this
small project.

No specific form of entertainment is at present
envisaged but it is hoped that in the course of it the
forces of Anarchy, Excitement, and Expressive Energy
latent in the most apparently sad persons shall be
given release.

----------------------------

MR. ARDEN also needs a number of helpers to come
back with him to Kirbymoorside to stay until the fifteenth of September, for whom he will be prepared to
Pay Expenses and provide Food and Accommodation.

----------------------------

COME TO KIRBYMOORSIDE AND HELP ARDEN
TO SPEND HIS MONEY LIKE WATER

("Appeal")

D'Arcy and Arden thus opened their home to the Kirbymoorside
villagers, local gentry, and everyone else who wished to come—
which unfortunately included various "London-theatre" types
and newsmen, so that the experiment did not have quite the
local character they had been striving for. However, it did
manage to produce a new community spirit amongst the
villagers who attended, although of course, certain villagers
looked upon the whole venture as a Bohemian caprice.

A typical evening might consist of a classical play put on
by an amateur group or by a professional company whom Arden

had got to pass through town; the plays would usually be put on in their living room, with an audience of approximately seventy to ninety people, though some of the helpers had cleared a corner of the garden as an outdoor stage. After the play, tea would be served by Arden and D'Arcy and then a second play put on by the villagers, or some other performance of local talent would take place. Ian Watson enumerates some of the various events:

> [T]here were readings and performances of Machiavelli, Brecht, Arrabal, O'Casey, Jarry, Livings, Owen, Jellicoe; the Mikron Theatre Company stopped off on its way to the Edinburgh Festival, to open the month with two performances of Charles Lewsen's *The Bubonic Plague Show*; poets wandered in to give readings of their work (young people from York found themselves accused by Jon Silkin of murdering Jews); Henry Livings performed; Chaplin, Fields and others shared the screen with the Kirbymoorside films and other documentaries; actors and local people improvised scenes around unusual newspaper stories (a classic one was Arden's own performance as the Army Sergeant who drove his wife to seek divorce by insisting that she tickle his feet for four hours per night); local artists, singers, groups, dialect story-tellers, and performers of all kinds found audiences for what they had to offer. (18)

Two of the most noteworthy events were the films that Arden had made. Watson describes them:

> The first shows a day in a life of Derek, a 12-year-old schoolboy and the son of a laundry worker. Derek is disenchanted, finds the town dull, lifeless, lacking in opportunities. The second quite simply portrays the various activities, and the lack of activity, of the town's inhabitants. The commentary, compiled by John Arden from historical works and incredibly frank recorded interviews with local people, is read by four people and achieves very much the same quality and comprehensiveness as a radio ballad. Those watching identify themselves and their friends

with glee, and are surprised at much of what they
hear. (18)

One interesting feature of the films is that Watson
pinpoints their effects as those of a ballad; another is that Arden,
through them, has had actual experience in this medium as he
often later uses both cinematic as well as documentary
techniques in his plays. That Arden has long been interested in
film was already apparent in his comments on *Sergeant
Musgrave's Dance*, the idea for which he partly attributed to the
film *The Raid*. The Kirbymoorside films were also instrumental in
making the villagers see themselves in a new light and creating a
feeling of community. Throughout the month, there were also
discussions of the various events; some people kept busy
painting or making pottery. The evenings usually ended with
turning the house into a discotheque where the "audience"
would happily dance until two or three in the morning. The
month thus became an all-inclusive happening.

Next to nothing has been written about the quality and
success of the individual plays presented, but this is exactly the
way it should be; the plays are not important in themselves, only
the overall texture of the experiment is. There can be no doubt
that "Kirbymoorside '63" was successful in the way in which
Arden and D'Arcy wanted it to succeed: they were able to
stimulate people. The moving spirit behind this experiment in
"communal" art was Margaretta D'Arcy; Arden claims that he is
"a writer of a solitary disposition" and that "although I
approved of it, I was never able to rid myself of a feeling that I
was not built for this sort of responsibility" ("Footnote" 21). But
even though the "entertainment" was mainly D'Arcy's idea, it is
completely in line with Arden's own principle of trying, through
drama, to bring a new vitality and unity to the people without
necessarily having any specific political message.

Though no doubt of leftist tendencies, the early Arden
does not possess quite the same abject veneration of the working
class and of pseudo-Marxist philosophy as Wesker does. Nor is
Arden primarily a didactic playwright as so many of his
contemporaries are, for example, Osborne and Wesker. Arden is
mainly interested in the intellectual joy, the mental and physical

energy, and the understanding of humanity that the true theatre is capable of generating in audiences regardless of their cultural or educational background.

It is interesting that in the advertisement Arden mentions that anarchy will be one of the creative forces in the experiment. He has always insisted on anarchy being one of the most human and necessary forces in life and has explored this idea in such plays as *Sergeant Musgrave's Dance* and *Armstrong's Last Goodnight*. Of course, it should be remembered that Arden means an "ordered" anarchy; he comments on his specific conception of anarchy in connection with the Kirbymoorside experiment:

> "Anarchy", as my wife had conceived it—I myself have always tended to run away from ideological abstractions—implied an artistic condition akin to that of a compost heap. In other words, throw a lot of people together and something will inevitably result without the necessity of authoritarian leadership. Perhaps: but in practise this resulted in a certain demoralisation of our assistants. . . . "Anarchy" is a tight-rope that can only be walked by a group of people all educated to keep their balance and not to flag in the middle. To what extent it can be a basis for theatre on a larger scale still remains a question. ("Footnote" 21)

Arden had already shown elements of this anarchical force in his playwriting. With the influence of Margaretta D'Arcy, it comes into full bloom in some of his more experimental plays. Even in his more conventional plays, Arden often has a fascination with anarchy as a thematic thread in the texture of the play.

For Arden the Kirbymoorside experiment was an important step in the evolution of his ideas about participatory theatre. Margaretta D'Arcy is the main impetus behind this particular direction in his playwriting. She has on her own created various events by working with local children in experimental and creative groups, very much along the lines of the developmental drama theories formulated by Brian Way and Peter Slade, which had become very important in the sixties and seventies. Their influences might also be discerned in Arden though on a different level. Way's and Slade's theories are mainly concerned with the psychological and creative development of the participants, who are usually amateurs or children, in order for them to achieve a greater awareness of themselves and their environment. Way and Slade are not really concerned with whether this "development" results in a play, whereas, of course, Arden as a playwright wants to use their theories in such a way that a "stageable" play will result. Thus he might use these ideas when working with amateurs in a rehearsal to make them aware of their own dramatic possibilities and to help them improvise. At Kirbymoorside, Arden managed in one way or another to involve most of the village and to break down a few barriers between the villagers. Some villagers took an active part in the plays, films, or other events, some participated passively as the audience but were usually drawn into discussions or at least the dancing, and some, of course, remained outside as critics but that, too, is a form of participation.

"Kirbymoorside '63" was an important and necessary step in Arden's development. It has helped him work out some ideas about a pragmatic and participatory theatre, though, as he says, he is not yet sure how these ideas can be applied to more conventional theatre, but certainly much credit is due him, for his family became personally involved both emotionally and financially.

These three early experimental plays all give indications of what was to come in his career: the visual elements, the emphasis on non-verbal communication, often ironically juxtaposed to the verbal communication, the pragmatic concern with evolving forms of stagecraft. On the thematic level, even in these relatively minor plays, there is the projection that life is anarchy—nothing is quite what it appears to be, chaos is the rule of the day—but it is a creative chaos out of which new ideas spring.

Much has happened in the theatre and in Arden's own authorship in the last twenty years; it is no doubt difficult to appreciate fully now how unusual and revolutionary Arden's ideas and dramaturgy were at the time of their first staging. He has always been a sophisticated and pragmatic writer, a man of tradition who obviously had a feel for his own literary history and very much a feel for the concerns and ideas of his time. It is a measure of his greatness and originality as a dramaturgist that much of his experimentation with form, and many of his ideas are now almost standard in the theatre and other arts of the nineties.

## Notes

1. The answer to the riddle is: "When it is ajar."

2. Some critics would now call this a mystery play as it deals with a Biblical incident, whereas miracle plays deal with the life of a saint; however, in the Middle Ages both types were called miracle plays.

3. In the twelfth century, the churches were also used as the setting for the miracle plays, which was even more convenient then than now because the churches contained no pews at the time and thus afforded a large fluid space for the action.

4. Cf. Arnold Wesker, "The Allio Brief" in *Fears of Fragmentation* (London: Jonathan Cape, 1970), pp. 52–62, for Wesker's own explanation of the ideology behind the creation of the Round House.

5. It is noteworthy that Arden used the Round House to mount *The Hero Rises Up*. During rehearsals of the play, he and his wife invited the neighborhood children in to view and discuss the play.

## Works Cited

Arden, John. "An Appeal by John Arden." *Encore* 10.4 (July–August 1963): back cover.

———. "Footnote by John Arden." *Encore* 10.6 (Nov.–Dec. 1963): 20–1.

———. *The Business of Good Government: A Christmas Play.* London: Methuen, 1963.

————. Preface. *Soldier, Soldier and Other Plays.* London: Methuen, 1967.

————. "When Is a Door Not a Door?: An Industrial Episode." *Soldier, Soldier and Other Plays.* London: Methuen, 1967. 153–174.

Parks, Edd Winfield, and Richmond Croom Beatty. Introduction. *The English Drama: An Anthology 900–1642.* New York: Norton, 1963.

Pollard, Alfred W., ed. *English Miracle Plays Moralities and Interludes.* 8th ed. Oxford: Clarendon Press, 1927.

Trussler, Simon. "Arden: An Introduction." *Encore* 12.5 (Sept.–Oct. 1965), 4–8.

Watson, Ian. "Kirbymoorside '63." *Encore* 10.6 (Nov.–Dec. 1963): 17–20.

# WHY READ ARDEN?

## Douglas Bruster

Why read Arden? An abrupt question, it is nevertheless one which—however varied our motives and expectations—the passing of time forces us to ask about all authors, including those with more claim to a place in the canon. What does Arden's work have to offer us that repays the labor of reading him? Of seeing his plays performed? Of producing his plays? In an attempt to provide an answer, I turn first not to Arden's work itself, but to David Lodge's picaresque novel, *Small World*, and a passage which, through its portrait of a middle-aged "Angry" and his writer's block, goes a long way toward capturing the special ambivalence we may feel over Arden.

Published in 1984, *Small World* is a comic treatment of the academy, full of professors and would-be academics from all areas of the globe. An exception is a character called Ronald Frobisher, a writer whose dust-jacket biography praises him as being a "leading figure" in the generation of Angry Young Men since the publication of his first novel in 1957. As described by Lodge, Frobisher is in every sense a composite "Angry," a writer—like Arden—whose popularity and productivity have long since come and gone, even given way to a kind of embarrassed silence. Yet the relevance of Lodge's writer to my argument lies not in the biographical parallels that make him resemble Arden (and many others), but in an incident which (as another character puts it) causes Frobisher to "lose faith in [his] style" (182).

Rehearsed by Frobisher over a tankard of authentic ale, the incident takes place at a redbrick university in an industrial town where he has been invited to receive an honorary degree. While there, he is taken to the university's "Centre for Computational Stylistics," where his writings have been chosen as the first to undergo computer analysis. With the push of a button, an overly enthusiastic computer programmer runs a complete stylistic analysis of Frobisher's *oeuvre* in his presence, showing the writer his "favourite" words, sounds, names, and literary situations. Then, not content with pointing out the writer's clichés to him on the computer screen, the programmer makes a printout of the analysis and gives it to Frobisher:

> "A little souvenir of the day," he was pleased to call it. Well, I took it home, read it on the train, and the next morning, when I sat down at my desk and tried to get on with my novel, I found I couldn't. Every time I wanted an adjective, *greasy* would spring into my mind. Every time I wrote *he said*, I would scratch it out and write *he groaned* or *he laughed*, but it didn't seem right—but when I went back to *he said*, that didn't seem right either, it seemed predictable and mechanical. [The computer programmers] had really fucked me up between them. I'[ve] never been able to write fiction since. (185)

Embarrassed by what he has just written because it seems "predictable and mechanical" (185), Frobisher functions as a portrait of the artist who has seen his style and subjects become clichés. Lodge's larger interest in and sensitivity to literary style is clear from both critical works such as *Language of Fiction* (1966), an analysis of novelistic prose style, and novels like *The British Museum Is Falling Down* (1965), the chapters of which successively ventriloquize various authors and the idiosyncracies of their literary styles. But in Frobisher Lodge pulls back, as it were, and shows us what happens when a writer *reads Language of Fiction* or sees his or her style parodied in a novel such as *The British Museum Is Falling Down*. The self-consciousness that arises blocks further writing. In pulling back here, though, Lodge does more than show us one character's psychological conflicts: he uncovers a general problem in recognizing patterns and the typical. This problem is *the* problem posed by many works of the fifties and sixties. Indeed, the writer's block Frobisher experiences when confronted with the particulars of how he writes and what he writes about— symbolizes what one could call the "reader's block" many people now feel over such works as Osborne's *Look Back in Anger* (1956), Colin Wilson's *The Outsider* (1956), and Arden's *Serjeant Musgrave's Dance* (1959).

By "reader's block" here I mean more than first-level historical estrangement from cultural objects: the sense of realizing that you don't know something you need to know to understand the work. I refer instead to a pattern of reception that sees one come to the work with adequate background for understanding it and subsequently find too little worth one's attention and sometimes much that one understands too well. Reader's block results from both boredom and embarrassment—the latter might well come from a sense that the book is part of a time one's culture has outgrown. Like an author looking over juvenilia, readers can regret an earlier part of themselves and their culture. The work's moves can seem too predictable, its sentiments uncomfortably familiar. Fredric Jameson captures something like the feeling I refer to when, discussing the experience of viewing an art-video from 1979, he ventures: "such is the tempo of the history of experimental video that insiders or connoisseurs are capable of watching this 1979 'text' with a certain nostalgia, and remembering that people did that kind of thing in those days, but are now busy doing something else" (211).[1] The end of Jameson's sentence—"that people did that kind of thing in those days, but are now busy doing something else"—describes the frustration many readers feel when taking up Arden and other writers of his generation over thirty years after their initial popularity.

Why, though? That is, what are the sources of the typicality that can make these works so hard to read, the sources of what Frobisher calls the "predictable and mechanical"? One source is the attempt by writers in the late fifties to communicate social estrangement frequently involved grounding their plots in the ennui of alienation; the desperate frustration which many of their protagonists feel is, intentionally or not, passed on to the texts' readers and audiences. What was once an anglicized quotation of Brecht's alienation effect, however, now operates in a different constellation of social and historical relations. If we are after the existential moment, we are also after the apocalyptic. The sense of impending deluge marking works of the thirties, forties, and fifties could be said to exist on the other side of a stylistic, thematic, and political break separating their world from contemporary audiences. Even in their own time, though, some of these works "wore" on their audiences. I am thinking here of a story which a friend tells about her mother's response to the celebrated New York production of *Waiting for Godot* in 1956: fifteen minutes into the performance, she turned to her companion and said "I get it. Can we leave now?" That the play was successful in wearing down an audience member is only half the point. It also anticipated the way many people now experience Beckett—and Arden.

*Godot* offers a useful contrast, as well as parallel, to *Musgrave* in that—unlike *Waiting for Godot*—in Arden's drama something happens; the play looks for its energy, in fact, to a shocking climax which develops logically out of what has gone before. Two "heavy wooden boxes"—and a box of another kind—function as the magic hats from which Arden produces this powerful moment. The play's plot—transpiring around 1880 and centering, finally, on the contents of these boxes—begins as follows: A band of army deserters, led by Serjeant Musgrave, travels to the "mining town in the north of England," the hometown of fellow soldier Billy Hicks. There they pose as recruiters.

After two acts of ominous development, the play reaches its peak in Act Three, scene one, when the soldiers start to open the magic boxes from a town meeting at the public marketplace. Miners, hungry and dissatisfied during a labor dispute, have joined the rest of the town at the marketplace to listen to Musgrave's "recruiting" pitch—a pitch that quickly turns into a diatribe on the social conditions and political system which led to their role in an oppressive occupation of a "Protectorate," the equally senseless murder of Billy Hicks, and the soldiers' bloody revenge on members of the local population not involved with his killing.

As Musgrave's speech continues, he has Attercliffe, a soldier, open one of the boxes and remove a Gatling gun. Attercliffe mounts this gun on its tripod and aims it into the on-stage audience—which, by extension, includes the play's audience as well. With his "urgency increasing all the time" (as a stage direction tells us), Musgrave ironically praises the gun:

The point being that here we've got a gun that doesn't
shoot like: *Bang*, rattle—click—up—the—spout—
what're—we—waiting—for, *bang*! But: Bang-bang-
bang-bang-bang-bang-bang-bang-*bang*—and there's
not a man alive in the whole of this market-place.
Modern times. Progress. Three hundred and fifty
rounds in one minute—*flat*!(82)

The scene grows steadily in the "urgency" Arden
describes, and Musgrave opens what could be called a "memory
box"; he tells the townspeople of the atrocities committed by the
British army in the wake of Billy Hicks's murder.

On his way home one night, Billy Hicks had been shot in
the back. The subsequent midnight round-up of citizens was
punitive and bloody; Attercliffe had killed a small girl in the
confusion. As Musgrave later puts it, "there's one man is dead,
but there's *everyone's* responsible":

We've *got* to have order. So I'll just tell you quietly
how many there were was put down as injured—
that's badly hurt, hospital, we don't count knocks and
bruises, any o' that. Twenty-five men. Nine women.
*No* children, whatever *he* says. She was a fully grown
girl, and she had a known record as an associate of
terrorists. That was her. Then four men, one of them
elderly, turned out to have died too. Making five. Not
so very many. Dark streets. Natural surge of rage. (87)

When Hurst, a soldier, points out "We didn't find the
killers," Musgrave quickly responds: "Of course we didn't find
'em. Not *then* we didn't, any road. We didn't even know 'em. But
*I* know 'em, now" (87). If the Gatling gun is not enough to
remind the play's audience of their complicity in colonial
politics, Musgrave's increasingly accusatory speech ensures that
they "get it."

The third box, out of which dangles a coil of rope,
contains the surprise which gives the play its impact. Arden's
stage directions tell its story:

*ATTERCLIFFE has nipped up the ladder, holding the rope.
He loops the rope over the cross-bar of the lamp-bracket,*

*drops to the plinth again, flings open the lid of the big box, and hauls on the rope.*

*HURST beats frantically on his drum. The rope is attached to the contents of the box, and these are jerked up to the cross-bar and reveal themselves as an articulated skeleton dressed in a soldier's tunic and trousers, the rope noosed round the neck. The PEOPLE draw back in horror. MUSGRAVE begins to dance, waving his rifle, his face contorted with demoniac fury. (84)*

A ritualized expression of ideological rage, Musgrave's dance revisits the sins of a culture upon itself in what is effectively the high point of the play. Yet it is more than that: because *Serjeant Musgrave's Dance* is arguably the best thing he has written, it is also the high point of Arden's career. The dramatic payoff, then, has to stretch not only over the whole of the play's slowly rising action but over the large amount of very mediocre writing that Arden has done since.

For this and other reasons, Arden is not an easy author to read or watch. If, unlike *Godot, Musgrave* has a dramatic payoff, it resembles Beckett's play in that it is about waiting; the Northern town in which the deserters wait for their capture is, like Beckett's stage, a kind of existential arena. Like theatres, however, cultures can sustain few intentionally tedious works for long. The novelty of "Angry" characters and plots—the undirected rage and unspecified contempt so powerful in the late fifties—no longer retains the shock value it once had. Instead, readers are left with the dramatic mechanisms of postponement. The impatience felt by audiences of *Musgrave* during the play's original run was compensated for by the title character's "demoniac" dance and the dramatic display of Billy Hicks's skeleton. Yet the dance and skeleton fail to provide the theatrical reward they once delivered. What remains—the dialogue of waiting, accusation, and revelation—is not enough.

Another block to reading Arden and many writers of his era has to do with the literature's representation of female characters. Politics aside, it is—ultimately—boring to read works committed to portraying women primarily as whores, betrayers, or both. Certainly it is more than boring to many people, but even (perhaps especially) those it enrages may find their opposition rooted in a certain kind of impatience. Behind the deployment of misogyny in the works of writers like Arden, Osborne, and even Pinter are dramatic imaginations rarely concerned with representing female characters with much depth, complexity, or even sympathy. The effort put into the characterization of the parts of Mrs. Hitchcock and Annie in *Musgrave*, Alison Porter and Helena Charles in *Look Back in Anger*, and Ruth in *The Homecoming* is remarkably slight in comparison with that devoted, for instance, to Musgrave, Jimmy Porter, and Max. Romantic at base, Arden's early plays—like those of Osborne—focus much of their energy on the emotional and social struggles of male protagonists. The result is plays which are aesthetically and socially lopsided.

A key word here is "romanticism." I am referring to Arden's (and writers of the fifties) adulation of the natural individual—read "working-class" and "Northern." While the "Old Cumberland Beggar" school of Romanticism had been exhausted by Orwell's generation, the economic situation of the thirties temporarily gave new life to sentimental narratives of the down and out—think here of the anonymous woman Orwell idealizes from a moving train in *The Road to Wigan Pier* (1937). Much of the literature of the late fifties can be seen, in fact, as echoing—even dreaming of—the thirties: the source of "Angry Young Men" as an epithet, significantly, came from Leslie Paul's narrative set in the political strife of the thirties, *Angry Young Man* (1951). But the second time is usually farce, and where Orwell's works still have an authenticity and purpose about them, Arden's romanticism is difficult to take as anything more than nostalgia of form. Perhaps not unrelated, his use of the past in works like *Musgrave, Ironhand* (1963), *Armstrong's Last Goodnight* (1964), and *The Non-Stop Connolly Show* (1975) invariably rings false. Arden often exercises his moral and political outrage at too safe a distance. Up close, people can— and do—tell writers to go to hell, as Arden and his wife, Margaretta D'Arcy, found out when they tried an agit-prop play on a very up-to-date topic.[2] To write the present is to open a conversation with those who can talk back; to write of a

Musgrave, a Connolly, or King Arthur can be to use the past (historical and legendary) as a source of romantic nostalgia.

Arden may have written his dramas of social voice in the wrong mode. A good case could be made for seeing the last four decades in England as a time of criticism, not literature. Here I am thinking about studies such as Richard Hoggart's *The Uses of Literacy* (1957), Raymond Williams's *The Long Revolution* (1961), and E. P. Thompson's *Making of the English Working Class* (1963). With its skillfully intertwined threads of narrative and its deft handling of separate registers of society, Thompson's study, for example, has always struck me as the modern, critical equivalent of the Victorian novel. Williams's *The Country and the City* (1973) and *Keywords* (1976), and the work of the Sussex cultural materialists are only a few of the writings which claim an energy (and audience) that many works of contemporary literature seem to lack. Retrospective analyses of British culture likewise focus less on strictly literary texts. A recent review of Alan Sinfield's *Literature, Politics, and Culture in Postwar Britain*, for instance, points out that in Sinfield's study "Margaret Thatcher has more entries in the index than Samuel Beckett, Iris Murdoch, and William Golding put together, while class mobility has more than poetry" (Baldack 457). As culture and history are with increasing frequency seen as texts which can be read and analyzed (something for which the "committed" literature of the thirties is at least partially responsible), the need for socially-committed literature as a source text—for audiences both inside and outside the academy—has decreased. Arden's work, like that of many other writers, is caught in this shift.

It may also be that Arden was working in a medium that took itself too seriously. Thinking back on the "serious" literature of the fifties and sixties, on the literature of The Movement, the Angry Young Men, the New Wave, it is easy to compare it unfavorably with the truly popular culture of England since the late fifties. Beside a film like David Lean's *Lawrence of Arabia* (1962), for instance, all of Arden's plays seem not smaller in scope of conception—for this is neither fair nor the point of the comparison—but less thoroughly thought out, less in control of their medium, and less honest about who is speaking and what is being said. The same might apply to

Arden's plays even in comparison with the works of John Le
Carré, Ian Fleming, the Beatles, the Rolling Stones, and the Who.

For me, Arden's primary virtue lies in reminding us of
what other writers have to offer. Brecht, certainly, has greater
mastery of the dramatic parable and the deeper messages of his
plays. An English author who proved a great influence on Brecht
(and, perhaps through Brecht, on Arden as well), was Kipling,
whose poetry and prose capture the registers of Britain—and its
ballads—in a way Arden did not. From Arden's era, the plays of
Pinter and Orton continue to hold up. Most of Philip Larkin's
poems, from *The Less Deceived* (1955) through *The Whitsun
Weddings* (1964) and even *High Windows* (1974), likewise deserve
attention, as do many of Stevie Smith's. Alan Sillitoe's classic
story, "The Loneliness of the Long Distance Runner" (1959)
remains powerful as well. J. G. Ballard's stories and novels of the
sixties, including *The Drowned World* (1962), *The Terminal Beach*
(1964), and *The Disaster Area* (1967), anticipate *The Atrocity
Exhibition* (1970) and make Ballard arguably the most influential
English writer of his time. A number of films from the period
under discussion also bear examination: in particular, two
directed by John Schlesinger from the early sixties, *A Kind of
Loving* (1962) and *Billy Liar* (1963), have always seemed to me to
possess a special energy and depth while displaying a level of
artistic talent that would elude Arden.

I began this essay with a passage from *Small World* that
implied, through its composite "Angry," that much of the
literature of the late fifties is too clichéd to take seriously now.
Much like the computer of his story, Lodge narrows in on a
composite style—here one which stands in for the literature of a
"movement." When we find out that the title of Frobisher's first
novel is *Any Road*, it is difficult to encounter Arden using this
expression—as he does, for example, in one of Musgrave's
speeches quoted above—without feeling that, with a few pages
of his novel, Lodge has managed to encapsulate both much of
what has characterized Arden's career and the experience today
of reading his work. Looking back at Arden, I feel his plays are
often too bound up in their own will-to-commitment to offer us
as much as works do which took themselves (though not their
audiences) less seriously. Culturally, tastes and reputations

always change. So it may well be that Arden's plays will, in the future, find wider acceptance. For this to happen, though, they will need to provide something that we are unable to get from other writers. What this could be is anyone's guess.

# Notes

1. Jameson's comments refer to a twenty-nine minute video entitled *AlienNATION*, produced at the School of the Art Institute of Chicago in 1979.

2. Here I am referring to the lawsuit for libel brought against Arden and D'Arcy after the controversial production of *The Ballygombeen Bequest* in 1972, where the "program included a seven-page manifesto with the name, address, and phone number" of a landlord who had allegedly evicted an "old widow" unfairly from her family's cottage in Oughterard, Ireland. Arden and D'Arcy ultimately settled out of court. (Recounted and discussed in Page 117–18.)

# Works Cited

Arden, John. *Serjeant Musgrave's Dance*. London: Methuen, 1960.

Baldack, Chris. Rev. of *Literature, Politics and Culture in Postwar Britain*, by Alan Sinfield. *Journal of English and Germanic Philology* 90 (1991): 456–9.

Jameson, Fredric. "Reading Without Interpretation: Post-modernism and the Video-text." *The Linguistics of Writing: Arguments Between Language and Literature*. Ed. Nigel Fabb, Derek Attridge, Alan Durant, and Colin MacCabe. New York: Methuen, 1987. 199–223.

Lodge, David. *Small World: An Academic Romance*. New York: Macmillan, 1984.

Page, Malcolm. *John Arden*. Boston: Twayne Publishers, 1984.

# AN UNDEVIATING PATH:
# MARGARETTA D'ARCY AND
# JOHN ARDEN

## Claudia W. Harris

Late on the afternoon of 20 August 1992, Margaretta D'Arcy and I went walking and talking along the Corrib on the north side of Galway. Wanting this essay to be as current as possible, I had driven from Dublin to Galway that morning specifically to discuss with John Arden and Margaretta D'Arcy their most recent work. They had invited me to spend the night and announced when I arrived that there would be a gathering that evening at their home with friends from the neighborhood as well as guests from Portugal, France, and Germany who were there in Galway because of interest in various aspects of their work. So after tea and a pleasant afternoon visit, when they talked to me at length about their present writing project—a radio play for BBC about Eleanor Marx, Karl Marx's daughter—Margaretta and I walked out together while John did the washing up and set out the cakes and drinks for the party.

The damp grass did not deter us as we strode across the fields toward the river. Clearly, Margaretta had taken this back way down alleys and through gates and over fences before. As we turned north along the east side of the river, not only was I trying to keep up with her pace over the uneven ground but also with her words turning over one topic after another. Her singleness of purpose again impressed me, even before we got to the road and bridge blocking our path and Margaretta scrambled up the steep slope. I followed slipping in the mud, unprepared for the terrain without proper shoes. We crossed the bridge to the west side of the river and Margaretta started to head down an even steeper slope. At that, I pointed to the cement steps leading down a hundred paces further on. She seemed almost surprised by their obvious presence but quickly dismissed the alternative, saying it wouldn't take us where we wanted to go and down to the riverbank she went with me sliding clumsily after. When we got back to the house, John asked how the walk had been. Wonderful, I said, but added that Margaretta according to her usual style had taken the hardest path, uncompromising and undeviating even in leisure. He laughed but she looked mystified by our exchange.

The evening was truly international as we heard recitations and songs from every represented country—a remarkably traditional Irish hoolie. The pleasure of the gathering was a perfect culmination to the day when I was again able to observe firsthand D'Arcy's and Arden's quite exceptional but rather misunderstood artistic collaboration which has actually spanned the three decades of their relationship. In her essay "Breaking Chains," D'Arcy explains the basis for their partnership: "When I met John Arden, our attraction to one another was based on our obsession with the theatre—also our dissatisfaction with it. We promised each other we would change it to accommodate what we wanted: those were the vows we made to each other" (*Corners* 131-2). Those early vows have continued to be the ongoing basis for their difficult but dynamic collaboration. When Arden emphasized for me the challenge of writing together and yet still maintaining amicable relations, D'Arcy said quietly, "You don't have to, John." They choose to collaborate, they say, because of the new ideas their working together produces, but another reason is, no doubt, because of the vitality and vibrancy writing jointly adds to their relationship.

Listening to them all day argue the same points, finish each other's sentences, fill in alternately the gaps in plot or approach or idea gives some sense of how closely they have become of one mind. Then listening to them discuss their differing writing styles, bemoan their ruthless but necessary critiques of each other's work, describe their final, careful shaping of the whole gives a sense of how thoroughly their working methods have become complementary. After they collect and study and discuss the material, D'Arcy says that she then goes away, isolating herself in her room, letting her subconscious work to identify what is most important and which approach to take: "It either comes in a flood or nothing comes.

And then, of course, John wants his subconscious to get going, but when John goes away, he goes away for three days. I have to do everything literally in five minutes, but when Arden goes into his subconscious, it takes him three days." My recorded tape from that afternoon is punctuated throughout with their laughter while exchanging amusing stories about the challenge yet, even so, expressing sheer delight in the creative process.

D'Arcy characterizes Arden as very competitive, which he does not deny. Arden compares offering their creative efforts to each other as a little like presenting school exams to their examiners: "Each partner disappoints the other with what he turns up with." At that, D'Arcy interjects, "I say nice things to John, and he never says nice things to me." But they both agree that it would be counterproductive to try to be sensitive to each other while discussing their work; they count on their mutual, merciless honesty.

> D'Arcy: I wake up and say, oh God, what am I allowing this man to do?
>
> Arden: Well, do you think I don't have those emotions, too?
>
> D'Arcy: Do you? Well, what do you think?
>
> Arden: Oh God! Where is she taking this play? I thought I had it all clear in my mind. And suddenly you have a brainwave and the thing is drifting off into an area of sheer horror. And I say, this sounds a little like a Margaret Drabble novel, and you say, well, I think that's rather what it ought to be. And you were taking the play to something I couldn't deal with, to some sort of Freudian relationship between Eleanor and Karl Marx. Working out a young girl's relationship with her father who thought she ought to be a boy is very difficult. It's part of the story, but it's something I want to shy away from.

Most of the conversation that day centered on the Eleanor Marx radio play. Set in 1898, the play deals with the complex, intertwining personal and political strands that led to Eleanor's suicide. Certainly, they want any play they write to have a clear focus and sound ideas, but nonetheless, this particular play is an

exciting departure for them. Although they believe all of their
plays are personally about them in a sense, this is their only play
exclusively about personal relationships, their sole domestic
play, their first play which is not an epic. That aspect has
confronted them in new ways. Not only must they understand
Marx and his problematic relationship with his daughter, but
they must also understand Eleanor and what led to her decision
to take poison that morning. The characters in this play came
first, and then they worked to find out how each one related to
Marx and to Eleanor—how they fit in and developed the story.
Writing becomes a process of elimination; they look and look
and look, again.

To show the importance of Karl Marx, to show this
extremely visionary, vital, witty man, to show him as an
integrated person is their goal and was Eleanor's goal as well.
When Eleanor could no longer maintain that view of her father,
when she could not control his papers, when she found out that
a long-term friend was really her half-brother, she decided she
wouldn't settle for less and killed herself. The play, according to
D'Arcy, is a statement about commitment, about not settling for
less. So the play is about charting that undeviating path. Even
this play is more like than unlike their other plays. On the
surface, their artistic direction might appear to be separate or
possibly circuitous; however, their radical, political drama has
provided a consistently direct route to their subject matter.
Keeping their vow to each other, they jointly see an undeviating
path to socially responsible artistic production no matter how
others might view the artist as obligated to somehow remain
above the fray.

Arden and D'Arcy are workers before they are artists. As
members of the trade-union-affiliated Society of Irish
Playwrights, Arden and D'Arcy have been on official strike
against the British stage since 1972. Their growing dispute with
commercially focused theatre finally erupted over the Royal
Shakespeare Company's staging of *The Island of the Mighty*. They
believed that the RSC production tempered the trilogy's anti-
imperialistic stance; when a meeting failed to address their
concerns, they withdrew and picketed the theatre. One of the
placards aptly expressed their point: "Playwrights are workers

before they are artists." At the preview, a few supporters interrupted the play, asking for a discussion; but the larger audience would not allow Arden to be heard. He left the theatre with D'Arcy saying, "We will never write for you again." Arden discusses the strike in his introduction to their book of essays, *Awkward Corners*:

> That RSC dispute has never been settled: and although we are no longer huddled with our placards outside the stage door of the Aldwych Theatre, we regard ourselves and our labour as still being "withdrawn" from the RSC and from any other theatre company that maintains the same invidious and overweening management practices. It was a very awkward corner in that back-alley of Drury Lane: all sorts of people theatrical and other, came to support and sustain us, but others came to revile, and the wind (it was in the early winter of 1972) was extremely cold, and the newspapers that reported our defiance did so, on the whole, with exactly the same insidious distortions and innuendo they were later to apply to much more celebrated industrial actions (3-4).

Their strike was not the frivolous, arrogant act described in press reports at the time. It was an act of conscience, committed only after they had pursued every other recourse. Feeling no control as playwrights over their artistic product in a world where the director reigns supreme, they did what workers do—they withdrew their labor. But not without great personal cost. According to D'Arcy, Arden enjoys the process of writing. And he agrees, "Up to a point." He is a playwright not a playwriter; he has the ability to craft the play to his vision and sees as ideal the relationship a Shakespeare or a Jonson might have had with his theatre company in a time when the word not theatrical effect took precedence. For them to have walked out of the theatre that night must have been extremely difficult; Arden was walking away from a successful career, from what he considered to be his life work. In discussing their dissimilarities, D'Arcy emphasizes Arden's pleasure in words: "John carefully puts down each word. He doesn't know what's going to happen; he doesn't see a scene before he begins writing. I don't write like that; I've always collaborated improvisationally. The whole thing comes in a flash, in a rhythm or movement, a flowing. But then, it's not bad the way John works because it slows the process down. When he's mythologizing his novels and short stories, he can take as long as he likes; he can be totally egotistical." [She means self-absorbed here, not egotistical in the negative sense.]

Arden has what is sometimes referred to as a primal, creative urge—he must write. And when they found themselves cut off from their audience, when radical theatres no longer had sufficient funds to mount their ambitious productions, when the heavily subsidized theatres blurred and distorted their anti-imperialist stance by cutting the text and changing the style and focus of their plays, Arden developed a new outlet for his creativity by writing novels. Arden cryptically explains the difference between playwrighting and novel writing as, "You've got to fill in the bits between the speeches":

> It doesn't necessarily take longer to write a novel, because a play can take a very long time. But a novel has more words, so I find that the amount of actual physical work at the typewriter rather than in the head is increased. It's also much more solitary because there's no element of collaboration at all. With a play, even if one writes it oneself, you end up collaborating with the actors and the producer. But the novel is all out of one's head and onto the paper. Writing novels has slowed me down. I've written two novels—*Books of Bale* and *Cogs Tyrannic*—without a drama in between, and I discovered, much to my dismay, that I was getting into a novelist frame of mind [with the Eleanor Marx play], wanting a lot of detail rather than jumping through, which one needs to do in a play. One needs to keep it elastic and alive for the actors.

Nonetheless, in spite of its tiring, solitary nature, novel writing has kept Arden actively producing work. And he sees no purpose to writing a stage play, anyway, because he sees no hope of getting a play produced by any of the people running theatres now. Besides he has not been asked to write a play by people who would value what he wanted to write or who would stage the text faithfully. Although he would like to write a film, he sees no opportunity there either. They wrote a film script about life in Galway a few years ago, and it was never made, regardless of numerous meetings about it. Despite his seeming discouragement, he admits that in the past he was always rather lucky in getting his plays staged; all have been produced. But he has no venue now. The American stage is out of the question because it is not accessible. And the Irish stage . . . At that D'Arcy interjected, "We've written a hell of a lot of plays and no one in Ireland or America has expressed any interest. Now if there were a body of people who expressed interest in one's work that would encourage one to write a play." So Arden has turned to novel writing, and D'Arcy has increased the time she spends as an activist for women.

D'Arcy and Arden are committed to the cause of the worker; as artists they feel deeply responsible to their society. Neutrality or objectivity in art is impossible; writers must choose to use their talents conscientiously or they will be exploited by the very power that oppresses society. D'Arcy and Arden are consistent and persistent in recognizing their artistic endeavor as a product which can be used to free women and men from exploitation and oppression or misused to obscure the historic struggle and render it mere capitalist entertainment. Although he is describing Brecht's theatre in *Marxism and Literary Criticism*, Terry Eagleton could just as well be describing D'Arcy's and Arden's; Eagleton uses applicable words like "formally uneven," "interrupted," "discontinuous"; he examines the disruption of "conventional expectations" and how the audience is then forced "into critical speculation on the dialectical relations between the episodes. Organic unity is also disrupted by the use of different art-forms—film, back-projection, song, choreography—which refuse to blend smoothly with one another" (65-6). In addition, like the Brecht plays Eagleton is describing, the text of a D'Arcy or Arden play is "always provisional . . . an experiment . . . The theatre ceases to be a breeding-ground of fantasy and comes to resemble a cross between a laboratory, circus, music hall, sports arena and public discussion hall" (66). D'Arcy and Arden are able to capture a Brechtian playfulness; the didactic impulse is present but so is the ludic one. But unlike Brecht, they make no attempt to alienate or distance; instead, they draw the audience into the action as students in the art class or as targets of the Gatling gun.

*Ars Longa Vita Brevis* (1964) demonstrates the provisional, discontinuous, unconventional qualities Eagleton discusses. In fact, in the introduction to their joint *Plays: One* (All references to *Ars Longa* will be to this edition), Arden and D'Arcy name this particular play as the one which taught them the most as playmakers (xv). This short play is an early collaboration and is the first where they list D'Arcy as principal writer. One night, 12-year-old Girl Guides knocked on their door in Yorkshire and asked them "to do a play with them." D'Arcy describes how the girls fought to put on the play despite the criticism: "it wasn't a *real play* [emphasis hers], there was no curtain, they made up their lines instead of having to learn them, wearing masks and wearing make-up was unsuitable for young females—but their joy in ridiculing the military-industrial complex and overturning all the taboos of family and thrift remains a delight in my mind, and has been more valuable to me over the years than all the stodginess and corruptions of the London theatre" (xi).

In the play, a newly hired art teacher forces his students to draw straight lines on graph paper, holding rulers in the left hand and sharp pencils in the right: "no freehand, no expressionism, impressionism, futurism, abstractism" (50). The students' laxity leads to a satiric military drill which culminates in the teacher's cry, "Order against chaos. Kill each other kill each other kill each other KILL!" (51-2). After the art master is fired on his first day, he receives no tea or sympathy from his wife: "Wait for your tea, you glutton, you sot, you stewed infusion, wait until I hear the truth—and then, if you still have stomach for it, I daresay you may eat" (54). Seeking discipline, he joins the Territorial Army only to be shot while disguised as a tree:

> Technology is confounded and art takes its place:
> For here I have received a real bullet in my face.
> Hardihood and discipline,
> Straight lines and repression
> Have today found their old true expression:
> I die for my duty and I die with a smile
> The Territorial Army has proved itself real. (58)

As the Headmaster explains: "He died in the knowledge that he was fulfilling his vocation. He was so still that we were certain he could only be a stag; had he moved we would have known he was a man" (59).

D'Arcy and Arden intend for this very funny and disturbing script to be "a framework for a performance." Saying the "little piece is not exactly a play," they refer to it as "A Theme for Variations." In the Foreword, they identify which speeches or scenes could best be improvised and which ones should perhaps be "played straight" (44). Symptomatic of much postmodern theatre, *Ars Longa* is decomposed during rehearsals and then recomposed during performances. The play therefore broadens the definitions of script, stage, actor, audience. Whether labeled art or politics, the committed theatre D'Arcy and Arden value is not just a simulation but an exaggerated performance of those interactions which are most problematic to a society and which would benefit most from the clarity that might come through practice. According to Richard Schechner, "Drama is not a model of all human action, not even most of it measured by time spent, but only the problematical, taboo, difficult, liminal, and dangerous activities. . . . Drama arises where clarity of signal is needed most: where the risk is greatest and the stakes highest, where redundancy is an advantage" (213-4). Drama of any type does not just mirror life but is an exaggeration, an intensification of life. It gives shape to life; it provides a window to view life through. Whether the undeviating path of D'Arcy's and Arden's drama entails a dramatic performance on the stage or their protest in the cold back alley of Drury lane or the "H Block" D'Arcy scrawled in red on the wall at a 1978 poetry reading in Belfast which led to her arrest and imprisonment in Armagh Gaol, the shape of D'Arcy's and Arden's dramatic window is simply unashamedly and overtly political.

When we were talking that August afternoon about a particular new play which I had just seen in Belfast and felt was singularly unsuccessful, D'Arcy immediately asked me what the playwright's politics were. In Ireland, what is called theatre and what is called politics are frequently indistinguishable on several important dimensions: scripts, writers, actors, audiences, and sometimes even settings. The relationship can be described as a convoluted analogy—theatre : politics : : politics : theatre. Theatre anywhere is a distinctive cultural product because it formally dramatizes much of what is true about a culture. But although political difficulties are epidemic throughout the world, Ireland is unique in a troubled world because theatre plays such a large part in the Irish expression of self. This interesting mix of politics and theatre makes the Irish and their difficulties more accessible than many other people with similar problems. The interrelatedness of politics and theatre also gives playwrights in Ireland a special role, even transplanted Englishmen like Arden. In fact, Arden and D'Arcy moved from England to Ireland to take a deliberate role in the Irish political-theatrical atmosphere.

In *From Ritual to Theatre*, Victor Turner discusses social drama, a term he invented to describe cultural performances not unlike *Ars Longa*. Turner explains that "there is an inter-dependent, perhaps dialectic, relationship between social dramas and genres of cultural performance in perhaps all societies. Life, after all is as much an imitation of art as the reverse" (72). Turner's four-step schema for social drama can be used to analyze either a stage drama or a political event. A *breach* becomes a *crisis*; a sacrificial victim is chosen; *redressive action*, usually in the form of a sacrifice, is performed in an attempt to heal the breach; and finally, *reconciliation*, reintegration, or agreement to differ occurs. The breach has usually existed for a long time, but some precipitating event occurs which leads to the crisis. The redressive action does not "make life comfortable for the heroes: they end up dead, maimed and/or exiled" (Schechner 189).

The *breach* between art and life implied by the play's title is defined in *Ars Longa Vita Brevis* by the Headmaster on the annual speech day when he deplores the lack of an art class in the school, which, of course, has led to the present *crisis*—the complete separation of art from the life of the school. Despite the dangers of encouraging unruliness, the Headmaster declares, "We must move with the times: dig it: be with it: in the groove: in not out: U not non-U. . . . An Art Master has been appointed. . . . I have no doubt he can be trusted to keep all our aspiring Picassos, Matisses, Rembrandts, Giulio Romanos, William Ettys, Bouguereaus, Aubrey Beardsleys, Gauguins, Bouchers and Goyas upon very much the straight and narrow" (48). The Art Master then is the sacrificial victim designated to control the impossible—the creative messiness of art. The *redressive action* involves the art master's firing because of his extreme methods as a teacher and then his killing because of his extreme discipline as a Territorial. He is reconciled in the end to the fact that the true expression of his art is as a dead soldier. This truly ironic *reconciliation* culminates in the final reintegration of society achieved by the money collected and given to his wife: *"With the money she buys clothes, food, wine, a new house and she enjoys herself in fast cars with innumerable young men, all more handsome and less confused than her late husband. In the middle of her enjoyment, she meets his funeral on the way to the graveyard"* (59):

> WIFE.
> I shed a tear upon his bier
> Because to me he was ever dear.
> But I could not follow him in all his wishes
> I prefer the quick easy swimming of the fishes
> Which sport and play
> In green water all day
> And have not a straight line in the whole of their
> bodies (59).

In thinking of the seminal theatrical experience they gained from *Ars Longa Vita Brevis*, Arden and D'Arcy do not refer to the RSC production at the LAMDA Theatre Club in London. Instead—

> We would think of the Girl Guides in Kirkby-moorside, of Albert Hunt and his students in Shropshire, of Robert Leach at Birmingham using five different groups of actors all interpreting it and improvising in different ways at the same time. We met a woman from Yugoslavia who told us of a production in that country in which she and her brother had taken part in the glorious heady days of student rebellion. It was broadcast into Greece to topple the Colonels' junta (which we like to think it did). And its ingredients contain the seeds of an entire

ideology which we have since arrived at in fuller and
more rational form—the recognition of women's
invisible work, women's power subverting the
military-industrial complex, spectators' power to
subvert the power of the actor where all activate and
none are passive, everyone becoming their own
script-writer, director, performer (*Plays: One* xv).

Turner delineates Barbara Myerhoff's description of
such cultural performances, saying they are "*reflective* in the
sense of showing ourselves to ourselves. They are also capable of
being *reflexive* [her emphases], arousing consciousness of
ourselves as we see ourselves. As heroes in our own dramas, we
are made self aware, conscious of our consciousness. At once
actor and audience, we may then come into the fullness of our
human capability—and perhaps human desire to watch
ourselves and enjoy knowing that we know" (75). It is a
consciousness of themselves as political performers that D'Arcy
and Arden demonstrate both in art and in life. They have vowed
to heal the *breach* between art and politics, at least in their own
work.

In *Tell Them Everything*, D'Arcy describes dramatically
her undeviating path toward fuller consciousness; the book is
subtitled *A Sojourn in the Prison of Her Majesty Queen Elizabeth II
at Ard Macha (Armagh)*. When D'Arcy, as an invited guest of the
Northern Ireland Arts Council, joined "a discerning audience, an
artistic audience, a caring audience of sensitive, special people"
(15) at a poetry reading at the Ulster Museum during the 1978
Belfast Arts Festival and heard poets reading poems dedicated to
dead dissident artists, she could not ignore the *crisis* in Northern
Ireland. An H Block protest parade had been banned the day
before because it might "unduly inflame passions. . . . Here, I
thought, were two dead artists being used by two living artists to
present an impression of radical protest against censorship and
the brutality of repression on the Falls Road; did the poets
believe that by merely mentioning the names they could avoid
all responsibility when the prisoners' families were not allowed
to march in the street? It was hypocrisy; it was disgusting. I leant
against the wall, took out a red marker and wrote H Block" (15-
16). Perhaps unknowingly, D'Arcy chose at that moment to play

the role of Turner's sacrificial victim and the central figure in the effort toward *redressive action*.

Her description of the outcome of her protest capitalizes on the drama inherent in the situation: "Except for the poet's words there was absolute silence at the time. The concentration, the dedication, the reverence to a poet. My marker squeaked; heads turned round; they registered—and they [those 'sensitive' people] opened their mouths and yelled. I was determined to finish off my 'picture' by putting a frame round it. I was dragged out by the museum attendants, taken downstairs and made to wait for the RUC" (16), or the largely Protestant Royal Ulster Constabulary. Arden had not yet arrived in Northern Ireland for the conference at Queens University accompanying 7:84 Theatre Company's performance of *Vandaleur's Folly* (1978) during the festival, so she was alone in her action and her punishment. "The Black Maria arrived, and a young steely-eyed RUC man tipped me in, hoping to break my neck. When I righted myself, he grinned—'How did you like that?' The dream was over, the illusion burst—here I was, staring at the reality of 'Northern Ireland'" (16).

No *reconciliation* or reintegration was possible. D'Arcy refused to cooperate or to recognize the court, seeing herself as an artist denied free expression. The charges were for "three assaults, breach of the peace, incitement to riot, defacing a public monument" (17). She was sent to Armagh to await trial and subsequently used her trial, in which she defended herself, as a way to "debate the role of the artist in a time of repression" (17). Arden had read her paper, "Theatre in an Age of Reform" [*Corners* 176-91], at the Queens conference while she was in prison. Ironically, D'Arcy had asked in the paper what might happen if artists painted protest pictures on walls near the Ulster Museum: "If the artists were caught arrests would no doubt take place. Who would defend them? Because they would not be working within the art-gallery cocoon, does that mean that their artistic credentials would automatically be rejected? And if so, why?" (*Corners* 184) D'Arcy discovered what would happen. Although fined £10 for each offense, which someone paid for her, and released from Armagh Gaol, she, like many others, was radicalized by her encounter with the Northern Irish court system. She would return again to Armagh for a longer stay, and she would become one of the Greenham Common protesters as well.

Arden in his essay "Drawing Blood in Galway," defines D'Arcy's protest as guerrilla theatre—"part-satire, part-protest, part-demo, a bit of all of them and yet not quite any of them. . . . It is intended to draw blood without warning. If it is tolerated, it has failed" (*Corners* 9). Among the many events he names as guerrilla theatre is "Margaretta D'Arcy, during a poetry-reading, carefully, seriously, embellishing the Ulster Museum with a framed 'H'block' logo at a time when that museum was censoring political paintings and H-block marches were being banned" (*Corners* 11). But then everything they do and write is intended to draw blood without warning. Their plays may be scripted more tightly than guerrilla theatre, but the purpose is very close. Turner's four-step schema for social drama can be found clearly expressed in everything they write. Making audiences aware of the *breach*, concerned about the *crisis*, participate in the *redressive action*, yearn for *reconciliation* is the aim of their art. They do not offer comfort but are committed to social change, and change is always very painful.

Unlike Margaretta D'Arcy, John Arden is outwardly a gentle man, almost taciturn. That August afternoon nothing seemed to irritate him—running out of cigarettes, failing lighters, cutting too soft bread. The only thing that ignited that radical spark in his eye was the thought that Margaretta D'Arcy, his partner and collaborator for thirty years, might not be accorded her due. Margaretta is a lightning rod whether she's working with *Duchas na Saoirse* [Artists for Freedom] in Belfast or Radio Pirate Woman in Galway. She is both tireless and uncompromising in her efforts as an artist, a woman, and an activist. Ignoring her, silencing her is impossible; she merely develops new ways to be heard. She readily scales that wall of indifference to her issues and continues passionately on her undeviating path.

# Works Cited

Arden, John and Margaretta D'Arcy. *Awkward Corners*. London: Methuen, 1988.

———. *Arden/D'Arcy: Plays: One*. London: Methuen, 1991.

D'Arcy, Margaretta. *Tell Them Everything*. London: Pluto Press, 1981.

Eagleton, Terry. *Marxism and Literary Criticism*. Berkeley: University of California Press, 1976.

Schechner, Richard. *Performance Theory*. Rev. ed. New York: Routledge, 1988.

Turner, Victor. *From Ritual to Theatre: The Human Seriousness of Play*. New York: Performing Arts Journal Publications, 1982.

# BRECHT—BRITAIN—BAKHTIN: THE BRIDGE OF *ARMSTRONG'S LAST GOODNIGHT*

## Susan Bennett

The history of post-war British drama is, in many ways, a history of the search for a social(ist) form which would engage with a new, more extensive theatre-going public. That early landmark year of 1956 brought not only *Look Back in Anger* but a first appearance in London of the Berliner Ensemble and, while John Osborne's play drew much public attention at the time, it is arguably those performances of Brecht's plays (and, more generally, an exposure to Brecht's ideas for theatre) which have facilitated the remarkable development of oppositional theatre practices in Britain. This has been, nevertheless, an undoubtedly slow process and, initially at least, British theatre professionals did not easily embrace Brecht's theory. Indeed, the model of epic theatre was particularly problematic—if not impossible—in a British mainstream theatre resolutely clinging to the conventions of naturalist representation.

First endeavours to be "Brechtian," exemplified in Osborne's *Luther*, were merely superficial and did not display an understanding of key elements such as the *Gest* or *Verfremdungseffekt*. Quite simply the plays looked Brechtian. John Arden, however, was perhaps the most successful at and perhaps the most interested in interrogating the Brechtian model and exploring its usefulness in a British cultural context. His early plays demonstrate an attempt to introduce dialectic presentation and to seek a politically sensitive theatre audience. Yet, as the reception history of *Armstrong's Last Goodnight* (1964) makes patent, the better the understanding of epic theatre, the more criticism a play received from the critical establishment.

The critical responses to first productions of *Armstrong's Last Goodnight* were hardly unexpected. John Arden's plays had already been identified as "difficult" or "problematic" and, as

Edwin Morgan put it, *"Armstrong's Last Goodnight* follows the now classic pattern" (48). Irving Wardle (in a defense of Arden's work) noted a less charitable reaction from one of his fellow critics (unnamed): "Writer? Writer? He [Arden] couldn't write bum on a lavatory wall. And if he could he'd write it in Gaelic!" (22) While this kind of critical insult was often leveled at Arden's work, re-reading this text at our own historical moment, almost thirty years later, it is easier to share Wardle's astonishment at such an implacable opposition to Arden's work.

Much of that specific hostility can, of course, be attributed to a wider (and somewhat enduring) hostility in English theatre to theory. Not only did Arden work as "the most Brechtian playwright that we have" (Wardle 22), but he ventured to have his own theories which adapted the practices of epic theatre and the traditions of Jonsonian comedy.[1] While Wardle offers "Brechtian" as a positive signifier, elsewhere it was a critical kiss of death. In Morgan's review of *Armstrong's Last Goodnight*, we are told "let him kick away the inapposite Brechtian scaffolding and get on with the task of developing character and situation" (51) and "this is an Arden play! Sympathy never develops very far" (50). It is true, of course, that in the nineteen-sixties Brecht's contribution to the development of modern theatre had not been widely recognized by the English-speaking world. The 1956 London performance by the Berliner Ensemble had been well received but only as "foreign" dramatic fare and not as a theatre which might have some relevance for new British playwrighting. Arden, however, showed both in his plays and his critical writings a detailed knowledge of and interest in Brecht's theory. *Armstrong's Last Goodnight*, in this context, can be read as an important threshold text. It stands between a British resistance to Brechtian practice in the fifties and sixties and a mainstage and academic canonization in the seventies and eighties of the German playwright's work.

*Armstrong's Last Goodnight* is evidently a concerted attack on the yet prevailing naturalism of the English stage.[2] Instead of setting the play's action in a room, then still much (over)used, Arden revives the medieval convention of mansion staging to afford a continuous, chronicle—in other words, Brechtian—structure. The radical nature of such a move (and one, of course, directly attacked by Morgan) is testified to in the careful instructions Arden gives in his preface to the *Armstrong* text: "If they [the mansions] appear too naturalistic, the production will appear incongruous and peculiar" (240). Like Brecht, Arden did not want to show his characters trapped in a determining environment. Thus the mansion staging, along with accurately realized working-class costumes, facilitated the placing of characters in social history as well as the exploration within the play of the processes and complexities of social relationships.

Despite Arden's desire to avoid the "peculiar," even the more positive critical responses were, in fact, provoked by the play's failure to fit within the prevailing and indeed very narrow dramatic convention. Frances Gray writes of *Armstrong* at Chichester as a "revelation":

> The characters did not, as they seemed to in most plays, simply walk on and say their lines or do their business and walk off; they created a whole pattern of energy on the stage so that not a moment was wasted. [O]peras and ballets and musicals, too, had given me a conviction that the theatre should look attractive, that music and colourful costumes were an essential part of a play, but most of the costume plays I had seen seemed rather tacky and trivial. *Armstrong* did not; the visual attractiveness was not just top-dressing, but was there to say something about the world of the play. (155)

It is tempting to add "and about the world of the audience."

*Armstrong's Last Goodnight*, read synchronically, was more or less a(nother Arden) failure. Read diachronically, it becomes one of a number of texts which challenged and, in certain ways, rewrote the conventions of British dramatic writing. While Arden has not escaped the label of "difficult," his early texts have been recovered from such status. Increased exposure to this new type of drama—anglicized Brecht—eventually produced new interpretive strategies for both theatre audiences and drama criticism. In 1962, in the first edition of *Anger and After,* John Russell Taylor wrote that Arden's "attitude to his creations is quite uncommitted" (84)—a line which has since and understandably provoked some amusement.[3] By 1969, however, in a revised edition of the same text, Taylor was able to point some solutions to the earlier confusion about Arden's work and these indicate an already shifting (accommodating) set of interpretive strategies. On *Armstrong's Last Goodnight*, for example, Taylor comments:

> Though in retrospect it seems to be one of the clearest and most completely achieved of Arden's plays, at the time it was widely received with mystification and resentment even from critics who had previously liked Arden's work. I suppose the first reason for this was the language. (102)

While the English stage had by the early sixties opened up to the "regional" dialects of the angry young men, the invention of a quasi-sixteenth-century Scots dialect was undoubtedly a bold and risky act. But, as Taylor goes on to admit, "the dialogue requires no special training in Scots" (102).[4] What Taylor does not consider, and what more clearly points to the mystification or hostility expressed by the play's critics, is the effect of Arden's strategy with language. It is not a question of comprehension, or lack of it, but of its purpose in laying bare significant social and hierarchical relationships. In *Armstrong*, shifts in linguistic competence and language systems signal shifts in power. As Gray suggests, "Arden does not want to absorb his audience but to hold a dialogue with them. Sometimes, indeed, the actors must speak the lines in such a way as to invite judgment on their characters" (39). This is particularly true of Lindsay's final speech which invites, if not provokes, judgement. Audiences are asked to take stock of contradictions and to reach their own conclusions. The inclusion of Gaelic in *Armstrong's Last Goodnight* was the most daring gesture of all. The irritation this caused the critical mainstream is captured in the comment cited by Wardle and quoted in my opening paragraph. Yet it is an effective strategy in pointing, in the world of the play, to language as ideological apparatus and, in the world of British playwrighting, to the hegemony of the Queen's English. Even more ironically the sixteenth-century

English of Shakespeare might be read against Arden's sixteenth
century Scots in *Armstrong*.

Audiences, accustomed to a role of polite passivity and
to the guidance of a narrow and determining set of dramatic
conventions, were indeed effectively trained to resist texts such
as *Armstrong's Last Goodnight*. Yet they, or at least the critics,
might have been more aware of Arden's particular interest in
Brecht. In 1964 he published a review of John Willett's
translation *Brecht on Theatre*, and his comments there are
instructive for readings of the contemporary *Armstrong*. On the
*Verfremdungseffekt* Arden notes:

> I take it as meaning that whatever is shown upon
> a stage, whether people, objects, or events, must
> be shown so precisely, so clearly, so transparently
> indeed, that it seems like a *new thing*: only then will
> the audience be able to understand its significance for
> their own lives—a moral, social, political significance
> which implies possibility of change, and which they
> ignore at their peril. (*To Present* 39)

The audiences of *Armstrong* were, it seems, quite able to
"ignore." What appeals to Arden in Brecht is evidently the focus
on both the understanding and pleasure of theatre audiences and
it is this effect that he is apparently striving for in *Armstrong*.
Later in the review he notes: "The word *Spass* (fun) crops up
time and time again. Brecht never forgot that the theatre must
entertain: but he knew that entertainment in the fullest sense
means more than whiling away two or three hours in
undemanding pleasure: it also means the improvement and
enrichment of our understanding of life" (40-1). As Gray's
response to *Armstrong* makes evident, on the mainstream British
stage at least, entertainment was marked in a much narrower
sense. Beyond this it is particularly interesting that Arden points
to the prominence of *Spass* in Brecht's theory, a feature which
other British readers have all but ignored. Arden's hopes that
audiences would experience that sense of *Spass* in the reception
of his own plays were, at that time, clearly unfulfilled.

While Arden was already interrogating Brecht's ideas,
the British theatre-going public and, especially, the theatre critics

were not. Critical commentaries reveal that the political import
of *Armstrong* was generally misunderstood and often entirely
missed. Any praise derived from the play's energy and not its
ideas. Indeed both audiences and critics showed themselves to
be remarkably resistant to Arden's attempt to have them think!
Clearly the theatre-going public of the early sixties did not
recognize themselves as politically constructed subjects. Arden
himself summarizes his audiences of the time in the Preface to
the collected edition of those early plays. He notes that they
responded "with a mute defiance and an obvious reluctance to
be impressed" (5). Yet one production of *Armstrong's Last
Goodnight* proved that not all audiences were so resistant to a
Brechtian mode of performance.

The première production of *Armstrong's Last Goodnight*
in 1964 was at the Citizens Theatre in Glasgow. Taylor noted that
the local audience had a "slight advantage" (*Anger and After*,
1969 ed. 102) in following the Scots of Arden's play.[5] But its
enthusiastic reception in Glasgow derived from more than ease
of understanding. Arden comments on the dialogue achieved
with that particular theatre audience:

> [T]he production—in comparison with the Royal
> Court or Chichester—was under-budgeted, unevenly
> cast, hastily-prepared, and yet there was a vigorous
> sharing of a lively experience with the audience—it
> was of course the experience of Scotland—of a
> discontented 'region' of the United Kingdom aware
> of its historical claim to its own unique identity
> and language, and aware of a theatrical reflection of
> that claim in the play upon the stage, a reflection
> consciously projected by the actors in response to a
> realized demand for it. (*Plays: One* 6)

Indeed, Michael Coveney, in his recent history of The Citizens
Theatre, describes *Armstrong* as "probably the best 'Scottish play'
ever" (57).

While Arden would probably dispute that the "best"
Scottish play could or should be written by an Englishman, there
is much in Arden's analysis of the success of the Glasgow
production for those local audiences which explicates its failure

elsewhere. Its production values were those of "rough theatre," the category Peter Brook was to evoke in 1968 as a post-Brechtian popular theatre which "saves the day" (73). The play's use of what English audiences saw as a "foreign" language, in combination with its music and realistic costume, made *Armstrong* a popular entertainment in Glasgow. The audience was one which responded to the play as immediate and local markers, which John McGrath has suggested are central in fostering an interrogatory, engaged, and working-class theatre public (*A Good Night* 57-8). In other words, *Armstrong's Last Goodnight* employed techniques which were outside the repertoire of the mainstream British theatre but were appropriate for the particular construction of that Glasgow audience.

Those "rough" production values did not disappoint an audience at The Citizens; indeed, resistant production values coincided with resisting viewers. This pointed, in microcosm, to the hegemonic cultural practice which made *Armstrong's Last Goodnight* incomprehensible to Southern audiences and which, not very much later, was to provoke Arden to work outside the mainstream of British theatre. Recent work in gender studies has reminded us again and again of the white, male, heterosexual "norms" that have policed society's "margins." In this way, dominant cultural practice, in part enacted in the discourses of the arts and arts criticism, could control a geographic margin such as Scotland. Thus the immediacy of the play's setting and its context of political disenfranchisement enabled an enthusiastic response to the play as a subverting agent which both exposed and challenged dominant culture. The discursive practices of the arts and arts criticism reiterated the centralized power of London in the rule of the nations comprised in the United Kingdom, while the production setting for *Armstrong* stated a territorial resistance. Even in its name, The Glasgow Citizens Theatre signifies its otherness to the mainstream model and its claim to an opposing cultural space. What *Armstrong* afforded, as Arden points out, was an unusual opportunity for the audience to see themselves and their history on the stage and in a form which made contact with them rather than repeating a cultural hegemony designed to enforce their marginality.

A contemporary reading of *Armstrong's Last Goodnight* affords us not only this ability to position the text as a site of contest in British culture in the sixties, but also the opportunity to read it as an artifact which predicts future developments on the British stage. As Taylor's revisions to his original position suggest, mainstream theatre began, by the late sixties to accommodate a more Brechtian theatre practice. That this trend continued is evidenced by the commission of Howard Brenton's *Weapons of Happiness* as the first new play for National Theatre stage (1976). Moreover, the Royal Court plays of the early sixties, including Arden's work at that time, can now be re-read as the facilitators of an expansion of mainstream repertoire to include a more politically aware drama. Similarly, large scale epics such as *The Romans in Britain*, *Nicholas Nickleby*, *Maydays*, and *Pravda* owe much to Arden's bridge between Brechtian practice and the mainstream English stage. Critical histories of post-war British theatre now, concomitantly, account for Arden's early plays as significant, important, and undervalued when first produced.[6] Yet Arden's career, now spanning more than thirty years, has not been recovered with the same enthusiasm. It tends, perhaps surprisingly, to be accorded somewhat less value. Malcolm Page, for example, notes simply that "his reputation appears to have declined in the 1970s" (137)

The apparent decline in reputation points to a parallel development in British theatre of which Arden has been a significant part. This is the development of a community-based theatre which is willingly outside the scope of much critical discourse. Looking back at *Armstrong's Last Goodnight* and its success with the non-traditional audiences that saw its production in Glasgow, there almost appears to be a "putting on notice" by Arden that his writing would be directed at communities engaged in the subject action of the text rather than at the obviously narrower community of mainstream theatre. In *Stages in the Revolution*, Catherine Itzin concludes her section on Arden with the following statement: "The question was . . . whether John Arden and Margaretta D'Arcy had much choice given their political commitment except to perform their own dramas off-stage in the public political arena?" (38).

*Armstrong's Last Goodnight* can now be re-read as participating in a group of texts which forced a change in the repertoire of conventions for the English stage. Nevertheless, neither it nor these other texts changed the stage itself. Since that time, however, Arden's drama, increasingly a partnership with Margaretta D'Arcy, has sought out ways of changing the construction of theatre. That, as *Armstrong* had suggested, meant a rejection of the critically important theatres and a development of work with community-based or touring theatres, ones which had as their mandate a non-traditional spectatorship. John McGrath, in an assessment of the effects of the 1944 Education Act, writes of Arden's career:

> Due to the hierarchy of genres, legit theatre was chosen as their [the beneficiaries of the Education Act who became writers] form, rather than any new or even old form. . . . An intelligent and tradition-conscious writer like John Arden, in his early plays, was bringing fragments of an older popular tradition into the framework of bourgeois plays. . . . But as time went by, Arden—now working with D'Arcy—began to turn over the form as well. (*The Bone* 154-5)

The experience of *Armstrong's Last Goodnight* in London and Chichester worked toward an inevitable rejection—by the critics of Arden's "reputation" and, more importantly, by Arden of the mainstream stage. Yet the production in Glasgow had taught that audiences could connect with a politically imaginative theatre.

In the "medieval" staging of *Armstrong* along with the play's exuberant Scottish identity the Glasgow community audience was offered both a celebration *and* a resistance and that has become the mandate of later community theatre in Britain. Mainstream theatre, despite or perhaps because of the success of the "angry young men," remains an elitist practice speaking almost always to a privileged minority. Social(ist) agendas have been accommodated into the plays performed, but the production and reception of those texts have facilitated an adjustment rather than a rejection of the cultural markers for theatre. Writers and audiences, particularly in the seventies, assumed an existing definition of theatre (what it was and what it could be) and experimented with the possibility of Brecht's ideas within that context. As the advantages as well as the limitations of a Brechtian model became better understood, so writers concerned with a radical rewriting and deinstitution-alization of the concept of "theatre" have looked to reconceive Brechtian/socialist drama. More recently this has meant a theatre which affirms its community base and which looks to create its art with that community and as a public resistance to the rigidity of dominant social structures.

As this community-oriented theatre has looked back to the origins of English drama and the production-reception con-tract of medieval theatre, so the model of carnival, explored through the work of M. M. Bakhtin, has become a useful agent in the interrogation of epic theatre. While Bakhtin's theory was not available in English at the time of writing *Armstrong's Last Goodnight*, that play does in interesting ways "predict" its later significance for non-traditional British theatre. Arden was already testing Brecht through his interest in Ben Jonson's plays, and it was, as a piece published in *Gambit* in 1972 evidences, Jonson's most carnivalesque text that had attracted Arden's attention:

> I went to see *Bartholomew Fair* at the Edinburgh Festival [in 1950], directed by George Devine. The production was not, I recollect, particularly well received by the critics—they claimed to have been *bored* by either Jonson or Devine. . . . This surprised me. There had, it is true, been a lot of long speeches, some of them almost incomprehensible: but the overall action of the play was so clear, the setting of the fair and its habitués so precise, that it didn't seem to matter. I cannot remember the evening in much detail—the main impression I retain is one of having actually *been at a fair* (rather than having seen a play about some fictional people at a fair), and a fair full of very curious happenings and juxtapositions of persons, which emerged, as it were, from out of the crowd and then sank back into it. (*To Present* 31-2)

This testifies to the impact of these transgressive elements for John Arden, an impact which is taken up in *Armstrong's Last Goodnight* and which afforded, for the Glasgow audience at least, the same kind of experience that Arden had had with *Bartholomew Fair*.[7] Much of Arden's later drama in collaboration with Margaretta D'Arcy has worked with the ideology of carnival, and once again *Armstrong's Last Goodnight* might be seen as a threshold text which, in this case, pointed to the potential for a simultaneous community celebration and resistance.

Increasingly the model for non-traditional theatre has been not only Brecht, but Brecht and Bakhtin to produce a drama which expresses the "'whole' human being, eating, drinking, defecating and copulating, as well as thinking, praying and wielding power" (McGrath, *The Bone* 153-4).[8] Bakhtin suggested that carnival "frees human consciousness, thought, and imagination for new potentialities" (49) and it is that possibility which emerges with the political impulses of Brecht's work to inform community-based modes of production. Thus re-read, *Armstrong's Last Goodnight* stands today not as a testament to the "superiority" of Arden's earlier plays but as a testament to the limitations of production within a mainstream definition of theatre. Early critical failure, ironically, enabled new directions for Arden and D'Arcy's writing in this new context of regional communities. The result has been playwrighting which affords celebratory excess alongside radical criticism.[9] *Armstrong's Last Goodnight* is read here not to prove the quality of Arden's early work; it is read to remind us of his and D'Arcy's immense and important contribution to the possibility of other—and contesting—theatres in Britain.

# Notes

1. See the preface to *The Workhouse Donkey* for an outline of Arden's ideas for a Dionysian theatre (*Plays One* 112–13).

2. Note the first sentence of the introduction to *Serjeant Musgrave's Dance*: "This is a realistic, but not a naturalistic, play" (*Plays One* 11).

3. Itzin describes Taylor's comment as "almost hilarious" (29).

4. In the context of language, Edwin Morgan's comments are interesting. He writes: "The fairly thick Scots language . . . will prove a severe challenge to the goodwill of English audiences. (As it did, though for a different reason, to the Glasgow audience. We in Scotland have had too many Scottish historical plays; we want plays in English!)" (51) the pervasive powers of cultural imperialism are ably illustrated. Morgan's ability to "speak" for the Glasgow audience is, however, thrown into some doubt, given Arden's comments on that audience's enthusiasm for his play.

5. Note 4 above has some relevance here. Again we are reminded that Morgan's reception of the play was not undertaken primarily as a "Glasgow citizen" but depended on a different set of critical strategies—that of the arts critic.

6. George Devine made much of the fact that while *Serjeant Musgrave's Dance* later became a school curriculum text, it had in 1959 lost a lot of money for the Royal Court Theatre.

7. The relationship of *Bartholomew Fair* to Bakhtin's theory of carnival has been explored in Peter Stallybrass and Allon White's *The Poetics of Transgression* (Ithaca: Cornell University Press, 1986).

8. The word "model" is used advisedly. As McGrath suggests about Bakhtin (*The Bone Won't Break* 153) and as I have suggested about Brecht ("Brecht and the British Playwright: Stages of Action" *Gestus* 3.4 (1989), 33–41), these models are interrogated and adapted rather than applying in any prescriptive sense.

9. I borrow these descriptions from Coult and Kershaw's summary of Welfare State International in the eighties. Arden and D'Arcy's work is, of course, different in many ways from Welfare State's, but many of the philosophic objectives are, I would argue, shared.

# Works Cited

Arden, John. *Armstrong's Last Goodnight* in *Plays: One* 237–350.

————. *Plays: One*. London: Eyre Methuen, 1977.

————. *To Present the Pretence*. London: Eyre Methuen, 1977.

Arden, John, and Margaretta D'Arcy. *Awkward Corners*. London: Methuen, 1988.

Bakhtin, Mikhail. *Rabelais and His World*. Trans. Helene Iswolsky. Bloomington: Indiana University Press, 1984.

Brook, Peter. *The Empty Space*. Harmondsworth: Penguin, 1972.

Coult, Tony and Baz Kershaw. *Engineers of the Imagination: The Welfare State Handbook*. Rev. ed. London: Methuen, 1990.

Coveney, Michael. *The Citz: 25 Years of the Glasgow Citizens Theatre*. London: Nick Hern, 1990.

Gray, Frances. *John Arden*. London: Macmillan, 1982.

Itzin, Catherine. *Stages in the Revolution*. London: Methuen, 1980.

McGrath, John. *A Good Night Out*. London: Methuen, 1981.

————. *The Bone Won't Break*. London: Methuen, 1990.

Morgan, Edwin. "*Armstrong's Last Goodnight*." *Encore* 11.4 (July–August 1964): 47–51.

Page, Malcolm. *John Arden*. Boston: Twayne, 1984.

Taylor, John Russell. *Anger and After*. London: Methuen, 1962. Rev. ed. 1969.

Wardle, Irving. "Arden: Intellectual Marauder." *New Society* 9 Dec. 1965: 22–3.

# THE PERSON OF A POET: JOHN ARDEN AND MODERN VERSE DRAMA

## Kayla McKinney Wiggins

Verse is not new to the stage, yet in a modern drama still largely dependent on the tenets of realism and naturalism, verse, along with other non-naturalistic conventions, has long been a source of contention for critics and playwrights. For T. S. Eliot and Christopher Fry, founders of the most recent "revival" of verse drama, verse became a cross hampering their critical reception. For John Arden, beginning his career almost a generation later, it became a tool, an unconventional element consciously utilized to heighten the unreality of his plays. Arden, like his predecessors Eliot and Fry, believes in the power, indeed the necessity, of verse in the theatre. Unlike these earlier practitioners of verse drama, however, he does not strive for a dramatic form that will integrate verse with the other elements. In his role as a dramatic poet, Arden uses verse, like other non-naturalistic elements, to call attention to the inner workings of the plays and the role of the poet, to encourage the audience to look beyond the surface-level reality to deeper human and poetic truths.

Once an accepted dramatic convention, the language of tragedy, of lofty emotion, of the aristocracy, verse was driven from the stage by a number of factors, among them the rise of the middle class and the concurrent emphasis on art forms for the common people. The realistic approach to theatre assumed the priority of ordinary language and resulted in dramas emphasizing naturalism. Relegated to the wings by prose, verse was in constant danger of disappearing from the theatre, or of being revived by poets with only a rudimentary knowledge of the stage. Early in the twentieth century, writers like John Masefield, Thomas Hardy, and Stephen Phillips tried their hand at large-scale historical works which brought scant recognition for their efforts and an even more ephemeral recognition for the new verse drama. Other early twentieth-century writers, among them William Butler Yeats, Gordon Bottomley, and Laurence

Binyon, made no attempt to compete with the realistic drama on the commercial stage, producing instead coterie-drama based on myth or history for select audiences in Yeats's Abbey Theatre and Masefield's Boar's Hill Theatre. Not until the thirties did dramatists make a consistent effort to establish verse as a modern theatrical convention by uniting the heightened expression of poetry with issues relevant to the modern world.

Modern verse dramatists quickly realized that if verse drama was going to compete with realistic drama on the modern stage, it was going to have to focus on the concerns of its own time and place. They, like prose dramatists of the time, were not dramatizing the experiences of kings and queens, but of individuals dealing with the dilemma of existence. Playwrights like T. S. Eliot and Christopher Fry were among the first to attempt a genuine revival of verse drama and were the most vocal in addressing the critical and theatrical questions involved. They saw verse in the theatre as a way to unite poetic truth with dramatic expression, thus ending the isolation of the poet, and creating meaning in an increasingly meaningless world.

"The search for a dramatic form embodying language as a part of structure and meaning" (Gerstenberger 26-7) caused these playwrights to break with realistic prose drama as inadequate to address the needs of the modern world . They recognized that the reality represented by naturalistic prose drama was a false construct. According to Christopher Fry, seventy years of realistic drama had resulted in a false view of reality, "the domestication of the enormous miracle," and only poetry, "the language in which man explores his own amazement," could properly express the true nature of existence ("Poetry in the Theatre" 18). Viewing the union between verse and drama as a way out of isolation for both the modern poet and the individual member of the modern audience, these playwrights broke not only with realistic drama and its "shallow apprehension of life", but also with a tradition of poetry which "had withdrawn into the realms of contemplation, or of croonings over nature" (Dobrée 582-3). Verse drama could speak to an audience, could make it possible for the individual to rediscover meaning in a mysterious and darkening world through the heightened expression of poetry:

> All would be well with my life of prose if there were
> not moments when action suddenly seems like a
> flame burning on the surface of a dark sea; when
> human behaviour dies upon itself for lack of
> nourishment outside its common experience; when
> the extreme diversity of life threatens to disintegrate
> altogether unless it can be unified in some place of the
> mind. (Fry, "Why Verse?" 137)

While Eliot and Fry shared a belief that dramatic poetry could, as Eliot put it, address an area of human experience "beyond the namable, classifiable emotions and motives of our conscious life" (*Poetry* 34), they took different routes to arrive at this ideal. Fry celebrated language, "that strange, brilliant, mature achievement of the human animal," and wrote without apology in verse, weathering a storm of critical protest but reaching acceptance with the public (Fry, "Poetry in the Theatre" 18). He looked for the "Highest Common Factor . . . the point to which common speech can be heightened without losing its identity" (Fry, "Poetry and the Theatre" 8-9). Eliot, on the other hand, sought to establish a verse form which would imitate common speech, believing that verse drama had to "enter into overt competition with prose drama" (26) and that "prose should be used very sparingly indeed; that we should aim at a form of verse in which everything can be said that has to be said" (Eliot, *Poetry* 14). Both playwrights believed that verse could express the underlying areas of human experience, and that verse in the theatre could make a difference in the lives of the members of their audience, that a theatre "where the persons and events have the recognizable ring of an old truth, and yet seem to occur in a lightning spasm of discovery" was "the province of poetry" (Fry, "Poetry in the Theatre" 33). They also believed, however, that the poetry had to be an integrated part of a coherent drama, to grow naturally out of the subject matter of the play. In this belief, Fry and Eliot were working within the naturalistic tradition, attempting to create a form of verse drama that would be accepted on the realistic stage. While sharing many of their views on verse in the theatre and its impact on both playwright and audience, John Arden does not share their concern that the verse be an integrated part of the overall theatre experience.

Quite the contrary; Arden uses verse along with other "unrealistic" elements to shake the audience up, to remind them that they are watching a play, a fiction, a false construct, in order to encourage their exploration of the underlying levels of that construct and of reality itself.

Arden wasn't alone in this conception of theatre. As Raymond Williams points out in "New English Drama," many of the plays of the fifties which appeared to be a return to naturalism were really a reach beyond "the resources of ordinary conversation" through the use of music, song, and speeches (35). Verse drama of this era moved away from plays written primarily in verse and into an "area of non-illusionist theatre, with a mixture of songs, music, verse and prose" (Leeming 22). A vital part of this movement, Arden utilizes a language and staging that consciously calls attention to itself. He has said that the "artificiality of the stage is one of its most important qualities," that people should come to the "theatre *because* of the artificiality, not despite it" (Page 77). He views the conventional theatre with its proscenium arch separating the audience from the action of the play as a less than ideal setting for his sort of plays (Arden, "Building" 35). The staging notes to *The Business of Good Government* (1960), a nativity play Arden and D'Arcy wrote for a local church, suggest that if the play is played on a proscenium stage, the proscenium frame, curtains, and footlights should be removed in order to facilitate a non-naturalistic staging (Arden and D'Arcy, *Business* 7-8). Arden also suggests that the actors should be seen on stage waiting for their cues throughout the action, a technique which helps to break down the barriers "between actor and audience, creator and participant" (Gray 24). When staging their children's play *The Royal Pardon* (1966), Arden and D'Arcy broke down the barriers even more by having the audience of children sit on the floor "among the feet of the actors," thus avoiding any attempt at illusion and allowing the children to enjoy the inner workings of the play, to share as equal participants in the creative activity (Arden and D'Arcy, *Pardon* 7). This sense of audience involvement in the creative product is vital to Arden's drama. He utilizes a number of nonverbal, nonnaturalistic techniques in order to achieve it, including stylized backdrops, masks, and background music. His verbal techniques include verse and direct address to the audience which comments on the action of the play. In *The Waters of Babylon* (1957), Krank's final verse speech, delivered as he is dying, forcibly reminds the audience that they are watching a play:

> So, only a few minutes to live,
> I must see can I not give
> Some clearer conclusion to this play
> To order your lives the neatest way . . . (96)

This tendency toward self-awareness is characteristic of postmodern drama, where "a critical language holds, as it were, the mirror up to itself" (Kennedy 16). This self-awareness invites the audience to reflect, consider, and, most importantly, participate. "Faced by a world that no one can fully understand," Arden and D'Arcy "hope to capture in the artificiality of theatre something of the complexity and perplexity that they see around and within themselves" (Brown 234). The result is collaborative efforts like *The Royal Pardon, The Non-Stop Connolly Show* (1975), and *The Island of the Mighty* (1972), which use non-naturalistic staging, costumes, and acting in order to draw the audience into the action of the play, to make them aware of the technique of drama, encouraging them to look beyond appearances in both the event and the message. Even in his early, more realistic plays, Arden employed staging techniques which would "constantly remind the audience that they are in a theatre, watching a play" (Blindheim 307). Thus in *The Waters of Babylon* "he proposes the use of sliding flats or drop curtains while the actors are on stage" in order to suggest locations and "manage quick scene-changes"; he also uses direct address to "extend the scope of the stage and reduce the barrier between actor and audience" (Blindheim 307). In his staging notes for *Serjeant Musgrave's Dance* (1959), Arden says that it is a "realistic, but not a naturalistic, play" and that scenery and costumes should be stylized, the properties only those things actually required by the action yet thoroughly realistic (Arden, *Musgrave* 11). He goes on to say that if a similar rule will govern the acting and direction, "the obvious difficulties, caused by the mixture of verse, prose, and song in the play, will be considerably lessened" (11).

This mixture of verse, prose, and song indicates the verbal variety present in Arden's work. Unlike Eliot and Fry, Arden is not interested in producing plays exclusively in verse. However, he believes that when verse is utilized in a play, it should call attention to itself, it should be "nakedly verse as opposed to the surrounding prose" (Arden, "Telling" 127). In a 1961 *Encore* interview he says, "I have always been interested in different experiments with verse and prose—I think that the assumption that a play must be one or the other is a very limiting one" (Arden, "Building" 22). Like Eliot and Fry, however, he sees verse as a way to express heightened emotion in drama. While he goes on to say that heightened emotion can be conveyed in lyrical prose without warranting a change into verse, he adds the caution that "[w]riting heightened prose is a dangerous pastime" and the observation that "[p]rose that scans is not prose but verse, and it should declare itself as such" (28).

Arden uses Annie's speech on the nature of soldiers and "love" in *Serjeant Musgrave's Dance* as an example of a speech of heightened emotion in verse. The most extensive passage of spoken verse in the play, this speech is, according to Arden, a statement of the theme of the play and is spoken out of an emotional pressure which allows the character to drop naturally into verse (Arden, "Building" 29). This use of verse for moments of heightened emotion occurs repeatedly throughout Arden's work. In *The Waters of Babylon*, characters speak in verse at moments of great sexual and philosophical tension. The main character's articulation of his desperate attempt to remain detached from the world around him is in verse and is spoken, according to the stage directions, violently:

> The world is running mad in every direction.
> It is quicksilver, shattered, here, here, here, here,
> All over the floor. Go on, hurtle after it,
> Chase it, dear Paul. But I choose to follow
> Only such fragments as I can easily catch,
> I catch them, I keep them such time as I choose,
> Then roll them away down and follow another.
> Is that philosophy? It is a reason, anyway . . . (81)

In *The Workhouse Donkey* (1963), the passages of heightened emotion come at moments of crisis in the lives of the characters like this terse verse in response to a moment of decision by the chief constable, Feng:

> Violence, damage . . . done already, done,
> All violence perpetrated, broken down
> In violence, brickwork cracked and fallen, damage,
> Responsibility . . . whose? (227)

Or the biblical echoes of another speech by the same character:

> I say . . . to another "come" and he cometh, and to my
>                servant "do this" and he doeth it . . .
> Not difficult to prevail but difficult indeed
> To live and hold that prevalence, yet live
> A social and communicating creature. (179-80)

In *Armstrong's Last Goodnight* (1964) the trauma of death and the triumph of sexuality warrant passages of verse when Meg laments the death of her lover and when the lovely courtier celebrates her ability to woo Armstrong from his speech defect (265-6; 308). In *The Royal Pardon*, verse is used to describe the young soldier's plight as a criminal escaping the law, as well as the constable's struggle to capture him and the dilemma of the Prince and Princess, destined to marry but forbidden to love:

> I intend to continue as I swore that I would start:
> I must not fall in love. Neither must you.
> Nevertheless one flesh must be made of our two
> (By the blessing of the Church): and by the blessing of
>                good luck
> Yours and no-one else's is the fruit that I must pluck. (73)

However, the most compelling passage of verse in response to intense emotion in this play comments, as in *Serjeant Musgrave's Dance*, on soldiers and war:

> And when we met we fought till none could stand.
> Our bodies now lie in a foreign land,
> Defeated, they have said. But we know better:
> We obeyed our general's orders to the letter.
> If blame there is to be—indeed we did not win—
> But blame those ministers, who sitting warm at home

Sent us across the seas, unfed, unclothed, alone,
To do our duty the best that we could.
We did it, sir, by pouring out our blood. (53)

Although he has said he uses prose to convey plot and character relationships and verse to comment on them, Arden sometimes uses verse to do the work of prose (Arden, "Building" 28). Verse passages help to establish characterization in *Serjeant Musgrave's Dance*, function as narrative bridges between episodes in *Left-Handed Liberty* (1965), and provide background information in *The Waters of Babylon*. However, these passages are more than simple exposition. They generally warrant verse because they still come at moments of tension and heightened emotion, as in this passage bridging scenes of conflict in *Left-Handed Liberty*:

Storm breaks in among the perfect circles,
Every day a puff of wind or a rumble of thunder
Declares some vain attempt to declare—what?
Very busy very busy very busy! (24)

*Soldier, Soldier* (1960) stands as something as a special case in the canon of Arden's earlier plays because it utilizes more spoken verse than any of the other works. Written for television, *Soldier, Soldier* was, according to Arden, an experiment to see if verse would work on the small screen. Arden felt that the experiment failed when he allowed himself "to fall into a more lyrical mood" because the lofty diction didn't work in a play intended to be a "low-life comedy" (Arden, *Soldier* 9-10). The story of a soldier who swindles an unsuspecting family and seduces a young wife, the play stands as an interesting experiment and, to an extent, an inversion of Arden's earlier use of verse for moments of heightened expression. While the other characters don't speak verse until moments of tension, the soldier talks verse virtually throughout the play, lapsing into prose at moments of decision.

Verse is used in a variety of other capacities in Arden and D'Arcy's plays. In keeping with the ancient dramatic tradition of verse in tragedy, the plays-within-a-play of their *The Royal Pardon* are in verse. In keeping with Arden's desire to present a melodrama in the traditional sense of a play accompanied throughout by music, *The Workhouse Donkey* utilizes a variety of song, dance, and verse routines reminiscent of the music hall as the characters stop to sing and dance and to deliver verse lines to the accompanying music (112). In the language and staging of *The Non-Stop Connolly Show* and *The Island of the Mighty*, Arden and D'Arcy were greatly influenced by Indian folk drama, which utilizes:

> extreme formality mixed with unexpectedly coarse realism; highly decorative costumes, make-up and/or masks with small relation to everyday naturalism; the regular use of music and dance as part of the dramatic structure; strongly rhythmical verse-narrative to link passages of action. (*To Present* 103)

The result in the case of *The Non-Stop Connolly Show*, a lengthy, ambitious theatrical event which attempts to dramatize the life and death of Irish socialist James Connolly, is a verse and prose drama utilizing iambic verse and what Arden calls "a brand of informal 'sprung-rhythm' verse with rhyme, assonance and alliteration" which was "intended as a vehicle for rapid vernacular speech" to quickly summarize long periods of historical fact (*To Present* 130). The result is a verse which succeeds at summarizing information about Connolly's philosophies and experiences but which is more effective and compelling when dealing with his private life and emotions.

Ultimately, Arden seems more at home at that bedrock level of emotion and narrative, of poetic truth, which is a component he identifies in the English ballad. Arden's early career was heavily influenced by the English ballad tradition. In "Telling a True Tale," he comments that the playwright's function is to "use the material of the contemporary world and present it on the public stage" (125). As an English writer for an English audience, he has been concerned, he says, with "the problem of translating the concrete life of today into terms of poetry that shall at the one time both illustrate that life and set it within the historical and legendary tradition of our culture" (125). He sees the answer to this endeavor in the ballad, the "bedrock of English poetry" (125). This interest in the ballad form helps to explain both the development of Arden's themes and the ambiguity in many of his early plays. According to Arden, grounding in the ballad tradition allows a writer to explore a wide variety of themes with the weight and impact of "traditional poetic truths" but not pat answers (128). The use of the ballad tradition forces audiences to draw their own conclusions because ballads themselves don't furnish answers to human dilemmas; they provide information and truths:

> If the poet intends us to make a judgement on his characters, this will be implied by the whole turn of the story, not by intellectualized comments as it proceeds. The tale stands and it exists in its own right. If the poet is a true one, then the tale will be true too. (129)

Ballads, both spoken and sung, play a vital role in a number of Arden plays, largely as commentary on love and loss. From Meg's lament on the death of her lover in *Armstrong's Last Goodnight:*

> John the Armstrang is to the hunten gaen
> Wi' his braid sword at his side
> And there he did meet with a nakit man
> Alane on the green hillside. (291)

to Mary's song of lust and betrayal in *Soldier, Soldier* and Mrs. Hitchcock's resigned commentary on the betrayal of men in *Serjeant Musgrave's Dance*, the women of the plays reveal a world-weary view of the traditional material of the ballads, the necessity of love, the inevitability of betrayal:

> The yellow-haired boy lay in my bed
> A-kissing me up from me toes to me head.
> But when my apron it did grow too short
> He thought it good time to leave his sport. (*Musgrave* 31)

In his preface to *Plays: One*, Arden comments that, when writing his scripts, he thinks of himself as preparing "a story which would be told to the audience" through the actors (5). Like the poets of the ballads, he strives to prepare a true tale which the actors can present and the audience can interpret. Yet balladry in its truest form creates truth out of known facts, suppositions, and that deeper poetic consciousness which is the basis of the form. In the interest of "truth" balladry doesn't hesitate to orchestrate facts. This tradition applies to Arden's plays as well. *Armstrong's Last Goodnight*, although based on fact, takes liberties with history, as Arden points out in his introduction (238-9). The sung balladry of *The Waters of Babylon* creates fact out of fiction. The protagonist of the play, Sigismanfred Krankiewicz, was a participant in the Holocaust as a guard in a German concentration camp. Yet his song of his past implies that he was a prisoner in the camp, inspiring a sympathy among the other characters and the audience that is never completely destroyed despite the eventual revelation of his amoral behavior and the "truth" of his past. Like many of the heroes of the traditional ballads, Krank is furnished a heroic status in fiction that he does not deserve in fact. The ballad may be a true tale, but it is a truth colored by popular opinion and community acceptance.

Ultimately, of course, it is the poet who tells the tale however it is changed by public repetition or, in the case of the verse dramatists, interpreted by an audience. The result of this telling of the tale in *The Island of the Mighty* is a verse which is more integrated and less self-conscious. This is due in part to the work's dependence on Celtic legend and its legendary setting as well as to its conscious investigation of the theme of the poet in society. This theme was not entirely new for Arden and D'Arcy. Their work shows a prior history of the awareness of the importance of language, of the power of poetry, and a consistent questioning about the contribution of the writer to the exploration and excavation of contemporary society. The person of the poet figures prominently in *Armstrong's Last Goodnight*, where the poet David Lindsay is the herald of the king. The power of language to shape and change society is explored in *The Non-Stop Connolly Show* when James Connolly recognizes that without words, ideas can never be realized, and that there is a force inherent in the spoken and printed word (I: 48). The same idea carries over to *The Island of the Mighty*, a play exploring the disintegration of Arthur's British kingdom. The play contrasts the freedom and mysticism of the Celtic way of life with the precision and formality of Arthur's Roman heritage. As Frances Gray points out, the theme explored throughout the work is "the relationship of the poet to society" (141), and it is the poets who are expected "to make political sense" of the warfare and bloodshed around them (135).

The Island of the Mighty is a play in three parts chronicling the downfall of Arthur, Roman institutions, and poetry as it was conceived in Roman terms. Two themes run throughout the work: the failure of rebirth through the Year King Ritual and the failure of poetry to make a difference in society. The first part deals with the conflict between the barbaric Celtic brothers Balin and Balan. Fleeing from the destruction of their village by English warriors, the brothers take different paths in their search for survival. Balan chooses to remain independent and becomes the king of a tribe of Picts as a result of defeating the old king in the Pictish version of the Year King Ritual, an ancient fertility rite promising yearly rebirth and renewal. At the price of being lamed, victory affords him the "love" of the Princess of the tribe for one year, until the relentless cycle of birth, renewal, and death demands a new victor and victim. Meanwhile, his brother goes to Arthur's court to become a Roman soldier, only to destroy his chances by hot-headedly killing the Priestess of the Pictish tribe who has come there under Arthur's protection. Ultimately the two brothers end by killing each other in a premature Year King Ritual that leaves the Picts with no king and no choice but to become Christian.

The poets in this first section of the play function primarily as bards. They have the responsibility of praising the heroes and recording the failures and triumphs of the warriors. They also serve in religious capacities, however. The Pictish poet is the voice of the Priestess, the Roman poets are ostensibly Christian, and the Celtic poets pass down the names of the gods. There is a power in poetry. The person of a Chief Poet is sacred and poetry is his armour. Merlin does not wield magic in defense of Arthur's kingdom, he wields advice and poetry. As he tells the hot-headed Balin, "I could turn you into a pillar of salt with one four-line stanza" (42). However, poets are by no means uncorrupt in Arthur's disintegrating world. They take more pleasure in women than in poetry, more in the physical than in the spiritual. As the Bondwoman laments:

> Chief Poet Taliesin did with me what he wanted.
> I might well have been contented
> Had he now and then made use
> Of my beauty for his verse.
> But he did not. I was for him
> His recreation and that was the end.
> Sometimes he would serve me up
> Like bread-and-cheese to a learned friend. (75)

In the end, the Chief Poets even renounce their role as bards. Under the shadow of the coming war with the English, Taliesin declares Arthur mad and exits, while Merlin regrets the loss of life, truth, and poetic integrity that the coming campaign will cost him and leaves the Pictish poet to finish the tale of Balin and Balan.

Part Two of *The Island of the Mighty* revolves around another version of the Year King Ritual, this time based on the legend of Bran and Branwen, an ancient Celtic god and goddess who protect the British Isles from invasion. It also develops more fully the characters of the three poets whose lives are the subject of the play: Taliesin, Strathclyde's Chief Poet; Merlin, Arthur's Chief Poet; and Aneurin, Gododdin's poet. Taliesin emerges as a poet who still believes in the power of his profession, Merlin as a troubled man who presents the appearance of a poet but who no longer believes, and Aneurin as a young poet with no pretensions who believes more in the old ways than the Roman ways and in the power of verse more as a part of life than as a part of politics. This section of the play opens with a College of Bards which has been convened to adjudicate the claim of Aneurin to be a Chief Poet. Required to produce an ode in a heroic metre on the legend of Bran, he recites instead a bawdy ballad about Bran's measures to guarantee the fidelity of his wife after his death. Questioned by a scandalized Merlin, Aneurin admits that the Prince of Gododdin uses him to write letters and add up money, not compose verse (105). Gododdin wants Aneurin to become a Chief Poet for the prestige it will afford his kingdom, but the young poet has a more basic view of the value of poetry. To him, it is important that people hear his verses. When Merlin reveals that one of Aneurin's songs has become part of popular lore, the younger poet is thrilled. To Merlin's

scoffing comment that the man who sang it had never heard
Aneurin's name, Aneurin replies, "Not important. Aha, he had
heard my song!" (106).

In developing the conflict between the ancient Celtic
beliefs and the Roman authority, Arden is developing the
conflict between superstition and religion, faith and practicality.
Arthur has for twenty years made a mockery of the ancient
Celtic belief that the skull of Bran protects Britain from invasion
because, unknown to his men, he dug up the skull and nailed it
to his standard. Britain is protected, according to Arthur, not by
Celtic superstition but by Roman might of arms (108). In the end,
this superiority fails, however, when Arthur's new queen,
Gwenhwyvar, discovers that she is the reincarnation of the
goddess Branwen and chooses Arthur's nephew/son Medraut as
the reincarnation of Bran. In the ensuing warfare between
Medraut's Celtic troops and Arthur's Romans, both Arthur and
Medraut are killed and Merlin is driven mad. Before his death,
Arthur reveals that he, too, was chosen by a Daughter of
Branwen, his own sister, the mother of Medraut. He, too, is the
lamed Year King whose reign, after twenty years, is at an end.
Celtic and Roman, the old music and the new, have destroyed
each other and left their world to the mercy of the invading
English.

The power of the poets breaks down along with the
disintegration of the society. Merlin can no longer think of a
reason to make a poem and all that is left is "Dead alliteration,
evaporated rhymes / That have hung in the cold air for a very
long time" (145). In the end, there are no more truths to hold on
to. Despite the power of words and the endurance of poetry,
legends can't be trusted and poets break faith. All that remains
constant is the memory of the people and the inevitability of the
cycle of death and rebirth. Only Aneurin's kind of poetry is still
possible, poetry built on the bedrock of popular culture. Even as
things fall apart, Aneurin is still there making his verse:

> I have been called
> A vagabond and worse
> By those who themselves destroy
> The poetry that they profess.

> I am still here none the less
> I am here: and I make my verse. (157)

And, as Morgan points out to him, it does not matter what he means by the verse, what matters is what it says and how the people interpret it (149). In applying a popular culture version of reader-response theory to the ancient bards, Arden and D'Arcy are holding the critical mirror up to the play and commenting on their own roles as poets.

Part Three of *The Island of the Mighty* flashes back to recount the events leading up to Merlin's madness. According to Gwenddydd, Merlin's estranged wife, he spent the eve of the battle questioning his own role as poet, aware that it was the function of a poet to promote peace and yet determined that Arthur should win and maintain Christianity (176). Impotent to act either to inspire Arthur or to deter him, Merlin can only rage against his own fate and then stand amazed when Taliesin, more sure of the validity of the poet, uses an ancient chant to disarm the combatants. Merlin bitterly scoffs at Taliesin's belief—"he thinks he can *forbid* the battle! He does believe that in this day and age there are warriors in Britain who will veritably respect the Authority of a Poet?"—and then stands amazed at the results: "In complete silence they stand still . . . and they listen to what he says . . . ?" (179). In his anger that Taliesin has interfered with Arthur's plans, and his jealousy that the other poet has done what he, the great Merlin could not, he defies the ancient tradition and destroys the last vestige of his honor as a poet; he lays hands on another Chief Poet, attempting to kill Taliesin with a spear. In retaliation, the older poet puts a curse on Merlin that he will run naked for the rest of his life, like a wild bird, and die at the point of a spear (180-1).

The battle over, Britain lost, the survivors see their only hope in the recovery of Merlin, Arthur's voice, the representative of good fortune, the poet necessary to inspire warriors to fight (184). They fail to see, as the other poets do, that fortune and God have forsaken them, or even that Merlin has been moving away from his poetry, away from his belief, for years:

> ANEURIN.
> You may think it took him but a moment

> To put out his hand and drive that spear.
> Great error. He had been in the doing of it
> Year after year after year after year—
> Driving his barb, you see, into his wife
> And into himself and into his poetry— (186)

In the end, Aneurin is forced to recover Merlin. Learning from Gwenddydd that Merlin has not always been a poet of formality, that he had once known the old songs, too, he leads the deranged old man back to the fortress not with promise of food or safety for Gwenddydd, but with poetry. In the wilderness, he watches Merlin waging a lonely battle to occupy a tree:

> Who could believe that a naked man
> Would fight and fight until he won
> His furious battle all alone
> Against the sword-blades of the naked thorn? (198)

When Merlin finally wins, he and Aneurin both realize how far he has come from the poet standing apart commenting on the action to the individual struggling alone to survive. They recite in unison:

> Here is my tree and I have conquered it
> It draws blood where I clutch it and blood where I sit.
> I used to stand aside and watch the battles from afar—
> Now I take part in them, I am both trooper and great
>     general,
> Proud wielder of Imperium, sole director of the war!
> (199)

Poetry and magic almost save Merlin, with the old sorceress, Morgan, completing Aneurin's work and restoring the poet's tenuous grip on reality. At the critical moment of recovery, however, modern science intrudes in the form of a doctor who reminds Merlin that he tried to kill Taliesin, reminding him also that Merlin only appeared to be a Chief Poet and that none of it was real (221). He runs mad in the woods again, eventually to die as Taliesin had prophesied, speared by a jealous husband when a woman, in Christian kindness and encouraged by a warrior turned priest, lures him back to civilization. He dies according to the curse, but not before he has found the basis of poetry again, the joy of sharing it with another, as he recites lines to the woman in mutual pleasure. We are left with the poet Aneurin who, with his conscious lack of poetic and politic formality, has been the groping voice of truth all along. When he first brought Merlin back to the champions desperate for his advice, Aneurin told them that a poet only wants to make the music:

> He has been used by far too many far too long.
> He desired to be a poet: he desired to make a song.
> He desired to make it for himself alone
> And for a girl, could he find one to love. (213)

However, at Merlin's death, he learns a greater truth. As Merlin plays out the last scene of his life, Aneurin addresses the audience from the corner of the stage, telling them that what he had said about the loneliness of the poet is not true, that "The poet without the people is nothing" (232).

Like that of *The Non-Stop Connolly Show,* the staging of *The Island of the Mighty* was influenced by Indian folk plays. The work is nonnaturalistic, utilizing a platform staging area with eight backdrops to represent various locales and events. The actors wait to act their parts in full view of the audience, at times addressing the audience directly, and the script makes extensive use of music, verse, chant, and song. Yet these elements seem more integrated than in Arden's and D'Arcy's earlier work, part of an organic whole, the recounting of legendary events about the death and rebirth of a society. It is a fitting subject for a bardic cycle and, consequently, the poetry seems integrated in a way that it hasn't in their work to this point. However, they have in no way abandoned his non-naturalistic aims for theatre; they have only rendered them more subtle. This play, even more than the others, comments on itself. The subject of this play is not the heroic and legendary deeds common to bardic poetry; it is poetry itself and the role of the poet in society. Merlin is not a magician making politics and policy through magic; he is a poet, ordering the world and failing to order it through poetry. In exploring the validity and nature of the poet, a subject definitely not suited to traditional bardic verse, the play holds a mirror up to its own action, asking questions about the validity of verse drama itself and refusing to give any clear answers.

In her preface to *The Island of the Mighty*, Margaretta D'Arcy mentions George Steiner's criticism of Arden for wasting his valuable talents on mythological subjects when he could be dealing with important contemporary themes and Arden's response that the Arthurian cycle was of "considerable contemporary relevance" (18). D'Arcy identifies the relevance of the finished script as an exploration of "the 'concrete phenomena' of eruptive social change" (20). While this is one of the prevalent themes of the work, equally important is its comment on the necessity of human communication, of understanding those underlying universal truths binding all cultures together. This kind of exploration, this sense of having something vital to say to a struggling world, this desire to "help us to see ourselves and the world freshly" has long been a quality of dramatic poets (Fry, "Poetry in the Theatre" 19). Poetry reaches beyond the surface level of reality to underlying meanings. In 1949, T. S. Eliot wrote that it was the "privilege of dramatic poetry to show us several planes of reality at once" (Eliot, "Aims" 16). In 1955, Christopher Fry added,

> It is no good asking poetry to tell us what it says; it simply is what it says. In the theatre it must have a direct surface meaning, an immediate impact of sense, but half its work should be going on below that meaning, drawing the ear, consciously or unconsciously, into a certain experience of being. ("Why Verse?" 166)

Six years later, Arden agreed: "If we are going to say anything in our plays over and above the surface meaning of the words, we can and must do it in verse" (Page 80). There is room in the theatre for verse. It is not always an easy form, but few would argue that drama which is intended to make a difference in the world, to communicate something about reality and the underlying levels of reality, ought to be easy. When we want basic facts, we read a how-to manual. When we want to explore the basic truths of human experience in a way that forces us to feel, to share, to think, we turn to Arden's brand of verse drama, a form of theatre which challenges all the assumptions of language, reality, and experience. In the person of the poet, we may not find easy answers, but we will find challenging questions.

## Works Cited

Arden, John. *Armstrong's Last Goodnight. Plays: One*. New York: Grove Press, 1977. 237–352.

———. "Building the Play." Interview. *Encore* 8.4 (July–Aug. 1961): 22–41.

———. *Left-Handed Liberty: A Play About Magna Carta*. New York: Grove Press, 1965.

———. Preface. *Plays: One*. By Arden. New York: Grove Press, 1977. 5–8.

———. *Serjeant Musgrave's Dance. Plays: One*. New York: Grove Press, 1977. 11–110.

———. *Soldier, Soldier and Other Plays*. London: Methuen, 1967.

———. "Telling a True Tale." *The Encore Reader*. Ed. Charles Marowitz, Tom Milne, and Owen Hale. London: Methuen, 1965. 125–9.

———. *To Present the Pretence*. London: Methuen, 1977.

———. *The Waters of Babylon. Three Plays*. New York: Grove Press, 1961. 7–97.

———. *The Workhouse Donkey. Plays: One*. New York: Grove Press, 1977. 111–236.

Arden, John, and Margaretta D'Arcy. *The Business of Good Government*. London: Methuen, 1975.

———. *The Island of the Mighty: A Play on a Traditional British Theme in Three Parts*. London: Methuen, 1974.

———. *The Royal Pardon or the Soldier who Became an Actor*. London: Methuen, 1967.

Blindheim, Joan Tindale. "John Arden's Use of the Stage." *Modern Drama* 11 (1968): 306–16.

Brown, John Russell. *Theatre Language*. London: Allen Lane, 1972.

D'Arcy, Margaretta. Preface. *The Island of the Mighty: A Play on a Traditional British Theme in Three Parts*. London: Methuen, 1974. 17–21.

D'Arcy, Margaretta, and John Arden. *The Non-Stop Connolly Show: A Dramatic Cycle of Continuous Struggle in Six Parts.* 1977. London: Methuen, 1986.

Dobrée, Bonamy. "Poetic Drama in England Today." *The Southern Review* 4 (1939): 581–99.

Eliot, T. S. "The Aims of Poetic Drama." *Adam International Review* 200 (1949): 10–16.

———. *Poetry and Drama.* London: Faber and Faber, 1951.

Fry, Christopher. "Poetry and the Theatre." *Adam International Review* 19 (1951): 2–10.

———. "Poetry in the Theatre." *The Saturday Review* 21 March 1953: 18+.

———. "Why Verse?" *Vogue* 1 Mar. 1955: 136+.

Gray, Frances. *John Arden.* New York: Grove Press, 1983.

Gerstenberger, Donna. "Perspectives of Modern Verse Drama." *Modern Drama* 3 (1960): 24–9.

Kennedy, Andrew K. *Six Dramatists in Search of a Language.* London: Cambridge University Press, 1975.

Leeming, Glenda. *Poetic Drama.* New York: St. Martin's, 1989.

Page, Malcolm. *Arden on File.* London: Methuen, 1985.

Williams, Raymond. "New English Drama." *Modern British Dramatists.: A Collection of Critical Essays.* Ed: John Russell Brown. Englewood Cliffs: Prentice Hall, 1968. 26–37.

# JAMES CONNOLLY: A FIT STORY FOR THE PLAYWRIGHT OF *SERJEANT MUSGRAVE'S DANCE*

## Tramble T. Turner

At the conclusion of his 1968 study of John Arden, Ronald Hayman speculated that the "only prediction it's safe to make about his future development is that it will be fascinating to watch." The uncertainty resulted, in Hayman's view, from the basis of Arden's career on a dual inheritance of traditionalism and experimentation: "[a]lthough he's the most traditional of all our playwrights, in the sense of being the one who is most deeply and most profitably in touch with literary and dramatic tradition, English and foreign, he also gives himself more freedom than anyone else, both from theatrical convention and from the precedent of his own writing" (76). Arden's plays since that prediction, and most especially the bold experiment of the six-part cycle *The Non-Stop Connolly Show* (1977-78), co-authored with Margaretta D'Arcy have renewed a controversy about his merits, a controversy much like that which greeted his first success, *Serjeant Musgrave's Dance* (1959).

Indeed, comments Arden made in responding to a 1964 obituary on Sean O'Casey eerily anticipate the issues raised by the critics most hostile to Arden's own later experiments. In putting forward the plea that O'Casey's later plays are by no means as "rancorous and rhetorically inflated'" as claimed in the obituary, Arden argued that "future judgements of O'Casey's work should be based upon the understanding that his later writing was continuously experimental in form, theme and vocabulary" (*To Present* 24). Content, technique, and artistic collaboration are all elements that have created controversy about Arden's later work. For example, Henry I. Schvey lamented that "[i]n Margaretta D'Arcy and John Arden's latest play, *The Non-Stop Connolly Show* (and it is significant that for the first time their names are reversed on the title-page), the Ardens continue the direction of using the theatre as a platform for their stand on the Irish question in particular, and on the necessity for Marxist revolution in general" (64). The collaborative effort of *The Hero Rises Up* (1968; first performed) was greeted with an even harsher response in the pages of *Modern Drama*: "[t]he coalition was not successful, for the play's heart was only half-heart, and the head was empty" (Clinton 56). For those who approach the Connolly cycle through Schvey's perspective, the principal failure is "the play's failed compromise between art and political propaganda" (65-6). A primary issue in Schvey's argument is the claim that through "the creation of Socialist Hero who is essentially perfect, Arden has completely repudiated his belief in the complex, flawed heroes who populate his earlier plays" (66). However, just as critical attitudes shifted toward the unconventional approach to character and staging in *Serjeant Musgrave's Dance*, the more recent play cycle also provides a firm basis for a shift from the critical perspective just cited, or rather for a furthering of the critical praise Albert Hunt has offered on the six play cycle.

The *Non-Stop Connolly Show* pivots, for dramatic interest, on the ambiguity of audience response to James Connolly, to other central characters, and to the use of type figures in contrast with more developed characters. By examining key scenes from the six-play sequence, the meaning of Arden's own assessment, that "'the whole story of Connolly was kind of inside-out version of my invented Black Jack Musgrave'" (*To Present* 155; qtd. in Schvey 66) can be seen in an alternative light. Examining evidence that Musgrave and Connolly are both complex, flawed heroes can result in a comparison that shows a continuity of concerns.

Such continuity would not be without precedent in Arden's writing. His 1975 lecture published as "Playwrights and Play-Writers" creates a dramatist's-eye analysis of Shakespeare's *Henry V*: "Shakespeare's technique in this play will by now have become clear. He regularly sets up a certain atmosphere of noble enterprise by means of evocative blank verse speeches, and without comment, deflates it through an alternation of scenes showing something very near the opposite" (*To Present* 202). Arden renewed his concern with the Bard's ambiguity in his

1988 historical novel, *Books of Bale*. In that fictionalized account of Elizabethan dramatists, the characters debate the merits of "a Henry-the-Fifth play" and therein reformulate Arden's points.

> That's what's wrong with Willy Shake-scene. He devises these clever tricks, and he does it so insidiously, some of the players will e'en accept it. Yes, *he* would be capable of bringing bewildered conscript ruffians, or Irish mercenaries even, into the battles of France, and killing the king's glory with their words, and they would not be clowns neither. Yet somehow the king's role would still seem to remain heroical. He divides his play this way and that till no-one knows what they mean. I believe he destroys our trade: we are at root but simple folk and our public is simple too. Good and bad, black and white, your father would have known. (396)

Despite such evidence of Arden's vivid interest in the ability to create both a critical perspective upon and a heroic response to a "hero" such as Henry V, D'Arcy and Arden's Connolly has been oversimplified by approving critics, as well as by those more hostile to their experiments. Malcolm Page, for instance, has written that "the Ardens" intended to present Connolly as "a hero without any tragic flaw" (123) but that their reliance on "detail risks swamping the portrait of Connolly as a true hero" (131). Such claims draw attention away from the center of dramatic conflict in the play, tensions within the Labour movement, while fostering expectations of a type of hero Arden has clearly identified as inappropriate to Socialist drama, or indeed to any challenging play. Following through on his assumptions, Page concludes that "some sections (particularly part 4 and the first half of part 5) are flat and relentlessly documentary" (128).

However, in the essay cited by Page, "A Socialist Hero on the Stage," the playwrights Arden and D'Arcy provide clear indications of how their hero is not presented as flawless. The relevance of the ambiguity of response to Shakespeare's "heroic" Henry V that Arden has argued for so consistently to his own "Socialist Hero" may be inferred from the authors' claim that "[t]here is no doubt that the events of Easter 1916 are as

immediately suited to the requirements of the stage as, say, the
Battle of Agincourt or the Siege of Troy" (*To Present* 96). The
serious questions raised about the latter two battles in the list
could suggest some irony; a more direct comparison of the
heroes can be established by showing that the Connolly cycle
evokes a heroic response at the end while nevertheless calling
into question the motivation and consistency of the title
character in the six plays.

Nor are critical pronouncements on the nature of
Connolly as hero the only issue that merits renewed attention.
The exploration of paradoxes, the standard by which Schvey
judges the "early" Arden successful and the "later" Arden as
lacking, remains at issue in the Connolly cycle, as may be
inferred from D'Arcy and Arden's definition of "modern
political theatre," a definition rarely quoted, as a theatre "where
ideologies must be explored and sophisticated economic
contradictions exposed" (*To Present* 101). Other comments in that
essay point toward some of the bases for acknowledging the
contradictory nature of the "hero" and the action of the play
cycle. By first looking at those passages and by relating them to
the contemporary responses to *Serjeant Musgrave's Dance*, an
alternative analysis of the Connolly cycle emerges.

Significantly the Arden and D'Arcy essay indicates that
the primary conflict lies elsewhere than in what has been
identified as being "their principal point of the necessity for a
socialist revolution. Thus capitalism is represented by a 'demon
king,' Mr. Grabitall, a personification of evil . . . [A]s Connolly's
adversaries change, the personification of capitalist evil takes on
a new name" (Schvey 66). The playwrights, on the other hand,
write of how they "found out very quickly that the essential
Conflict of the fable, which ostensibly was that between Capital
and Labour, seemed often lost in the tributary struggle between
opposed factions of the latter: and that this struggle in itself
could time and again be summarised as the Fight between
Revolution and Reform—an archetypal *agon* for the dramatist,
comparable to such emblematic battles as *Carnival v. Lent, Sacred
v. Profane Love, Idleness v. Industry*" (*To Present* 98). While
emphasizing the importance of the distinction between what is
"ostensibly" the conflict and what is presented as the conflict

within Labour might seem a foregrounding the "tributary struggle," the contents of the plays and of the essay indicate the validity of such an approach. Though the essay identifies *"Capital v. Labour"* as "the overall context for the secondary conflicts" (98), a limiting focus, the essay also establishes Connolly's flaws within the perspective of international labour. For the playwrights "the minutiae of party-caucus-meetings and inter-union bickerings . . . these small-scale events would have to be treated as though they were dynastic quarrels of Renaissance princes in Jocobean [sic] tragedy" (98).

D'Arcy and Arden indicate a potential conflict for their title character when, in writing of Sean O'Casey, "an international Socialist," they note that historically O'Casey "regarded Connolly as a man who had mistakenly replaced the red flag by the green and thereby betrayed the true cause of the workers" (117). A more explicit comment on how Connolly's stance is elevated and yet is called into question invokes O'Casey's role as a dramatist, social activist, and critic of the Rising: "As readers of history and students of modern politics, we believed that he [Connolly] had no choice but to take part in the Rising: as dramatists we were aware that his decision was questioned then (by O'Casey, for instance) and has frequently been questioned since" (127). The playwrights' willingness to explore the basis for such questioning, their use of a dream sequence about "Prohibitions" that Connolly violates, and the challenges to Connolly's stance raised through such characters as O'Casey and Rosa Luxemburg are all grounds for arguing that the play cycle involves a complex achievement.

By looking back to controversies surrounding Arden's first major success, *Serjeant Musgrave's Dance*, we may gain perspective on the Connolly cycle. Indeed as critical discussions still focus on that 1959 play, it seems a necessary starting point. (MLA bibliographies for the eighties almost invariably list either no entries on Arden or the publication of a new analysis of *Serjeant Musgrave's Dance*.)

Albert Hunt's 1974 study of Arden's work (and of Arden's collaborative productions with Margaretta D'Arcy) provides an excellent introduction to the history of Arden criticism to that point. Indeed, his treatment of *Serjeant*

*Musgrave's Dance* identifies key critical issues of Arden and D'Arcy's more recent work. Hunt notes that the play that "has been canonized by being made a part of the English Literature 'A' level syllabus" (52) was not always considered a success: "[w]hen the play was first produced, it was greeted with critical abuse" (53). More significantly, Hunt identifies audience expectations about the central character as the source of such hostility: "among the expectations is included an ability to identify oneself with the man who appears to be the hero: Musgrave himself" (55). This observation seems particularly important when analyzing Arden and D'Arcy's later plays, for it establishes two key issues—the concept of the hero and the issue of the degree to which the audience is encouraged to identify with the characters.

Another general basis for examining the ongoing critical debate about the latter plays has been suggested in Frances Gray's comment that "Arden is now attacked chiefly for the matter rather than the manner of his plays; throughout the 70s he has been moving towards a clearly defined political position and his newer work, whether written in collaboration with Margaretta D'Arcy or alone, expresses this position. The widespread critical dismay this has caused has a slightly farcical air, since many of the attacks begin by paying tribute to the early plays that were so relentlessly derogated in the 50s" (15). Lest Gray's claim seem unsupported, an examination of specifics from criticism of the *Musgrave* play and of the *Connolly* cycle may be appropriate. Harold Hobson's 25 October 1959 *Sunday Times* review, cited by Gray, gives a sense of the strength of the criticisms (and the assumptions upon which they were based): "another frightful ordeal. It is time someone reminded our advanced dramatists that the principal function of the theatre is to give pleasure. . . . It is the duty of the theatre, not to make men better, but to render them harmlessly happy" (4). Ronald Hayman's more extensive critical commentary raised issues of structure and characterization: "Nothing at this stage could save the play because the confusion is right in the heart of it. It's a play in which Arden couldn't afford to ignore individuality and motivations in the way that he does. The areas within which the writing succeeds and the areas of failure can be clearly defined.

It succeeds where the emphasis is on the group or on the social, political or economic background. It fails when individuals step into the foreground" (28). Another critic has lamented that whereas in the "early plays the conflict was left unresolved, and the audiences left the theatre discontented with received beliefs and forced to question themselves," the later works show a playwright "who has increasingly grown ashamed of his own intellect" (Schvey 68). A similar point has been raised in the claim that audiences for the later plays "do not see the hovering neutrality of the early plays, but find instead a vigorous directness in which a blatantly stated political point is developed through the utilization of superficial stylistic elements from Brecht's Epic Theatre—elements appropriated on a scale unparalleled in Arden's earlier works. Songs and placards giving plot information proliferate, as do expository speeches directed to the audience" (Clinton 55). Such approaches hold only if the playwright can be shown to have simplified his materials and to settle for "simple solutions in life."

Yet in claiming that "little or no mention is made of Connolly's repeated belief 'that one could be a Marxist in politics and a Catholic in religion without any question of conflict'" in order not to "tarnish his image as a 'Socialist Hero'" (66), Schvey overlooks an example of the paradoxes that D'Arcy and Arden build into their play cycle. An analysis of the six plays that begins with the particular details of the Catholic material can be developed based on the model of Albert Hunt's comments on the play that proceeded it, *The Ballygombeen Bequest* (1972): "if the world-view of the play is simple, the detailed analysis—the way in which the Ardens show the tangled structures of Irish society—is both subtle and masterly. The Ardens start from a clear-cut position. . . . But the Ardens don't simply make an assertion, assume that it's self-evidently right, and leave it at that. As much as in the earlier plays they take care to show everybody's motives, to explain the reasons behind everyone's actions" (155).

Connolly's Catholicism, like his Irishness, could have led the original 1975 Dublin audience into self-examination. Part Four, Act One, scene four introduces Connolly's Catholic background as an element in the factional battles in American labor. The lines about religious differences could provide perspective at a distance on the Irish conflicts that grew out of such responses: "My reputation a little bent, / I discovered, by my being Irish. Dan De Leon, it appeared, / Had conveyed a general aroma that all born catholics were men to be feared" (12). Rather than little being made of it, Connolly's Catholicism becomes one instance of what the playwrights termed "an intertwining arrangement of repeated themes running through all parts of the cycle" (*To Present* 127). While in Part Four Connolly's background serves as one of the motivating factors for Dan De Leon's maneuvers—"[i]f James Connolly is not an undercover Jesuit, the only other thing he could be is a complete and blundering idiot" (57)—other plays in the cycle draw on the biographical detail to create conflicts of a different nature.

In Part Six, Act One, scene eleven, an Ulster-based Irish Catholic leader, "Wee Joe Devlin of the Belfast branch of the Nationalist Party" (32), takes issue with Connolly by recalling the supposed cause for the failure of the 1913 Strike: "[y]ou had nothing to offer good catholic folk but your godless German socialism" (32). The two characters argue over a leaflet "alleging that King Billy of the Boyne was a papist in disguise" (32). Connolly's reply outlines a plea for a careful examination of history and of how history is influenced by political and religious biases. In considering the impact of such lines, it's important to remember that the play was performed in The Republic and in Northern Ireland during a heated period of the ongoing Troubles. Of a similar decision to produce *The Ballygombeen Bequest* first "in the Falls Road, Belfast, at the height of the conflict there," Albert Hunt has written, "[t]his was theatre *in* a political situation used not for repeating familiar propaganda slogans, but for teaching people, through entertainment, to understand more clearly the complexities and contradictions underlying realities of their own situation" (156). Such complexities and contradictions emerge in the cycle via a number of issues. The continued conversation between Connolly and Devlin about the influence of Catholicism in the North serves as an example.

> CONNOLLY: Politically it suited the Pope to give thanks for the victory of the Boyne, which he construed as a Dutch victory against the imperialism of France, to which he was hostile. A perfectly accurate small lesson in history. I'm surprised you should be so furious at it.
>
> DEVLIN: It confuses my catholic people.
>
> CONNOLLY: You mean it informs them (33).

By challenging the bases for popular historical interpretation, Connolly challenges the basis of Devlin's power. By having the character even suggest that the emotional associations with the Battle of the Boyne could be defused, Arden and D'Arcy risk alienating some audience members.

Nor are Parts Four and Six the only instances in the cycle where D'Arcy and Arden use the detail of Connolly's Catholicism to create moments of conflict. Rather than ignoring the paradoxes created by Connolly's multiple allegiances as an Irishman, an Internationalist, and a Catholic, Arden and D'Arcy exploit the potential complexities by alternating scenes where Connolly responds to Catholic-baiting and Red-bashing. The uses of religion to create a basis for rejecting Socialism are dramatized in confrontations in Part Three, Act One, scene four between Connolly, who presents his new manifesto for Ireland, and representatives of the forces that came to dominate the Republic and Northern Ireland.

> NATIONALIST QUESTIONER: Does not the Catholic Church teach that private property is ordained by God?
>
> CONNOLLY: The private property of the money-changers who were driven out of the temple—what does the church teach as to the rights and wrongs of that?
>
> NATIONALIST QUESTIONER: The socialist ideology is alien to the Gaelic race.
>
> CONNOLLY: And what d'you think St Patrick brought here but an alien ideology? Why, you argue like a pagan druid! And moreover from the same premises—the ultimate identity of church and state.

*Exit* NATIONALIST QUESTIONER.

And there you see the potentiality of your middle-
class revolution. (7)

While that exchange represents the ongoing questioning of the
effects of an alliance between business and clerics on the
Republic (a topic long an issue in the plays of O'Casey), the same
scene also shows how religion could serve as a basis for
separating Ulster Protestants from the Republican and the
Nationalist causes.

A Unionist Questioner, who is soon to exit like the
Nationalist Questioner, proclaims, "The beginning of social
revolution in Europe was the protestant reformation of the
sixteenth century: the trade union movement of Great Britain is
the legitimate inheritor of the puritan conventicles of the
seventeenth century: and only by securing ourselves firmly to
that movement can labour organisations in Ireland expect and
enjoy the solidarity they require. Republicanism is a red herring"
(7). That mention of the "puritan conventicles" provides a clear
instance of the Connolly character encountering an alternative,
conflicting image that identifies the church and Labour. The
rapid repetition of two challenges to accept inherited notions
that would exclude others seems to undercut any possibility of
taking seriously the positions presented. Emphasizing a
Cromwellian inheritance of British union officials undercuts the
Labour solidarity offered, and the potential resentment that
could be expected in Connolly is not presented, though it is
developed earlier in the cycle.

Indeed, conflicts over ideas about the connections
between religious, national, and class identity are raised as early
as the first two parts in the cycle of plays. In Part One the young
Connolly is shown deserting from the British Army, discovering
a possible interest in socialism, and meeting his wife, Lillie
Reynolds. The scenes that dramatize their romance and life
together create a counterpoint and stand as a challenge to the
sectarianism that dominates much of the scenes about Labour
and politics. That contrasting function of those scenes is
established early in the Part One scenes of courtship.

CONNOLLY: (*takes a step or two backwards*) That's a Protestant name. She's a Protestant. I'm a Catholic. This ends here.

LILLIE: He told me his name.

CONNOLLY: Connolly.

LILLIE: He's a Catholic. I'm a Protestant. Does this have to end here? (27)

Yet the romantic image of a couple finding new answers is not presented in an idealized, simplified light. Rather, the ambiguous attitudes Connolly expresses in the Part Two wedding scene add to the texture of complexity in later scenes with labor leaders, like the one with Devlin, where Connolly is baited about his religious identity. To the Scottish socialist leader John Leslie's question, "Is she strict in her religion, the lassie?" Connolly replies, "She has a colour of a prejudice, as why should she not? I have one myself, don't you see? (36). That confession of an internal flaw results in a series of speeches that bring to life the interwoven threads of Irish political and church history while sparking an awareness in the audience of the self-restraint or reeducation that must be shown in Connolly's Part Three and Part Six confrontations over religion.

After Connolly rejects the possible "solution of a service in a Protestant church," he announces:

*My* wedding. Mine. My decision: no-one else's. The point is: I am an Irishman. Look at it how you like, the Church and the people are the one thing—all together. It may not make very good socialist sense: but, a Protestant minister—to my mind—would be—
He'd be Oliver Cromwell at Drogheda gate
With the Book in his hand and red blood upon each
                                                                    boot!
I could never agree to it" (37).

The Part Six confrontations over the inheritance of King Billy thus could show the individual evolution of an individual consciousness, while the Catholic-baiting of De Leon may serve to suggest that Connolly never rejected or reconciled contradictory systems. Yet even in the scene about planning the wedding, Connolly contradicts his initial lines of religious bias.

That speech occurs, however, only after Lillie gives voice to another martyrology that fosters hate. Though Lillie's lines could agitate an Ulster audience, the scene allows Connolly to distance himself from the faith after insisting on a church wedding:

> LILLIE: A Catholic priest with the mass wafer held
> on high
> Is the smoke of the fires of Smithfield and the cry
> Of every Protestant in old England who walked forth
> in chains to die
> As a martyr for the truth of God and his free
> conscience before the Lord.
> How can I not think of that before I give my word. (37)

Yet after the Scottish Bishop says, "your children belong to us in a land full of heresy," Connolly, speaking to the audience, announces, "My children will be the children of mankind— / Determining their free future through the freedom of an aroused mind" (37). Though such a concern with religion-centered dynamics is not central in *Serjeant Musgrave's Dance*, there are dynamics within the scenes just discussed that provide bases for comparing the plays.

Hunt cites Arden's comments in an interview on the earlier play, "'Which character are you supposed to sympathize with in *Ghosts*? . . . The trouble arises in the first performance of such plays, because the audience still looks for the character they are supposed to sympathize with'" (55). In choosing a known story, the career of an internationalist whom many sought to distance themselves from during his life and whose political inheritance has been held at arm's length in the Republic of Ireland, D'Arcy and Arden already have a potential distancing effect in their choice of subject. As Simon Trussler has noted, "a prior acquaintance with the story is implicit in the nature of chronicle plays, and Arden's acceptance and utilization of this fact may help to explain why he is the one modern playwright apart from Brecht who has been able to dramatize history into more than hopefully intellectual costume dramas" (45). In addition to ambivalent responses to the historical Connolly, the points on religious controversy just quoted would be likely to establish alternating flows of sympathy and antipathy between audience and character. Such ambivalence suggests the applicability to the Connolly cycle of Craig Clinton's praise for Arden's interpretation of one of his models, Brecht: "Brecht can create a situation in which a character's actions or argument are at complete odds; the pervasive strength of each position is equal, and thus the upshot is conceptual stalemate" (Clinton 50). Yet, unlike Clinton, I believe the Connolly cycle renews that dramatic structure. Other examples of internal inconsistencies within the character Connolly occur in key scenes involving the debate over nationalist separatism and over the need for party discipline.

Scenes that dramatize the contradictions for international socialism of nationalist or ethnic separatist movements raise questions about the validity of Connolly's self-sacrifice in the cycle's final action. Rosa Luxemburg speaks most directly of such contradictions in Part Three, Act Three, scene four. The scene, like the play cycle, assumes an interest in the drama of intellectual debate. Luxemburg, introduced as the author of *Reform or Revolution* (an implicit link with the sources of conflict within the Labour movement as identified by Arden and D'Arcy in *To Present the Pretence*), is initially identified by the Irish delegates as speaking "with the very voice of Jim Connolly himself" (62) after her rejection of the politics of compromise. In the debate that follows over the recognition of split delegations, she introduces issues about the impact of national separatism that the playwrights chose to leave unresolved in the final action.

> ROSA LUXEMBURG: (*gets up on to the platform despite the* CHAIRMAN) At an international socialist conference it is important whether *Poland* is truly represented by him—or by him—? Nonsense! What do we suppose Poland—as a concept—has to do with scientific socialism, which extends beyond frontiers and recognises only *classes* as the fundamental structure of the present state of the human race? Why, Poland, as a concept, does not even exist! The nation, as we all well know, is divided out and ruled by Germany, Austria, Russia, as subordinate provinces of their three respective empires. Why else have I come here as a member of a *German* party?

STEWART: Now wait a moment: I've come here as a member of an *Irish* party! By your argument, ma'am, 'tis the *British* delegation that my friend and meself had ought to be attached to?

ROSA LUXEMBURG: That is so: yes.

TOM LYNG: But—but—but here, wait a moment— it's for that very reason that we voted against Kautsky!

ROSA LUXEMBURG: I hope not. If you think that revolution can best triumph over reformism by invoking these national differences, then let me caution you both to examine your position. (63).

As the shifts in Eastern Europe and the former Soviet Union show the significance of such concerns with the forces of nationalism and revolution, Luxemburg's speeches take on fresh relevance. Nor does the cycle's dramatization of the problems with nationalism end with that one speech. While speaking for an idealist position as a socialist, Luxemburg also serves to introduce concepts that call into question Connolly's Easter 1916 actions that lead to his death.

ROSA LUXEMBURG: We who are convinced that the proletariat is not in a position to change political geography, nor to reconstruct bourgeois states, but that it must organise itself on existing foundations, historically created, so as to bring about the conquest of socialist power and the ultimate socialist republic, which alone will be able to liberate the entire world! *There* should be the true meaning of this word you use—republican.

STEWART: Sure she talks like an Orangeman out of Belfast . . . I've heard the very same argument put forward by labour organisers in the North who are after nothing more than the supremacy of their own religious sect over everyone else in the province!

ROSA LUXEMBURG: Ah, religion . . . ! It goes hand-in-hand with national sentiment, as always! . . . Do not think of yourselves as catholics, nor of others as protestants, nor of any of you as Irishmen: you are proletarians or you are nothing: and your interests are

> identical. . . . The man who is half a nationalist will
> always join a national army when his patriotism is
> invoked (64).

Were the playwrights solely interested in ideological purity, this sympathetic speech would have to be undermined so as not to call into question the "hero's" death as the head of the Irish Citizen Army.

However, Connolly's speech that ends Part Three, Act Three, scene four calls the audience's attention to the need for clarifying an issue that is left unresolved at the end of the play.

> CONNOLLY: In her place, quite clearly, national
> sentiment is of small value: but the Irish question's
> different and we judge it by different rules. The next
> time we go to one of these international affairs, we are
> going to have to work out much more thoroughly our
> particular philosophy and explain it with great care
> (65).

Though Connolly's speech encourages the audience to accept as serious the issue Luxemburg raised, the cycle shows no evidence of an attempt by the character to resolve the contradiction. The playwrights thus leave an alert audience with an active challenge to puzzle over. Indeed, through the character O'Casey (a dramatization of a man whom Arden has declared his admiration of), the playwrights renew the issue in a scene that shows conflict within the movement. When O'Casey proclaims in Part Six, Act Two, scene nine that "the Volunteers in their efforts and aims are inimical to the interests of labour" (54), he raises a challenge that remains behind after his departure from the dramatic action. And though O'Casey's hero, Jim Larkin, refers to the departed playwright and Secretary of the Irish Citizen's Army as "a minority out of a minority out of a minority," Larkin nevertheless continues the challenge, asking Connolly "is it true you've been signing political statements on the same paper as Arthur Griffith?" (55). That scene, the tenth, ends with the central debate about the merit of Connolly's involvement in the Rising, the action that will end the play cycle:

> COUNTESS (*in support of Connolly*) Supposing it did
> prove possible to proclaim a republic, and it turned

> out in the upshot that our movement had played no
> part in it?
>
> LARKIN: On his present form Arthur Griffith would
> have played no part either.
>
> COUNTESS: And is not that exactly what we are
> calculating upon?
>
> LARKIN: (*in disgust*) Sure a slogan is one thing—but
> republicanism, secret societies . . . boy-scout pass-
> words in the night . . .
>
> CONNOLLY: Jim, there is more than that, five
> hundred times more than that—! Will ye not listen to
> what goes on! (56).

Scene fourteen in that same act of Part Six keeps the concerns
about republicanism raised by Larkin and De Leon before the
audience when Connolly himself decides to challenge Pearse,
"what are you playing at?

> Hole-and-corner hugger-mugger
> Secret societies, the wink-and-the nod— (64).

In that final play of the cycle, the end of Act Two
culminates with a dream sequence that includes "a great red
BIRD" who emerges from a shell to challenge Connolly with
violating Prohibitions and, through such accompanying shapes
as O'Casey, De Leon, and Larkin to recall the earlier objections to
Connolly's direct action. This Gethsemane-like sequence ends
with D'Arcy and Arden's most daring exploration of Connolly's
motivation. The lines that follow show the playwrights creating
a character who conflates personal and political motivation in
what remains a speech centered on human passion.

> Very well: I am a man who will hazard his whole life
> And those of his friends, because he knows his wife
> Has got from him alive such little good.
> Very well, perhaps I do shed blood
> Perhaps I do make war
> For no-one else but her—
> What's wrong with that: she is a legion, I can't count
> How many of her there are . . . (72-3).

Of this scene, the playwrights have written that the bird represents "perhaps the voice of Scientific Socialism" by outlining "the things that ought not to be done by a Socialist Internationalist in a crisis . . . collaborating with the nationalist Volunteers; ignoring the reality of working-class Unionism in Ulster; setting a military adventure afoot without a proper basis in the work-class mass-movement." Connolly's rebuttal of the cautions, however, they describe as "some attempt at argument—but even at this late stage there is little of what one could call 'dialectical strength'" (*To Present* 127). Though the playwrights themselves have thus called into question as logic the emotional appeal of the argument, the force of Connolly's self-justifying speech about Lillie serves well as an emblem of the motivating dynamic Arden and D'Arcy sought to explore: "[w]e also felt sure that in the terrible tensions of 1916 he must have been activated as much by deep emotion and intuitive response as by any carefully thought out programme of reasoning" (127). By creating an emotionally appealing motivation for an action that so frequently is called into question in the play, the writers sustain dramatic conflict and interest.

Nor is the argument over the validity of the Republican Rising the only time that splits within the leadership of labour provide a center of dramatic interest. By examining how sympathy for and force in such characters as De Leon and Gompers is created in the extended conflicts within Labour, the play's renewal of Arden's early dramaturgic principle of creating from each character's point of view can be claimed. Like the conflict with the Ulster Catholic leader, Devlin, Connolly's encounters with the fragmented American Labour movement in part result from attempts to control knowledge. Samuel Gompers enters Part Four, Act One singing, "No, Sam Gompers has a trickier way to go: / When the working class knows nuth'n, boys, there's nuth'n for them to know—" (7). Part of the force of the character Gompers (like that of the merchant figures Murphy and Grabitall) results not from the depth of characterization but rather from the power exerted by the historical individual. As with their choice of central character, the playwrights, in placing Gompers on the stage, have a character to whom the audience can already assign some

significance. Yet Gompers is not presented solely as a simplified
villain.

Though the early acts of Part Four present Gompers as a
corrupt labor official in cahoots with management, as one who's
willing to "fix the election" (31), and capable of sexually
harassing Elizabeth Gurley Brown (Act Two, scene one), he is
also shown as a pragmatist who forces the bosses to recognize
the role of unions: "[t]he working class don't make no slump.
And when slump comes, the working class is gonna fight against
it, hard. Remember—*my* membership could be that man's
membership tomorrow lunchtime—and if it is, I weep no tears"
(45). When he speaks against the rising influence in the
American labour movement of Eugene Debs, significantly the
lines he is given express his fears through pragmatic appeals:
"the delicate balance between organised labour—*my* organised
labour—and the representatives of big business will be thrown
into the melting-pot. The American working man is *not* a
socialist—he is an unfulfilled capitalist—and to save for him his
hopes and dreams I add my voice—'Stop Debs!'" (76-7). Arden
and D'Arcy thus maintain Arden's long-standing approach of
giving force to the arguments of opposing characters and so
renew the approach to play-writing that Arden has been faulted
as leaving behind.

Albert Hunt made those early comments on play-writing
more generally accessible by reprinting Arden's comments from
an interview printed 30 August 1963 in *Peace News*.[1] In that
interview Arden remarked, "I never write a scene so that the
audience can identify with any particular character . . . I try and
write the scene truthfully from the point of view of each
individual character" (Hunt 78). Since Arden has been
collaborating with Margaretta D'Arcy, the charge most often, as
we have seen, is that the works have moved from "paradox to
propaganda," that Arden would no longer say, as he had in
1963, that "if you dramatize a conflict and you say, one side in
my opinion is white, the other side is black, and you underrate
the strength, integrity and commonsense of the black side, then
you will give your side an easy walkover. Well, you wouldn't be
writing the play if your side had an easy walkover. It wouldn't
be necessary to make this propaganda if there wasn't a serious

struggle involved—therefore why not be fair?" (Hunt 80-1). The scenes that focus on the conflict between forces guided by Connolly and those guided by Gompers derive their ability powerfully to convey conflict from the historical reality of "serious struggles" that Gompers engaged in. That Gompers was no "walkover" in endeavors such as his attempts to discredit the I.W.W. makes it hard to dismiss the character as an exaggerated caricature.

That Arden and D'Arcy have not abandoned interest in creating dramatic conflict also may be established by turning to the section of "A Socialist Hero on the Stage" that has as a title "Dramatic Conflict in the Life of Connolly." There the playwrights observe that a "struggle between persons becomes interesting to an audience by reason of the passions and *inner emotions* it gives rise to, and the skill of the dramatist is traditionally shown in the way he or she relates the action of the struggle to the personal passions" (*To Present* 95). As Dan De Leon most often serves as Connolly's adversary in the Labor conflict, focusing on evidence that the dramatists worked to create in De Leon a character with inner motivations can show that the playwrights have continued to make use of Arden's earlier practice of presenting the action through the perspective of each character's inner passions. By Part Four, Act Two, scene four, the pattern of conflict between the two has been established and De Leon reacts to news of Connolly's establishment of the Newark Italian Socialist Federation and an Irish Socialist Federation as follows: "Ha! The Irish faction-fighter smelling blood on the end of his old shillelagh" (42). The playwrights' ability to interweave a point from one part of the cycle through a different perspective in another part is seen in De Leon's objection, "And of course, as we well know, the Irish predilection for secret societies is even worse than the Italian. Are you familiar with the history of an occult cabal called the Irish Republican Brotherhood? Its 'secret melodramatic conspiratorial methods'—I quote Karl Marx" (42). That De Leon's objection to the IRB establishes the point that Jim Larkin, the Labour "hero," will raise in the final play of the cycle is one of several instances where the scenes set in America provide another context for conflicts to be developed in the scenes set in Ireland.

De Leon and Connolly clash primarily over issues of party discipline and the control of access to publication in the party paper. If Connolly is intended to be flawless, it could be expected that De Leon's position would have been shown to be totally without merit by the time that Connolly charges in Part Four, Act Two, scene ten that "it was more than time that *somebody* discussed the central oligarchy of the party and the . . . the dictatorship that they imposed!" (54) However, though Connolly's machinations are shown to be intelligent, they are also shown potentially to undermine not only party discipline but also the revolutionary potential of groups such as the IWW.

The first confrontation over letters to the Socialist party newspaper, *The Weekly People*, shows De Leon's tendency toward control, yet it also shows him initially willing to allow an airing of Connolly's ideas, while warning of the potentially divisive nature of the younger man's approach:

> first the master, then the disciples, then the completely informed and corrected nucleus of activists and agitators: and finally, the masses, in control of their own destiny. There is a flaw in it, what's the flaw? I will tell you: the very make-up of the masses themselves upon the moment of their arrival: they unwittingly succumb to the anarchic laissez-faire of the American way of life, within the very context of the socialist theory itself. . . . [W]e will publish this letter—without amendment. It does come from a paid-up member: and by open controversy alone can such gross errors be corrected . . . Fragmentism, economicism: this fool could split the party just like it was split before! (14)

As De Leon's move toward control escalates, so does the basis given to the audience for having some degree of understanding and sympathy with his motivation.

During a scene that clearly shows De Leon's manipulation of official party minutes in order to regain control over access to the party paper, De Leon justifies himself by saying, "Was *I* here when *my* business as editor of the newspaper was discussed at the last meeting?" (56). Furthermore, though his own unattractive bias toward Irish Catholics is shown, a partial basis for understanding De Leon's motivation is provided when he speaks of the roots of his suspicion about a Jesuit plot: "my own family lived in just such a society—we were Sephardic Jews, if you please, in Spanish America" (57). While that partial explanation of motivation is provided in the play, De Leon is presented more directly as angry because "the National Executive Committee—*my* committee—the policy-making body of the foremost revolutionary force in the entire western hemisphere—has been manipulated into denying itself access to its own newspaper!" (55) In such incidents, the "very tediousness and seeming hopelessness of the eternal wrangling" found in the source material was converted into human drama (*To Present* 99). And while the anger at being outwitted may partially explain the highhanded response of shutting Connolly out from the newspaper, the clearest instance of the play being written to establish some sympathy for De Leon occurs as the character exits the play.

De Leon enters the I. W. W. Convention of 1908 in Part Four, Act Three, scene seven to demand "the dismissal of that man Connolly from his post! I am appalled he is still here with his sectarian Irish propaganda in his hand!" A willingness to listen to his pleas for order is created through Connolly's own line: "these men here today have so crowded in with such rage into their convention that I cannot believe they can ever get out of it without throwing away almost everything brought them together in the first place. They begin by throwing away the very framework of their procedure—" (73). As De Leon exemplifies an emphasis on such "rules and regulations," he becomes the butt of cries to "[g]et the politicians out of it—spring ourselves clear of the goddam intellectuals—crack the eggheads outa the outfit" (73). Even the Chairman's response to the cries, "Just ain't no good going on, boys, without we do it *orderly*!" validates De Leon's emphasis on the need for order. And if that is not sufficient to lead the audience to question whether De Leon's opponents don't show the value of some of his emphasis on discipline, the bigotry shown in the dialogue that follows seems intentionally to distance audience sympathy from the workers,

DE LEON: Comrade Chairman—

3RD VOICE: Will ya can that comrade bullshit! We're one hundred per cent Americans here and we don't want no fucking European faggot-talk: 'fellow-worker' is the word we use, Dan, and you shape it up our way or you ship out, professor! (73).

Soon after, an anarchic response results in De Leon's being voted out of the organization. Initially, D'Arcy and Arden might be faulted for portraying De Leon as a villain through the opening act of Part Four, which shows De Leon's plan for gaining control: "In the Industrial Workers of the World, the one party involved that possesses a precise doctrine will be the one and only party in the end to achieve the allegiance of this hitherto amorphous mass" (23). Yet the subsequent rejection of De Leon's plea for recognition is scripted to sound like that of an unfair mob: "This is nineteen oh eight, not nineteen oh five—get wise, man. What happened in nineteen oh five is dead and deep down under—we ain't bound by none of last year's structure, tear it out" (74).

That the rejection by the mob may be structured to create sympathy for De Leon seems likely as the scene recalls the disarray seen at the end of Part Three, where Connolly returns to find an Irish Socialist Party that has degenerated into a drunken, insolvent group. The scene is staged to show a "licensed bloody bar, a prank of a joke, and a printing-press in hock" (73). That the scene is developed to show the importance and value of party discipline, and thus to provide a frame for the Part Four confrontations between Connolly and De Leon over discipline is clear. That framing function is established in the third play when it ends with Connolly praising De Leon for having created "a strong, theoretical, permanent nucleus of very well-disciplined members" (76).

Such moments in the play cycle as Connolly's confrontations with Rosa Luxemburg and Dan De Leon and his Part Two speeches that show religious intolerance establish a frame for audiences to recognize the flaws of the title character. That possible distancing is encouraged by Arden and D'Arcy's daring combination of mythic pageant material (not unlike the pageant about Cuchulain staged by Pearse in his days before)

with their people's ballad theatre material. The Prologue to Part
Six, entitled "King Conaire and the Prohibitions," enacts briefly
the story of a king who dares to break the three prohibitions
placed on him by the Druid priests. Speeches at the end of the
prologue outline the action.

> 1ST DRUID: King Conaire's reign from now on is
> accursed
> Because he stepped from underneath his sacred
> crown
> And tried to turn the whole world upside-down
> (5). . . .
>
> RAGGED WOMAN: He broke his prohibitions and
> he died.
>
> MOTHER: And in so doing he left the Irish land
> With greater life and hope than from any other hand
> (5-6).

Those speeches, like the apple tree ballad at the end of *Serjeant
Musgrave's Dance*, provide a frame for the central action of
Connolly's life. By making the comparison of Conaire and
Connolly explicit through the Act Two dream sequence of the
red Bird, the playwrights simultaneously invoke the lines of the
Ragged Woman and the Mother as possible commentaries on the
death of James Connolly. In siding with the Nationalist
Republicans, he breaks assumptions (the prohibitions) of the
international socialists. Likewise, in marrying Lillie and not
promising to raise their children within the faith, he breaks with
the prohibitions of his faith. In taking up arms he breaks with the
pacifism of British Labour allies. While each of those actions may
embody the "new spirit" that the Bird speaks of at the end of the
Prologue (6), the meaning of the comparison may be considered
unsettling when one recalls the fate of Conaire and his men after
their battle with the pirate invaders: "[t]hey themselves were all
killed: it was the woman alone who escaped" (6).

But is there more to the six-play cycle than dramatizing
the party politics and political history of Ireland? Another
parallel with the early Musgrave play, the cycle's ballad
structure, creates entertainment of a type like that praised in
Tom Stoppard's *Travesties*. The work's pace and structure

resulted in the following praise from Robert Leach: "[i]t is the
image, not the surface reality, with which the play is concerned.
All this goes back through that strand in twentieth-century
theatre best represented by Meyerhold (whose disciple
Eisenstein was) to *commedia dell'arte*. . . . *The Non-Stop Connolly
Show* is a remarkable fusion of comedy and epic" (Page, *File* 57).
During Part Four, Act Two, one of the sections most dense with
the minutiae of party politics, Connolly undergoes a music hall
transformation much like that of Joyce in the Stoppard play. In
scene three, set in a library, the stage directions call for Connolly
*"rapidly to change his appearance"*:

> Gotta go there like I look like I know everything that I
> do not know:
> Razzmatazz, go get it, boy, go get up and go!
> *He puts himself into a loud checked jacket, clip-on bow-tie,
> flat straw hat etc., and caps the effect with a cigar* (36).

Nor is that brief moment the only instance of music-hall
technique. In the second scene of Act One, Connolly's arrival in
America, complete with immigrant's luggage, is presented in
song:

> CONNOLLY (sings)
> With a song upon me lips and a pack upon me back
> I have travelled o'er the ocean upon me weary track.
> From the coast of Erin's isle to the harbour of New York
> Rambling Pat across the world comes looking out for
> work! (8).

In Part Four, however, such music-hall business serves not only
to enliven the action that some critics have found tedious, but to
bring to mind the stage Irish tradition. Images of that tradition
are brought to the fore through the attitudes of the Irish-
American boss, Slattery, who speaks of "The Harp that once
through Tara's halls" before announcing "these two things I
have no time for: that's atheism and protestants" (50). Thus the
music-hall technique contributes to cycle's strategies for calling
into question such intolerance.

    Now that nearly two decades have passed since the
publication of Albert Hunt's study of Arden's plays,

reexaminations of the playwrights' career, via the major cycle of six D'Arcy and Arden plays performed as *The Non-Stop Connolly Show*, can demonstrate that the writing team of John Arden and Margaretta D'Arcy have continued experiments to develop more fully the precedent established in Arden's first major success, *Serjeant Musgrave's Dance*. Besides a central character who provides a basis for contradictory responses, and the use of the ballad tradition, the plays offer additional grounds for comparison.

Arden's own comment on the relationship of the plays stresses their historical origins and ongoing topicality: "In January 1972 thirteen people were shot dead by the Paras in Derry, while industrial trouble raged in the coalfields on a level unknown since the 1920s. While this was happening, I was at work with D'Arcy on an early draft of *The Non-Stop Connolly Show*: in a sense the whole story of Connolly was a kind of inside-out version of my invented Black Jack Musgrave" (*To Present* 155). Yet in that same collection of essays, *To Present the Pretence*, which was published shortly before the Connolly plays, Arden identifies how his collaborations with D'Arcy were found faulty by some established members of the theatre community and how, through funding grants, there came to be an attempt to control his work.

> In my case it has been incontrovertibly passed on to me (though never put down on paper in so many words) that any work of mine done in collaboration with D'Arcy (which in effect means all my Irish material) is altogether out of line with the requirements of more than one subsidised theatre . . . that a new play could be commissioned—provided that it was *a genuine Arden work*. . . . It occurred to me later that there was possibly another way of interpreting the cryptic phrase: that "a genuine Arden work" in fact meant "a play like *Serjeant Musgrave's Dance*, which does not come to any very positive conclusion"—whereas *non-genuine Arden* would be "Arden at last affirming from his own hard experience the need for revolution and a Socialistic society: and moreover convinced that his artistic

independence and integrity will be strengthened
rather than compromised by so *doctrinaire* a stance"
(157-8).

The relevance of that Irish material and the collaborations with
D'Arcy to Arden's ability to more fully explore his preoccupations developed in his first success has been an underlying
assumption in this essay.

The central moment of passion occurs in *Serjeant
Musgrave's Dance* when the Serjeant and his troops realize that
the entrance of the Dragoons will put an end to their efforts to
confront the community with the reality of Billy Hicks', the
native son's, fate. The young soldier Hurst pleads for more than
his life when he asks the crowd to protect him from the
Dragoons: "if you let 'em be, then us three'll be killed—aye and
worse, *we'll be forgotten*—an the whole bloody lot'll start all over
again!" (100; my italics). That concern with the soldiers' place in
the communal memory (and the impact of that memory) is
emphasized more clearly in Musgrave's plea, "For God's sake
stand with us. We've *got* to be remembered!" (100), which is
echoed in Mrs. Hitchcock's line "One day they'll be full, though,
and the Dragoons'll be gone, and then they'll remember" (108).
That concern with the living force of memory and the
paradoxical basis for audience response toward Musgrave are
crucial elements in demonstrating the continuity of the later play
cycle with Arden's early work. While Musgrave's determination
to confront society with the cost of sacrificing soldiers may be
admirable, his willingness to turn a Gatling gun on a civilian
crowd creates outrage and awe. However, this point of recalling
a sacrifice and its cost that creates the strongest similarity in
theme and structure with the closing play of *The Non-Stop
Connolly Show*. There the final speech is delivered by the actor
playing Connolly (though the historical execution has already
been enacted) and, like Musgrave, he pleads for a reassessed
place in memory: "We were the first to feel their loaded gun /
That would prevent us doing it any more— / Or so they hoped.
We were the first. We shall not be the last. / This was not
history. It has not passed" (106). That speech perhaps most
explicitly declares the purpose of the living enactment of the

historical events in the play. Drama is alive at the moment of enactment and the play revives and reexamines the events of the Easter 1916 Rising in Dublin.

     While Hunt's study points toward an aspect of the Arden and D'Arcy collaborations that takes center stage in the *Connolly Show*, the "extrovert, circus-like quality of the Ardens' script" (159), Hayman's earlier predictions about the directions that the collaborative team might take also highlight concerns for future discussion of the play cycle: "if he [Arden and D'Arcy] can go on to bring off a play which combines the seriousness of *Serjeant Musgrave's Dance* and the sweep of *Armstrong's Last Goodnight* with the density and humour of *Ars Longa* . . . it will be a great play" (77). While the "density" of the cycle's plays has been generally accepted, it is evidence of "seriousness" and "humor" that have most often been dismissed in discussions of *The Non-Stop Connolly Show*. By reconsidering aspects of how the cycle brings to life the contradictions and paradoxes in Connolly's career and by assessing the merits, via stage performances, of the music-hall elements of the cycle, critical assessment of this epic may undergo a shift similar to that which has occurred in the case of *Serjeant Musgrave's Dance*. For that to occur, critics may first need to be willing to examine the evidence that Arden himself practices the technique he described in 1975 as Shakespeare's means for creating a "secret play" in *Henry V*: "[h]e regularly sets up a certain atmosphere of noble enterprise by means of evocative blank verse speeches, and without comment, deflates it through an alternation of scenes showing something near the opposite" (*To Present* 202). The goal of this essay has been to initiate such a reexamination of the way alternating scenes in the Connolly cycle call into question the meaning and significance of the central character's actions.

## Notes

1. "A Theatre of Sexuality and Poetry." Reprinted as "On Comedy." *Encore* 12.5 (Sept.–Oct. 1965): 15.

# Works Cited

Arden, John. *To Present the Pretence*. London: Eyre Methuen, 1977.

———. *Books of Bale*. London: Methuen, 1988.

———. *Serjeant Musgrave's Dance*. In *John Arden: Plays: One*. New York: Grove Press, 1977.

D'Arcy, Margaretta, and John Arden. *The Non-Stop Connolly Show*. 5 vols. London: Pluto Press, 1977–1978.

Clinton, Craig. "John Arden: The Promise Unfulfilled." *Modern Drama* 21 (1978) 47–57.

Gray, Frances. *John Arden*. New York: Grove Press, 1983.

Hayman, Ronald. *John Arden*. London: Heinemann, 1968.

Hunt, Albert. *Arden: A Study of His Plays*. London: Eyre Methuen, 1974.

Page, Malcolm. *Arden on File*. London: Methuen, 1985.

———. *John Arden*. Boston: Twayne Publishers, 1984.

Schvey, Henry I. "From Paradox to Propaganda: The Plays of John Arden." *Essays on Contemporary British Drama*. Eds. Hedwig Bock and Albert Wertheim. Munich: Max Hueber Verlag, 1981. 47–70.

Trussler, Simon. *John Arden*. New York: Columbia Univ. Press, 1973.

# THE NON-STOP CONNOLLY SHOW: THE ROLE OF A NON-TRADITIONAL AUDIENCE IN A NEW THEATRE TRADITION

## Catherine Graham

Why do Margaretta D'Arcy and John Arden's Irish stage plays receive so little attention? Have their politics damaged their dramaturgy since their break with the "legitimate" stage after the 1972 London production of *The Island of the Mighty*?[1] While the neglect of the Irish stage plays is certainly inspired in part by a reluctance to deal with controversial issues like the British occupation of northern Ireland and a socialist response to British colonialism in that country, I believe that it is also due to the methodological difficulties involved in the study of popular political drama. To find appropriate methodologies for this task, I think we must start from the assumption that the playwrights' goals are not as simple as critics of didacticism would too often have it. D'Arcy and Arden have never limited their political agenda to "selling" particular political issues or activities. In fact D'Arcy specifically criticized "one-issue" politics during a 1977 symposium on "Playwriting for the Seventies" sponsored by *Theatre Quarterly*:

> The weakness of "progressive" politics in this country
> [England] is reflected in the political theatre of this
> country—which is always on single issues. That is the
> way the capitalists stay in power. They let us all waste
> our energy pursuing these issues in isolation. (49)

Arden, when discussing his decision to take sides in writing political plays, has always done so in terms of point of view more than in terms of convincing people to take particular actions at particular moments. The title he chose for an essay where he discusses his opposition to British imperialism in Ireland is telling; Arden speaks not of a particular political action

but of a "Shift of Perspective" (*Corners* 13-20). In this sense both
D'Arcy and Arden are part of the new tradition of political
popular theatre, which challenges not only the articulated
ideologies of Western cultures but also their dominant models of
knowledge. Nowhere is this new tradition and the resistance to it
on the part of some drama critics more clearly expressed than in
the performance event that was *The Non-Stop Connolly Show.*

The most striking thing about D'Arcy and Arden's first
major work after their break with the legitimate stage is its
length. The *Non-Stop Connolly Show* is a cycle of six plays, which
were first presented as a continuous twenty-six-hour-long
performance on Easter weekend 1975 in Liberty Hall, the Dublin
headquarters of the Irish Transport and General Workers Union
(Marsh 133). While D'Arcy conceived of this style of presentation
as a "kind of giant 'pop festival' for the Left—a long night of
plays, films, etc." in the spirit of the Angry Arts weeks which
were held in New York and London during the Vietnam War
(D'Arcy and Arden, "Socialist" 118), critics viewed it as a test of
endurance. Subsequent performances in Belfast and elsewhere in
Ireland were cut to a "mere" twelve hours (Archer 40) and a
series of lunchtime presentations in London in 1976 presented
the texts in fourteen fifty-minute-long episodes. Many critics
seem to assume that the length of *The Non-Stop Connolly Show*
was an expression of the self-indulgence of propagandists who
put their message before their art. Henry Schvey is among the
most virulent in his attacks on the artistic value of D'Arcy and
Arden's efforts. After informing his reader that such a lengthy
performance "must be lively, emphasize visual action, and not
be too intellectually demanding or dependent on a complicated
plot" (65), he asserts that

> the Ardens' [sic] interest in a dogmatic approach to
> Connolly's life clearly outweighs their concern for the
> spectacle as a work of art or even as effective
> theatrical propaganda.
>
> Judged by the standards of conventional
> drama, the plays rely almost entirely on caricature,
> cliché and slogan to make their principal point of the
> necessity for a socialist revolution. (65-6)

This succinct expression of the critic's standpoint on both aesthetic and political questions in theatre criticism provides a valuable guide to interpreting even the reactions of more sympathetic critics, because it foregrounds some of the basic assumptions about popular political theatre which underlie their critiques too. One of these assumptions constructs a hierarchy of discourses within which academic or other professionally institutionalized discourse has the highest power to understand all others and concludes that material with which the academic critic has difficulty must be completely incomprehensible to any other audience. Even a sympathetic critic like Kane Archer falls into this trap when he characterizes the Dublin performance as "didactic and insufficiently clear-cut, confusing even to the mind trained to pick out the thread of academic discourse"; it is worth noting that Archer found De Leon, who is portrayed as a dogmatic intellectual, the most captivating character in the Dublin performance text (40). Yet there is no reason to believe that academics were the ideal audience for whom D'Arcy and Arden wrote this piece. The choice of performance setting, theme, and theatrical style all indicate that D'Arcy and Arden wrote *The Non-Stop Connolly Show* for Irish trade unionists or for people involved in left-wing political groups that respected both Irish and working class traditions of thought. D'Arcy and Arden insist on this point when they cite intertwining Celtic serpentine motifs as one of the inspirations for the form of this play ("Interstates" 11). A further Celtic influence may be seen in the portrayal of wishes which come true and yet have unforeseen consequences (e.g., Connolly's return to Ireland), as happens in so many Irish fairy tales. Many passages participate in trade-union discourse: for example, in Part Six we see a rowdy union meeting in which the only thing on which Larkin and O'Casey can agree is that questions of personality cannot be considered relevant to a trade union debate (396). Once these factors are taken into account, the crucial question becomes not "How does this play correspond to Schvey's 'standards of conventional drama'?" but "What standards of dramaturgy does this way of knowing demand?" In other words, an understanding of the dramaturgy of *The Non-*

*Stop Connolly Show* must proceed from an understanding of the ways of knowing particular to its ideal audience.

A first step in defining any way of knowing is the identification of its presuppositions, including what it considers to be relevant thematic questions and sense-making strategies. For instance, as noted above, in trade union discourse questions of personality are not considered relevant themes for evaluating the success or failure of any particular action. As this stands in direct contradiction to the standards of conventional individualist drama, which demand character development through the exposition and resolution of crises in personal values, new conventions must be found to express this way of knowing on the stage. Further, these conventions must take into account the preferred sense-making strategies of the ideal audience. In the case of trade unionists, an important role in knowing the world is attributed to direct personal experience, and this in itself may partly justify D'Arcy and Arden's choice to lead the audience through a twenty-six hour marathon in order to demonstrate the problems of long-term political struggle. When the professional critics complain of exhaustion induced by such a lengthy presentation, we must consider the possibility that working-class audiences may construct quite different meanings from the same physical sensations. One of the important features of *The Non-Stop Connolly Show* is the portrayal of Connolly's determination to continue the struggle for workers' rights despite his own exhaustion and in face of overwhelming odds. Whereas a traditional intellectual and middle-class audience would generally state that their sensations of exhaustion undermine the credibility of this portrayal, workers in the audience might well find that their own physical sensations in the theatre setting help them better understand Connolly's situation. This, in turn, could only enhance the credibility of images of exhaustion and regeneration in the fictional world Connolly inhabits.

Desmond Hogan lends credence to this conjecture when he describes his experience as an actor in the first Dublin performance, and recounts not mainly the "message" the critics were so eager to track down but what Raymond Williams calls a "structure of feeling": the sense of "irony" at leaving Liberty

Hall at about the same time as the strikers had during the original Easter Rising, the cold of the hall, the determination of the actors, the dynamic climax, the "uncanny tension which locked these scenes together, a poignancy for those of us who were educated on the sanctity of 1916" (552). In another instance, D'Arcy and Arden's reference to Celtic serpentine motifs evokes a strategy of sense-making alien to the Cartesian intellectual tradition of structuring an argument as a linear development. Those familiar with the Celtic strategy might well prefer to organize the information presented in the performance text by constructing patterns of contact and rupture instead of sequences of cause and effect. This in itself would make a cycle structure more accessible because it would allow for inattention and even temporary absences on the part of individual audience members, provided they followed enough of the narrative (directly or through reports from other audience members) to construct an overall pattern.

Two of the dramaturgic strategies which D'Arcy and Arden chose correspond to these alternative ways of knowing. In the first place they approached the Connolly story as a story of collective social actions rather than one of personality. In their own words: "The conflict of his life was on the whole *impersonal*—it is only to be discovered in the conflict between his class (the working class) and the classes which oppressed it" ("Socialist" 96). Further, the development of this conflict is not structured as a chain of battles leading directly and inexorably to the Easter Rising of 1916 but "as a series of digressive stage-presentations of the events of his time which influenced his political views and consequent actions" (*Connolly* v). Second, they reject naturalistic conventions in favour of an overtly fictional theatricality which they describe as "not so much the *real truth* as a reconstructed *emblem* of it" ("Socialist" 94). In this light, it becomes clear that *The Non-Stop Connolly Show* functions in much the same way as the semiotician's Possible World: it presents the audience with a counterfactual model in which a possibility (in this case armed resistance of the working class to bourgeois power) is verified by the imaginary creation of the conditions necessary for its existence (or falsified by their absence). It demonstrates that such a strategy makes sense given a certain set of conditions, and thus proves that it is a possible strategy in the struggle to ensure social justice for working men, women, and children.

The six major sections of *The Non-Stop Connolly Show* are all framed by direct presentations to the audience which focus attention on the question of defining what is possible and under what conditions. The cycle starts with a prologue in which Connolly's mother presents the values underlying a socialist world-view as self-evident presuppositions and then directs audience attention to the conditions which must prevail in order for these values to be put into practice:

> It is the right of every man on earth
> (Who for his life must bend his back and work)
> To own, control, and finally enjoy
> The produce of his labour at its greatest worth.
> Did I say every man? Each woman, girl, and boy
> Is equally entitled to such a right—
> If not, why do we live? But yet we have not got it:
> Through all of history it has been withheld:
> Though frequently, after a fearsome fight,
> Some grudging portion has been slowly granted
> Only because the mighty were compelled
> By greater might of those whom they oppressed.
>                                         (*Connolly* 1)

When she is interrupted by the capitalist "demon king," Grabitall, who warns the audience that to take such discourse seriously is to endanger his domination, Mother Connolly reacts, not by denouncing his values but by asserting the possibility of winning social justice in face of Grabitall's dire predictions of the cost of struggle: "you *can* and shall be beaten!" (my emphasis) The play ends with this same emphasis on possibility. In its last speech Connolly, tied to a chair and shot by Grabitall's men, does not try to justify his armed revolt nor to understand its immediate failure. Neither does he preach about what must or should be done. Instead, he discusses his actions in terms of the possibility of positive change for oppressed peoples: "We were the first to show the dark deep hole within / *Could* be thrown open to the living sun" (448, my emphasis).

The key question in a cognitive strategy whose aim is to examine possibility is: "How could this come about?" Throughout *The Non-Stop Connolly Show*, audience attention is directed to social conditions as a locus where an appropriate response to this question can be found. In contrast to individualistic and naturalist drama, the audience is not encouraged to search for a tragic flaw of character which prevented Connolly from achieving his goals, and the cycle's individual plays do not encourage a concentration on the evolution of desire in individual dramaturgic agents by surprising them in mid-action. Instead, each play begins with a formal presentation of the state of affairs (analogous to the "set of conditions" of Possible World theory) which the protagonists must transform if their desires are to become realities and with a simple statement of the values which will be tested in the ensuing action. Far from taking a dogmatic approach to the ideals Connolly embodied, D'Arcy and Arden use *The Non-Stop Connolly Show* to subject them to a pragmatic test. This process culminates in Part Six when a prologue, in folk-legend style, on a separate stage demonstrates that while broken prohibitions may lead to the end of the state of affairs the prohibitions were designed to protect, this end (and by extension any change of state) should not be assumed at the outset to be negative for all participants (343-8). Shortly thereafter the Bird confronts Connolly with a series of prohibitions appropriate to a doctrinaire socialist consciousness. Connolly rejects each of them with references to the problems of carrying them out in the world in which he lives. When told to look for strategic advantage "on the next full page" he replies that "the book is closed and glued / With soot of cordite / And with blood" (411); when told he must win the support of Protestant workers he replies, "I piped to them, they did not dance. / It is too late: they now must take their chance" (413). Finally he sends the Bird away because it has no positive plan, and he is convinced that "to do nothing / Will do nothing to relieve their pain" (415).

Prohibition is one of the ways in which the necessary conditions for the success of the hero's quest are expressed in legends and folktales, and D'Arcy and Arden's choice of this form to model the problems in Connolly's Possible World of rebellion is significant. Whereas in the traditional folktale it is quite clear that the magical helper has the wisdom and authority to articulate the conditions of the hero's success, the new political parable calls for pragmatic questioning. Ideals, even socialist ideals, can no longer be accepted on the basis of the authority of the speaker. Instead, every ideal must be tested in terms of conditions which must exist in order for it to be put into practice. After subjecting the Bird's prohibitions to such a test, Connolly must reject them because he deems the social conditions they require to become reality politically unacceptable.

Of course such a test must not be taken as a literal expression of historical reality. As Teun van Dijk points out in *Text and Context; Explorations in the Semantics and Pragmatics of Discourse,* in Possible World testing we are dealing not with an actual physical state but with a structure of meaning (29). This is a particularly important distinction in the study of theatre, where the physical presence of human beings who act out a narrative before an audience could lead one to assert intuitively that the Possible World is actually physically present on the stage. In fact, as numerous semioticians have pointed out, even when endowed with three-dimensional presence, the map is not the territory, and stage activity must be taken as a map which serves to induce the Possible World in the minds of the spectators. Umberto Eco provides a particularly valuable description of this process of meaning-creation in his discussion of theatrical signification as *ostension.* He points out that the theatrical sign is not actively produced in the way a word or drawn image is produced but is instead picked up from existing physical bodies, then de-realized or de-semanticized by showing it to an audience in a manner which reduces it to those of its features which are pertinent to the signification of a whole class of objects. It is the showing of this de-realized object to an audience which constitutes ostension, the most important theatrical form of signification (110-11). In this light the agents, objects, and relationships on the stage are signs, chosen for their ability to evoke a reality other than the actual physical reality of their presence. In their capacity as signs they cannot, by definition, have the same ontological status as agents, objects, and relationships in the empirical world. So the Possible World is an abstract construct and not simply the "world" enclosed in the physical space of the stage. Further, the spectators' creation of the Possible World is not, in fact cannot be, constituted only from information presented on the stage. If Eco's reference to classes of objects is to be realized, then we must posit the ability of the spectators to organize objects into classes on the basis of information they already have when they enter the theatre. Since different audiences enter the theatre with different information and different ways of organizing that information, a serious attempt to discuss new traditions of dramaturgy must look at the specific models which are likely to be operating in the case of a given ideal audience.

The dramatic model D'Arcy and Arden chose to organize their emblematic theatrical strategy was the Mystery play, a pre-individualist form of drama. In the European Christian tradition, it was originally performed by amateurs on religious occasions, such as Easter, to inculcate basic teachings of Christianity by leading the faithful through a series of tableaux representing the major events leading up to and in Christ's life. In this form of drama, significance is attributed to events exclusively in the public sphere, and every action is understood in terms of its role in "the grand scheme of things." D'Arcy and Arden refer to the Hindu Mystery plays they witnessed during their 1970 visit to India as the source of the theatrical style of *The Non-Stop Connolly Show* ("Socialist" 103). However, it seems virtually certain that Irish audiences would best be able to structure the information in the cycle in meaningful ways by reference to the remnants of the Christian mystery cycles in such religious activities as the liturgical year in general and processions through the Stations of the Cross in particular. That D'Arcy believes in the possibility of re-functioning these religious rituals (in the Brechtian sense of *"umfunktionieren"*; cf. Benjamin, "Der Autor als Produzent" 691) is implied in her essay "The Voice of the Bitch Goddess," where she discusses the pre-Christian images of the Goddess carried in the processions in honour of the Virgin which were held in the Dominican convent where she was educated (69-70). Reference to the Christian death and resurrection myth is quite explicit in Connolly's last speech, where he uses imagery of the opening of Christ's tomb on Easter Sunday: "We were the first to roll away the stone / From the leprous wall of the whitened tomb" (448). Michael Etherton makes direct reference to the Stations of the Cross in his analysis of *The Non-Stop Connolly Show*, where he suggests that the backcloths used to set each scene allow the audience to follow the evolution of the narrative in much the same ways that painted panels guide the Christian through the Easter story in the Catholic ritual (221). D'Arcy and Arden specify in their preface to the printed text of *The Non-Stop Connolly Show* that the intended function of these backcloths is to encourage the audience actively to create the Possible World in which particular actions will be meaningful:

> We have suggested a series of backcloths which can be fixed singly or two-at-a-time to give the overall atmosphere of each section of the cycle. . . . The style we have in mind should be based on the formal emblematic tradition of trade union banners, and should be carried out in bright colours with no attempt at impressionism or naturalistic representation. The cloths should include appropriate slogans and captions. (vii)

The scenes portrayed are not simply landscapes but montage-like images that focus attention on the basic contradictions against which new possibilities are tested and that give the audience clues as to the scope of the Possible World they must create in order to make sense of the scenes played out before them. Scenes between Connolly and his wife Lillie, for instance, must be interpreted as events of public significance when they are played out in front of backcloths which do not portray the interior of a home but an emblematic image of the society which governs their domestic relations, as is the case in the pauper's Christmas scene of Part III, which is played before a banner showing

> *converging processions of demonstrators representing socialist and nationalist ferment from different parts of the world, in a variety of costumes and with a variety of slogans on their banners in many languages. The whole*

> *contained within a border of watchful police of no particular nationality.* (123)

Instead of reinforcing the dominant viewpoint that desire is a personal and psychological phenomenon, this contextualization encourages the audience to identify the ways in which the Possible World determines the forms personal relations can take, and obversely to view personal relations as constitutive of the conditions that allow a given Possible World to function. In a song at the end of the cycle, Lillie verbalizes the ways in which personal relationships can be structured to maintain unjust social conditions, telling the audience directly that she would "rather let him roam / With the wildest in the world / Be they women or be they men / Than lie beside me night by night / With broken heart and frozen brain— / For the life of his wife he must go to sleep again?" (435). For his part, Connolly demonstrates how one can attribute meaning to personal relationships by putting them in a social context. In the dream sequence in which he weighs the pros and cons of involvement in the Easter Rising, he replies to the Bird's prohibition against deceiving himself that he is justified in making "private wars" by referring to Lillie's sufferings on his behalf: "Perhaps I do make war / For no-one else but her— / What's wrong with that: she is a legion, I can't count / How many of her there are" (415).

Whereas backcloths give the audience visual clues as to the scope of the Possible World needed to make sense of the action, costumes in *The Non-Stop Connolly Show* give indications of the degree of precision necessary in creating the agential relations of the proposed Possible World. In their description of masks and costumes D'Arcy and Arden divide the dramaturgic agents of *The Non-Stop Connolly Show* into three (sometimes overlapping) relational classes: figures which are essentially social functions (military, ecclesiastical, bourgeois-political, and judicial); agents who represent groups (members of the working class and national liberation movements); and well-known individuals (Connolly, Countess Markiewicz, Larkin, etc.) The first group wear stock masks and uniform, the second are unmasked but show a uniform-like similarity of costume, while in the third case (with the exception of Connolly, who was made up to look like historical portraits) "there was some attempt at accuracy of *atmosphere* rather than precision of detail" ("Socialist" 129). Following Eco's suggestion that ostension in theatrical performance functions by inducing the identification of a class of objects familiar to the spectator, we may conclude that, in this emblematic style of costuming, the degree of individualization indicates the degree of precision to be attained in determining the class to which the particular performance refers. In some cases it is important to identify an agent with a particular historical person, in others the agent serves only to describe the conditions in which the protagonists must test their ideals. In this sense it is important to note, as does Schnabl, that the degree of historically individualized reference indicates the agent's position in the main conflict of the cycle: "On the socialist side there are historical persons, whereas the capitalist side is peopled, with the exception of the politicians, by types like employers, officers, preachers, and by the monstrous archetype Grabitall" (111; my translation).

While critics like Schvey react negatively to this type of emblematic presentation, others, like Archer, appreciate the stylistic devices which ask the audience "to accept exaggeration for what it is" and which make the authors' standpoint clear (40). Such an appreciation must be based on the understanding that dramaturgies can be founded on sets of presuppositions other than those that govern conventional bourgeois drama. The question then becomes: "Where are these presuppositions generated?" In the case of *The Non-Stop Connolly Show*, these presuppositions are not defined by dogmatic political doctrine but drawn from such diverse sources as trade-union discourse, Celtic artistic traditions, popular culture, and Catholic religious ritual. In this light it would seem difficult to argue that D'Arcy and Arden's dramaturgic range has narrowed as their political commitment has deepened. In fairness, we must acknowledge that these playwrights have in fact *expanded* their repertoire of sense-making strategies and dramaturgic devices in order to respond to non-traditional theatre audiences. Far from being an unfortunate weakness in their later work, this is, perhaps, their greatest contribution to the new tradition of political popular theatre.

# Notes

1. A review of standard bibliographies conducted in 1991 turned up twenty-seven texts on *Serjeant Musgrave's Dance*, but only ten articles dealing specifically with the post-1972 Irish plays. Further, a good part of the general criticism of the works of these playwrights seems not simply ill at ease with D'Arcy and Arden's more radical political commitment since their move to Ireland but also to consider it as either irrelevant or detrimental to their dramaturgies. Of the five books on Arden (D'Arcy's contributions are always subsumed under her husband's) published since 1968 only two, those by Albert Hunt and Frances Gray, identify political commitment as an important positive factor in determining Arden and D'Arcy's dramaturgy. Malcolm Page and Glenda Leeming are more cautious in their assessments. Page praises the later plays but tends to be apologetic about Arden's political commitments, while Leeming doesn't mention Arden's political views at all in her discussion of the post-1968 works. Hayman, who published the earliest book-length assessment of Arden's work in 1969, clearly believes that political commitment has damaged the playwright's work; in a BBC interview in 1980 he stated "Arden hasn't given up writing plays. He's just given up writing good ones." (quoted in Gray, 16).

# Works Cited

Archer, Kane. "Dublin." *Plays and Players* 22.10 (July 1975): 40–1.

Arden, John, Margaretta D'Arcy et al. "Playwriting for the Seventies: Old Theatres, New Audiences, and the Politics of Revolution." *Theatre Quarterly* 6.24 (Winter 1976–77): 35–74.

Benjamin, Walter. "Der Autor als Produzent." *Gesammelte Schriften*, II.2. Ed. Rolf Tiedemann und Hermann Schweppenhäuser. Frankfurt: Suhrkamp, 1977. 683–701.

D'Arcy, Margaretta. "The Voice of the Bitch Goddess." *Voices of the Goddess; a Chorus of Sibyls*. Ed. Caitlín Matthews. Wellingborough: Aquarian Press, 1990. 67–84.

D'Arcy, Margaretta, and John Arden. *Awkward Corners*. London: Methuen, 1988.

———. *The Non-Stop Connolly Show*. London: Methuen, 1986.

———. "A Socialist Hero on the Stage." *To Present the Pretense*. London: Eyre Methuen, 1977. 92–138.

Eco, Umberto. "Semiotics of Theatrical Performance." *The Drama Review* 21.1 (March 1977): 107–17.

Etherton, Michael. *Contemporary Irish Dramatists*. London: Macmillan, 1989. 209–30.

Gray, Frances. *John Arden*. New York: Grove Press, 1982.

Hayman, Ronald. *John Arden*. London: Heinemann, 1968.

Hogan, Desmond. "The Beating Down of the Wise." *New Statesman* 11 Apr. 1980: 552–3.

Hunt, Albert. *Arden: A Study of His Plays*. London: Methuen, 1974.

"Interstates Left." *Guardian* 22 May 1976: 11.

Leach, Robert. "Connolly Reclaimed: Arden and D'Arcy's *The Non-Stop Connolly Show*." *Platform* 5 (Spring 1983): 12–15.

Leeming, Glenda. *John Arden*. London: Longman, 1974.

Marsh, Paddy. "Easter at Liberty Hall." *Theatre Quarterly* 5.20 (Dec. 1975–Feb. 1976). 133–41.

Page, Malcolm. *John Arden*. Boston: Twayne, 1984.

Schnabl, Gerlinde. "Margaretta D'Arcy/John Arden, *The Non-Stop Connolly Show*." *Historische Stoffe im neueren politischen Drama Großbritanniens*. Heidelberg: Carl Winter Universitätsverlag, 1982. 107–19.

Schvey, Henry. "From Paradox to Propaganda: The Plays of John Arden." *Essays on Contemporary British Drama*. Eds. Hedwig Bock and Albert Wertheim. Munich: Hueber, 1981. 47–70.

Van Dijk, Teun A. *Text and Context: Explorations in the Semantics and Pragmatics of Discourse*. London: Longmans, 1977.

# JOHN ARDEN'S *PEARL*:
# HISTORICAL IMAGININGS

## Mary Karen Dahl

For the past few years I've been looking at playtexts and performance occasions that propose images of citizenship in contemporary nation-states. If, for example, one takes seriously notions of the de-centered subject and couples that with an awareness of "the expansion and diversification of state activity", which Italian sociologist Gianfranco Poggi captures in his descriptive phrase, the "invasive state" (120), how can individual citizens take part in the political operation of western liberal democratic states like the United States or the United Kingdom? Or in today's critical language, what does personal agency look like in the complex web of social and political relations that characterize postmodern society?

   In thinking about citizenship, my focus has been on playtexts designed to be staged in traditional theatre houses, and I have necessarily repeatedly come up against questions about what kinds of playtexts will achieve production, and how extensive and diverse an audience those productions will reach. In staging his play *Racing Demons* at the National Theatre, for example, does David Hare speak to a constituency that can effectively change the Anglican church? Has Hare chosen his subject because his audiences already constitute the class that not only is invested in the institutions that dominate British society but also can revise, revitalize, or revolutionize them? Has he left other subjects aside because he knows his constituency? That is, does the constituency dictate the subject? What is the relationship between the structures surrounding production and the text the spectator receives? Now these are rather ordinary questions and concerns in the tradition of performance criticism, and my way of posing them merely reflects this moment's postmodern discursive currency. But the stakes involved emerge in sharp outline once I turn to a specific playwright who not only writes about the state and the economic and social institutions associated with it but who has confronted and found it necessary to resist those institutions as they affect his work.

John Arden's radio play *Pearl* (broadcast on BBC Radio 4 on July 3, 1978) is a gesture towards critiquing and defining the role theatre plays in social change. *Pearl* was written at a time when, according to Arden's own account, he and his partner Margaretta D'Arcy had "withdrawn" their labor from not only the Royal Shakespeare Company but from "any other theatre company that maintains the same invidious and over-weening management practices" (*Corners* 3). He seemed to have found in radio drama relative freedom from producers' and directors' distorting interventions. He has since written novels, migrating to a form that relies still less on others to mediate the text the writer communicates to readers and offers less opportunity for even the most well-meaning tinkering (*Corners* 44).[1] *Pearl* proposes critical questions about the relationship between the form in which ideas are transmitted and the ideas themselves. The play depicts interactions between playwrights, actors, and spectators in a complex political and social situation and, by tracing the characters' decisions in that situation, implies the choices facing contemporary theatre workers in the United Kingdom.

*Pearl* is set in England "some time around 1640" (5), just at that historical moment when parliamentary resistance to the absolutist monarchy of Charles Stuart is building towards what will be the Civil War. A mysterious woman called Pearl has traveled from Scotland and Ireland into Northern England to invite a disaffected nobleman, Lord Grimscar, to join forces across with rebel leaders from those regions. Grimscar has been pursuing alliances of his own across religious and class lines. He has arranged a performance of Shakespeare's *Julius Caesar* "to teach some of us that the worst despot in the world is yet vulnerable to the aroused outrage of honest men who love their country" (16). He hopes to convince local Puritans, led by Gideon Grip, that they can make common cause against the King, and that theatre is a valid educational medium. Grip and his fellow sectarians, however, do not wait to be convinced. The sight of boy actors playing female characters outrages them (14, 18-19). They disrupt the performance but not before Pearl has discovered that her heart's desire is to perform in stage tragedies (24).

The two efforts at forging alliances come together when Grimscar decides to mount a play in London. His poet, Tom Backhouse, will write the text. In collaboration with Pearl, Backhouse develops a script designed to show Puritans that the stage can be a sober, yet rousing, revolutionary medium and that its noble patrons, like Grimscar himself, can be worthy allies. When it comes to staging the play, however, their design is betrayed. The production ends in chaos. Arden's play concludes with Grimscar discredited, Backhouse badly wounded, and Pearl blinded, scarred, and thrown out onto the streets. In a voiceover she tells what followed: England broke into civil war; Parliament tried and beheaded the King; Oliver Cromwell ruthlessly suppressed Irish rebels; and theatre suffered a final divorce from the common people that has endured from that day to this.

The play relies on an interplay of historical, religious, and dramatic texts to create its commentary. The expectation is that auditors are familiar with English history and the other textual sources, and part of our imaginative work during and after hearing or reading the play is to think through the implications of the juxtaposition Arden has arranged.

Each of the two plays within the play concentrates on individual resistance to an abuse of power. In the first, *Julius Caesar*, Brutus fears Caesar may have the desire and popular support to take the crown and become sole ruler of Rome. He becomes embroiled in a conspiracy and (although Grip interrupts the performance before it comes to this point) kills Caesar. As noted above, Grimscar thinks that *Julius Caesar* provides an inspiring model for revolutionary conspirators. We who listen, however, may have a more ironic appreciation of the play in this setting. We know that Brutus's revolt provoked a general civil war and ended in his defeat and suicide. Antony replaced Caesar, in fact, so that the authoritarian rule Brutus feared came into being at least partly because of his own rebellion. On one level, then, Shakespeare's play can be understood as a warning against killing a king, a suggestion that chaos follows the overthrow of authority. While Arden's play unfolds, Shakespeare's conclusion may not be present in our consciousness. But as the radio play closes, Brutus's end reverberates in Pearl's description of what will come for Britain. Recollections of the play just concluded and the one aborted earlier combine to produce a redoubled image of catastrophe.

The second play within the play modifies the seemingly conservative implications of the first. Backhouse and Pearl create a play based on the book of Esther in the Hebrew Old Testament. According to the story, Haman, who was an agent of Ahasuerus, the King of Persia, persecuted and conspired to eliminate the Hebrew tribes living under Persian rule. Esther and her people are portrayed as loyal subjects even though they serve a god other than the king's. Esther resists Haman, and through her courageous action, she unlocks the king's benevolence. He needed only to be awakened to his agent's abuses. He has Haman hanged and permits the Jews to destroy all who have conspired against them.

Pearl selects the source book and story herself, and, as she articulates her reasons, she proposes ideas about theatre's role in changing social and political structures that are then tested within the course of the action. Pearl chooses to base the play on Grip's "own book" to persuade him and his followers that theatre can speak for them about their concerns (46-7). She assumes that theatre relies on identification: "out of his own book an acted play: out of his own politics a victorious struggle" (46). She further assumes the importance of the means of theatrical representation: it must mirror the values of its audience, "the production must follow exactly the manner and style we have determined for it" (52). A play that effects identification can overcome the boundaries that religious and class prejudice create and transform political alliances: Pearl believes their "play is so powerful and unprecedented that any Puritan who sees it will immediately reverse his whole attitude to the English theatre. They will thoroughly accept [the nobleman] Grimscar as speaking through his poet with the true voice of the common people" (52). Their conversion will clear the way to the partnerships she and her collaborators envision.

In addition, Pearl expects that dramatic performance can model the political goals and actions of these new partnerships. The playtext she helps Backhouse craft targets the English king's clerical and military allies. Depicting a successful inversion of power relations will suggest that the King's Lord Deputy, who prosecutes a war against Scottish Presbyterians with an army raised among poor Irish Catholics, can fall from favor and receive punishment at the hands of those he now persecutes and oppresses. Disgrace and dispossession will follow for all other enemies of Parliament. By setting out this sequence of events, the play can reinforce opposition beliefs and even set in motion spectatorial agency.

Other evidence from within Arden's play affirms Pearl's view of theatre and its potential contribution to social change. The chain of events she desires is the same feared by others. The most politically astute royalist, the Duchess, explains that she doubts the King's steadiness. He will "give way" under pressure; their sons and husbands will be killed or exiled and their lands "sequestrated" (56). The assumption that theatre can help produce such pressure motivates her effort to subvert Backhouse's production. The play might strengthen the King's opposition—Grip confirms the possibility (68-9)—and undermine his commitment to the royalists; therefore, it must fail.

The techniques the royalists use to betray Backhouse's production confirm Pearl's view that theatre attacks or affirms spectators at the level of deeply held values. Captain Catso, the experienced mercenary soldier called upon by the Duchess to "mine" the production, does so not only by eliminating "crucial speeches", but by adding "bare-breasted women . . . where they were not wanted" and "tag-lag fal-de-lals" to scenery and costumes (71-2). Most damningly, he hijacks the performance's conclusion. Pearl and Backhouse have planned that she, who has been playing Esther, will suddenly appear dressed as a sober Puritan maid to deliver a secretly written and rehearsed epilogue calling for the public indictment of each and every person who has "sought to fix upon this realm the chain / Of bondage everlasting" (66-7). Catso surprises Pearl in her costume change and exposes her half-naked before the spectators. Even a messenger's announcement that the King's Lord Deputy has been defeated by the Scots—news that should finally have catapulted Grip and Grimscar into a revolutionary alliance—

cannot upstage this image for the Roundheads in the audience. Catso's theatrical effect outweighs news of military events and irreparably alienates Grip from Grimscar.

The assumptions about theatre's potential political and social function that set the play within the play in motion carry over to Arden's radio play as a whole. Arden uses techniques that invite the listener to draw out these comparisons. For example, the radio play's primary characters duplicate those in the play within. Pearl draws attention to this phenomenon by identifying herself with the heroine of the story she selects for Backhouse to dramatize. If Pearl is like Esther, then the Lord Deputy is like Captain Catso, and Charles I is like King Ahasuerus, with the significant difference that Arden's royalists base their political actions on knowledge of the King's weakness rather than on his fairness or benevolence. Arden will provide his listeners with not even a fictional image of sympathetic authority in his history of English kings.

For the character Backhouse, however, the most obvious parallel points outside the play to another set of relationships. Backhouse is like Arden; Pearl, like D'Arcy. In this roman-a-clef search to draw correspondences between *Pearl* and its own broadcast context, the immediate referent for Catso's destructive manipulation of Backhouse and Pearl's production might well be the 1972 production of Arden and D'Arcy's *The Island of the Mighty* by the Royal Shakespeare Company. Once made, this link suggests a broader application: the processes the radio play depicts, Arden suggests, are much like those that generally constrain theatrical production today (*To Present* 156-8). From this point of view, *Pearl* points forward, not back.

I am proposing what Anthony Giddens and others would call the "historicity" of Arden's radio play. The strategy directing the play as a whole doubles that propelling the play within. Pearl's search for a story assumes that Puritans accept the Old Testament as a true history. She aims to "use" the past, in Giddens's phrase, "to help shape the present." Her choice of the specific text, Esther's story, suggests her analysis of the current political situation and ways of setting it right. Like Pearl and Backhouse, Arden and D'Arcy may have had certain expectations dictating their selection of historical sources for

*Island of the Mighty*. The failure of the one may reflect or comment upon the experience of the other. Arden's construction of *Pearl* exemplifies Giddens's observation that historicity "does not depend upon respect for the past"; rather it "means the use of knowledge about the past as a means of breaking with it" or "only sustaining what can be justified in a principled manner" (50). The dramatized tale of artistic misjudgment and disappointment, then, links past errors with the present and opens a discussion about how artists and citizens can break with the past.

The character Pearl who is the named subject of the playtext exemplifies the play's technique as it structures correspondences between historical and contemporary problems and possibilities. Pearl functions synecdochally for the problem of individual agency, first, at the personal and, then also, at the political level. Pearl both performs the self she has created and, in her recognition of theatre as a site for self-presentation, concretely suggests how art can address both an individual's specific and society's more general needs.

First, on the level of personal agency, the character presents herself as an individual who is defining and discovering her own subjectivity: "I turn over and over one question: just who I am, / Who is the one who is thinking my thoughts, / Who is this woman who turns and turns at the mill of my brain?" (24) She never discloses her true name (48). She visibly constructs her identity for the onlooker as a response to specific circumstances (35). In the situation the play relates, Pearl constructs herself as another Esther. She too is "A young woman out of nothing chosen forth by pure chance to stand all on her own bolt-upright under peril of death to perform this great mercy" (48). She selects a history that is congruent with her political goal; she conceptualizes and arranges the platform from which she will present herself; she directs Backhouse's writing and revisions of the text she will utter. In the process of rehearsing and enacting the role she has selected, she has "hauled myself forth . . . into the centre of the world: I have built myself with my own two hands my humanity for myself: and I shall not let go of it . . . !" (66)

The radio play links Pearl's drive for personal agency with her public action in the theatre and with her political effectiveness. Pearl sees herself as Esther; the play identifies her with the oppressed of Ireland, Scotland, and North America. She comes to stand for populations who have been subjected to British imperialism and who have sought to define themselves under conditions of domination. She is the child of two continents. Before Pearl was born, her mother was the concubine of an Irish chieftain from Connemara. The King's Lord Deputy sent dragoons against him, she was captured and sent in chains to one of England's colonial outposts in the new world. Named Virginia in honor of the queen "for purity and growth and hope," this outpost was instead a "place of chains and whips and misery and rape" (34). There she was again taken captive, this time by a native chief. Pearl is the daughter of their union. They live happily until white men come out of the forest and destroy the village.

As an exemplar of individual agency, the character Pearl includes two components, race and gender. She potentially occupies the lowest position in a hierarchy of oppression, first of the colonizer over the colonized and, within that, of male over female. As Pearl tells the story, each stage of her mother's journey is precipitated by male conquest and plunder. Whether the Lord Deputy's dragoons, the indigenous people of North America, or English settlers in the new world, men are the agents of violence. Pearl sums up their actions in one sentence—"They burnt and they killed and they captured"—which she repeats like a choral refrain to punctuate her story and emphasize the pattern of history (33-5). Woman's place in this history consistently is as an object of conquest, whether sexual or economic.

Pearl's position offers up images of a double oppression, but she identifies herself with both her dark-skinned father and her slave mother against European and British invaders. She tracks the course of male violence and oppression, notes that her mother saw the similarity between the two villages, but distinguishes her mother's position in the tribe by describing it more fully and as marked with "high honour and regard." She remembers her father's affection for them both and notes that her mother was "a red man's wife and glad of it" (35). She wears her mother's "short bone-handled" knife to betoken her joint heritage. The fact that it is a woman of the colonizing class who uses that very knife to mutilate her justifies her choice. Male may subjugate female, but the urgency of the desire to preserve class and economic privilege outweighs any potential gender-based solidarity.

Pearl sets out to defy the power relations her parents' history illustrates. She reverses her mother's journey, returning to the Old World not as a victim but as the agent of her own actions: "Then year after year, ever changing my shape, back to Europe from the New World a Conquistador in reverse" (35). She takes the knife her mother wore and uses it like her father to revenge her mother against the white men who defiled and killed her. She defines herself as standing both within and without her heritage. She follows neither the faith of her mother in the Virgin Mary nor that of her father in the "wild spirits" of nature. She asks how either religion could serve "a woman like me" (35). She tells her story, placing herself within her cultural history at the very time that she creates herself anew in the old world.

Even her decision to take to the stage enacts her politics. Grimscar and his fellow conspirators attempt an alliance based on their belief in the individual citizen's right to liberty (39). In their view, liberty is bound up with religious freedom and their right to own and protect property. Backhouse and Pearl attempt revolutionary aesthetic tactics as well. They attempt to redefine theatrical practice in England by putting women on stage; that effort produces a combined image of artistic and political agency. Pearl determines the story, role, and platform on which she will express the goals she has also chosen and defined during her self-propelled journey through Great Britain and Spain, the colonizer's world. Because of the nature of the identity the character has articulated in the course of the play, Pearl's demand to represent her own "heroic" vision in her own person extends to women and people of color their individual rights to self-definition and public self-representation, on stage and off.

Pearl's voiceover in the play's final moments extends the connections she has made with oppressed peoples from time and places past into the present. Blind, maimed, tapping with a stick Tiresias-like, Pearl transcends history. Those who have disfigured her have crippled the peoples she stands alongside; they have defaced the values the character has come to signify: freedom, self-definition and self-determination. The policy of using British troops to enforce order in Northern Ireland since the troubles broke out in 1969 is only the most immediate referent. The rights Pearl chooses and performs belong to all who have been enslaved or colonized.

These linkages pointing beyond the play extend to Arden and his peers in contemporary Britain the critique the play develops of Pearl's collaborators. Decisions that Backhouse makes which Pearl only reluctantly accepts lead directly to her mutilation and death. Pearl argues against working with the actor Jack Barnabas, knowing he will "abhor" the play's message once he discovers it. Backhouse believes he can "inveigle" Barnabas, trusting the part of Haman he has written for him to pique the actor's vanity sufficiently to blind him to the play's message. When Pearl argues that rehearsals will disclose their purpose, Backhouse refuses to change actors: "He's the best actor in England: I will work with none other: and he *respects* me" (53). He insists she learn the role of Esther two ways, one of which they rehearse in private against the moment of performance (65-6). Pearl believes their success rests on her ability to substitute the interpretations. Events suggest, however, that the production's disastrous conclusion results directly from opportunities the mechanics of carrying out their deception presented to their enemies. Backhouse can see that Grimscar has confused and conflicting objectives (37), but he fails to see that his own interests are just as conflicted and will destroy him and ruin the project. He might have done better had he rearranged his priorities, subordinated his desire to work with the best actor in England, and produced the play as he wrote it, message intact, however inadequate the artistry (65-6).

The play's critique, then, encompasses a specific diagnosis of reasons why artistic attacks on political and social oppression fall short of their goal. *Pearl* seems to say that, like Backhouse, both Arden and his peers have at one time or another deluded themselves that they could outwit the regime's representatives or subvert productions mounted on its stages with its financial support. They have thought they could work within, or at least alongside, the establishment. They have underestimated the forces they were attacking. They have compromised and put artistic integrity ahead of political and social goals. In his notes to the play, Arden writes,

> so long as our writers today . . . remain unable to decide whether negotiations over royalties with the state-supported National Theatre, for example, should take priority, as an immediate issue for agitation, over state-supporting torture in the Ulster police-stations . . . there is still good reason for re-examining an earlier period of history when disastrous decisions were taken for the most plausible motives. (5-6)

In other words, a narrow focus on personal achievement, wealth, and welfare prevents individual writers from taking effective action against large-scale institutionalized political oppression. Backhouse is an example for today.

With this in mind, Pearl and Backhouse's efforts to reunite the common people with their writers in the theatre takes on increased significance. The failure of their project results not only in political disaster but in muddy art that does not address its public and a public that has no tragic art to speak its deepest values and dreams. Again the character Pearl functions as a synecdoche. The failed tragedy finalizes the divorce of the people from their artists, which leads in turn to the deformation of theatre as an artistic product. The chain of effects wounds the people, as Pearl says, "deeper" than body and bone, "within the soul" (76). The character's fate is both a consequence and a confirmation of the mutilation that results in the body politic.

Not only the artists but the common people themselves are responsible for allowing this state of affairs to continue. As Pearl says, "Let them live with it" (76). Arden does not, however, rest content. He addresses the issues and the people directly through one of the most democratic public media available to him, radio. As described by scholars writing near the time the play was aired, BBC drama provided an artistic venue even more accurately characterized by the term "national" than other state theatres (Rodger 152-5). David Wade observes that 700,000 spectators attended the National Theatre during its first season on the South Bank; each single afternoon broadcast of radio drama over the BBC was likely to attract that same total number of listeners ("British Radio Drama" 219). Wade and others note that the broadcasts were comparatively accessible: neither the cost of the ticket nor proximity to London restricted listening (219). Portable radio technology meant that shut-ins, students, typists, pieceworkers, and homemakers could listen in. Insiders designated one category of scripts as "plays to hoover to." (222).

Although it reaches a wide and diverse public, radio is a peculiarly private medium (Imison 290; Druker 334-5). Surrounded as I am by books on radio drama and others by and about John Arden, at this distance (both spatial and temporal) I can only speculate on the effect of first hearing the play. The play's merit was recognized immediately—it was nominated for a Giles Cooper Award for best radio play of 1978—but critical response to the original broadcast reminds me that my own assumptions about the "correct" or "reasonable" understanding of the play, especially the priority Arden places on its political implications, are conditioned by my own preoccupations as a student of political theatre. Neil Hepburn, reviewing the play in *The Listener* of July 13, 1978, admitted himself to be "puzzled":

> the places where I expected [Arden] to be most effective, as in the scenes of collaboration between Pearl and Backhouse, were least convincing, and all the vitality, the passion, the splendid rhetoric went into the Irish grievance, the Puritan or Levelling prosecution, and Pearl's passion for the theatre. (in Page 64)

What was confusing to him is simply necessary to me: the personal is subordinate to the political. Pearl refuses Backhouse's romantic overtures until they have finished the playtext. The relationship matures within and as a result of their political activity rather than motivating it. But the message is, of course, shaped by the receiver's inclination and historical situation.

Arden exploits those attributes which potentially allow the medium to bridge the gap, to heal the divorce between writer and the general public. He seems to be at pains to provoke active, engaged listening. The vigor of the narrative propels the listener along, whether or not all allusions and implications are immediately apparent. Backhouse and Pearl (and their opposition) assume a vitally responsive spectatorship. Puritan and royalist spectators to the plays within the play give vociferous reactions which in turn may arouse excitement and emotional engagement in radio listeners. At the same time that it can isolate (Brecht 52), radio also allows for an intimate approach, a direct route into the listener's mind through the ear without the mediation of the theatre's usual physical apparatus. Pearl narrates much of the action, and the experience of her voice may engage each of us more deeply in her passion for theatre, her determination to play Esther well, her frustration and anxiety at the strategy Backhouse has chosen, her grief and pain as she tells how her own knife was used to cut her nose and cheeks and blind her. Such engagement may instigate in the individual listener first identification, then the kind of *"thoroughgoing, constitutive reflexivity"* that Anthony Giddens assumes characterizes the current historical moment in general (50-2, 149f).

The script structures opportunities for considerable individual imaginative activity on the part of the listener. *Pearl* plays on the internal field of the listener's imagination and produces images that are particularized, stamped with his or her own history, experience, and values. Arden's appropriation of two canonical texts that have their own interpretative history to create a new fable potentially gives longer lasting and deeper resonance to the listener's experience of the performance. The intertextual activity may provoke listeners into tracing, recalling, re-reading, re-thinking texts, productions, and their critical reception. Judging from descriptions of the BBC's role in distributing documentary programs, canonical texts, and historical information, it may be that, despite *Pearl*'s "extraordinarily challenging" text (Drakakis 18), BBC listeners were well prepared to knit together the references Arden provided.[2]

If Arden prompts the listener to stage in his or her imagination two stories of rebellion against authority in order to tell yet another, what kind of political activity might this constitute? As noted with regard to interpretation, the answer again is as variable as individual listeners, their knowledge (of Arden, Ireland, England), their experiential history, and so forth. I found that Arden uses the network of literary and historical identifications that stretch across the play as a whole to initiate another set of exploratory identifications with its wider context, the United Kingdom and its world of artistic production and political frame. The process of tracing cross-references and making roman-a-clef connections drew me into placing myself alongside the characters and discovering parallel situations, first in the United Kingdom, then in the United States. The notion of action in the theatre began to function metatheatrically, as an image of civic action in general.

Writing, rehearsal, and performance are subject to censorship, intervention, distortion, and betrayal; from this point of view, theatre can stand for collaborative public activities of many kinds. The inability of political factions to understand even the use of women actors on stage to represent women characters (which is the basis of Grip's rejection of theatre as a valid cultural activity) begins to look like a metaphor for contemporary political activists' inability to rise above tactical differences and make common cause on substantive matters. In "A Shift of Perspective," first published in *The Connacht Tribune* in 1985, Arden asserts:

> Censorship, politically-fixed justice, hysteria against "subversion," the denigration of civil liberties, are all part of a system left in this country [Ireland] by its former occupiers and rulers. The struggle against that system is the same struggle as the one that expelled (to some extent) those rulers. They are still not expelled from the control of Britain. They cannot be got rid of from one side of the water alone. But if the Irish work against them solely in Ireland and the British in Britain, I am sure that complete understanding—and hence co-operation—can never be achieved. (*Corners* 20)

And of course, what Arden observes of the United Kingdom might well be said of the United States. *Pearl* addresses me directly on the intimate stage of my imagination in order to shift me, however minutely, into re-considering history, its mistakes, and my present opportunities. Through radio's intimate address, Arden invites me to walk in Pearl's shoes, in the expectation that I will take part in her journey, trials, disappointment, and death, and come to understand her personal and political goals. His observations about theatre carry over into the public arena as a whole. If individuals making up the factions of the political opposition could be induced to see beyond their artistic, religious, and political differences to their common goal, Backhouse's vision might be realized at last: "Why, Cassius and his conspirators would be nothing to it . . . pit and gallery of all England would be shook like a watchman's rattle!" (36) *Pearl*'s sequel is waiting to be written.

# Notes

1. Radio avoids some, but not all, of the pitfalls of working in the theatre. Arden recalls that a BBC producer sought to commission a radio play on the condition that it be "genuine Arden"—that is, without the contaminating influence of D'Arcy (*Corners* 56–7).

2. *Pearl* was "originally broadcast in the popular *Monday Play* series on Radio 4" and later rebroadcast on Radio 3, which is generally "associated with 'more esoteric and demanding plays'" (Drakakis 18). David Wade attempts roughly to categorize the content of radio programs according to their audience appeal. On the relatively more "popular" Radio 4 drama he exempts the *Monday Play* where *Pearl* was originally broadcast ("Popular Radio Drama" 92). But he then goes on to complicate the categories, saying that at the time of his attempting the description, there was increasingly less difference.

# Works Cited

Arden, John, and Margaretta D'Arcy. *Awkward Corners*. London: Methuen, 1988.

Arden, John. *Pearl: A Play About a Play Within the Play*. London: Methuen, 1979.

———. *To Present the Pretence: Essays on the Theatre and its Public*. London: Eyre Methuen, 1977.

Brecht, Bertolt. *Brecht on Theatre*. Trans. and ed. John Willett. New York: Hill and Wang, 1964.

Drakakis, John. Introduction. *British Radio Drama*. Cambridge: Cambridge University Press, 1981. 1–36.

Druker, Don. "Listening to the Radio." *Theatre Journal* 43 (1991): 325–35.

Giddens, Anthony. *The Consequences of Modernity*. Stanford, CA: Stanford University Press, 1990.

Imison, Richard. "Radio and the Theatre: A British Perspective." *Theatre Journal* 43 (1991): 289–92.

Page, Malcolm. *Arden on File*. London: Methuen, 1985.

Poggi, Gianfranco. *The State: Its Nature, Development and Prospects*. Stanford: Stanford University Press, 1990.

Rodger, Ian. *Radio Drama*. London: Macmillan, 1982.

Wade, David. "British Radio Drama Since 1960." *British Radio Drama*. Ed. John Drakakis. Cambridge: Cambridge University Press, 1981. 218–44.

Wade, David. "Popular Radio Drama." *Radio Drama*. Ed. Peter Lewis. London: Longman, 1981. 91–110.

# EXEMPLARY DRAMA: ARDEN'S SHIFTING PERSPECTIVE ON SIXTEENTH AND SEVENTEENTH CENTURY PREDECESSORS

## Michael Cohen

That the function of theatre and of the playwright has preoccupied Arden throughout his career is clear from the way he has returned to considering it almost as often during the fifteen years or so since he and D'Arcy gave writing for the stage as previously. For the novelist in later middle age writing *The Books of Bale* (1988), as much as for the young playwright of thirty years before, the raison d'être of theatre is a consuming question, but his perspective has shifted considerably. It would be misleading now to treat this development in terms of two stages as we did at one time, conscious as we were of the emergence of a very different Arden in middle age. There are obviously the more recent, non-theatre years to consider. Equally, the political terms in which his earlier periods were contrasted, such as "from liberal to marxist," were not always helpful, as has been argued elsewhere.[1] I will attempt here to analyse Arden's development less in relation to specific political categories and more in terms of his shifting valuations of those sixteenth- and seventeenth-century precursors and ages of drama to which both his works and his theory have regularly returned. The periods in question can be defined as the pre-Elizabethan sixteenth century decades on the one hand and the Elizabethan/Jacobean ones on the other. The latter of course make up what is still commonly referred to as "The Age of Shakespeare" though, for Arden, it has usually been as much that of Jonson. His perspectives on the two eras for drama will be separated into three phases: "earlier," "middle," and "later." These phases are necessarily inexact as Arden's changes of attitude, like anyone else's, are sometimes inconsistent and within an apparently new outlook, there may be residues from the old, continuities as well as discontinuities.

The earlier Arden was distinguished from other notable figures who emerged in the post-1956 movement in British theatre by a number of characteristics, but perhaps the most important one was the intensity of his preoccupation with the past literature of the British Isles. In one of two much-cited essays published in 1960, "Telling a True Tale" (the other is "A Thoroughly Romantic View"), he explicitly distinguished himself from key contemporaries by virtue of his quest for a drama which would deal with the contemporary world but by setting it "within the historical and legendary traditions of our culture" (125). In this essay he focussed chiefly on the ballad, not so much as an "influence" but as an *exemplum*, as the "bedrock" on which he proposed to build himself. Among various authors who had also supposedly done so he listed three who recur in his writings and who will figure in this discussion: Skelton, Shakespeare, and Jonson (126). In the second essay he refers to another, Sir David Lindsay, whose *Three Estates* had made such a deep impression on him when he saw it as a young National Serviceman in Edinburgh. This had *actually* suggested to him the possibility of a modern drama which would deal with the ills of the present world without renouncing "the excitement and splendour of the old theatre I had been brought up to believe in" ("Romantic View" 13). "Actually" is emphasized because this writer, even after seeing *The Three Estates* again at the 1991 Edinburgh Festival, remains unsure of how Lindsay's play could actually have served much as a model for Arden, even in the apparently obvious case of *Armstrong's Last Goodnight* (1964). But the essential point here is that it *did* and that the sheer unusualness, the degree of cultural heterodoxy, of a contemporary dramatist whose proclaimed influences and precursors go back to the earlier Stuart and Tudor periods, or what some might classify as the late Middle Ages, has probably been insufficiently emphasized.

At this stage there is no suggestion of any difficulty in making such an appropriation of past conventions in drama for contemporary purposes. The differences in political and ideological situations, in relations between drama and audience, playwrights and authority, appear not to have been considered to any important extent. Arden's primary interest here would seem to have been in conventions which could be employed as part of the anti-naturalistic theatre which he felt was best equipped to portray the modern world, conventions that is, in Williams's most restricted sense of, "only a method . . . which facilitates the performance" (6). "Convention" in a more complex sense was to prove more of a problem.

So far as the Elizabethan era is concerned, Arden was already making emphatic distinctions between the examples offered by Shakespeare and Jonson when he was asked to pay tribute to Shakespeare in *The Guardian* newspaper on the day of Shakespeare's quatercentenary in 1964 (11). Young playwrights were advised to take Jonson rather than Shakespeare as their model because he, unlike Shakespeare, offered models of play construction which might actually be emulated. Shakespeare was essentially inimitable, breaking the classical "rules" at will and offering nothing "impersonal" which could be taken away and used for his own designs by the prentice playwright, nothing which had not been "impregnated with his unique character" (11). To readers only of middle and later Arden this might come as a surprise offering as it does what is by the standards of its time rather a conventional tribute to an inimitable genius, though elsewhere he makes it clear that, like his other early exemplar Jonson, he admired Shakespeare this side of idolatry. What is still farther removed from his later views on Shakespeare and on the goals of theatre is the tribute's contention that the Bard had set an example to all future workers in the theatre by making the best of its perennially unsatisfactory conditions, which resulted above all from the necessity "to appeal to an *audience* rather than individuals" (11; emphasis added). This necessity was seen as the major obstacle to achieving perfection in drama.

The influence of Elizabethan models generally on the earlier plays was acknowledged by Arden in what have also become very frequently quoted statements. Specialists will be only too familiar with his remark that he had written *The Waters of Babylon* (1957) as "a kind of cross-breed between two Elizabethan pieces—Jonson's *Alchemist* and Chapman's *Blind Beggar of Alexandria*" ("Romantic View" 14). It may be that such observations helped to ensure the academic interest that the early work always had even when critical responses were uneven. The Chapman reference could have suggested a play–wright who was not only at ease in corners of Elizabethan drama normally only explored by scholars, few of whom would remember much about *The Blind Beggar of Alexandria*, but one who could turn even the obscurer territory subsumed under the heading of "English literature" to creative purposes.

However, there is the danger that we shall focus too much on the teller rather than the tales. The extent to which the plays of this period actually correspond to Arden's statements of intent is debatable, never more so than when these remarks referring to the respective influences of Jonson and Shakespeare are considered. With justification, he stressed the Jonsonian elements in *The Workhouse Donkey* (1963), but in retrospect arguably the Shakespearean ones are stronger. If we isolate the issue of construction for a moment, it is broadly true that Jonson's comedies usually lack *The Workhouse Donkey*'s sheer number, variety and speed of location changes, reminiscent of Shakespeare at his most fluid.[2] In Act 1 alone there are nine different changes of scene, and subsequently almost as many per act.

The free-wheeling narrative technique of *The Workhouse Donkey* seems to owe more to Shakespeare and other sixteenth century playwrights (including earlier ones) than it does to the more classically "correct" Jonson, though in *Bartholomew Fair*, a play admired by Arden (*To Present* 31-2), Jonson developed a quite varied open stage style. The development of a flexible narrative convention by Arden in his social comedies was linked with similar objectives in the form of his political dramas whose resemblance to aspects of Brecht's "epic theatre" comes less from direct influence than from the two playwrights' *independent* interest in Elizabethan and other earlier theatre models.[3] This convention was in turn a product of his interest in the history play, a central genre for Shakespeare of course, but not on the whole for Jonson, unless we count the Roman plays whose model is closer to Senecan tragedy.

Ideologically and programmatically too the political dramas seem to have a greater affinity with Shakespeare in this earlier phase, though this is a complex issue to deal with in limited space. If we say that the moral universe of these plays is not un-Shakespearean, many questions are begged, especially in an era of cultural materialism. They will remain begged for much of this outline of Arden's development, but it is hoped that some of the crucial ones are at least addressed later. The earlier Arden is, like Shakespeare, a less openly didactic dramatist than Jonson. The interest—for some the irritation—of *Serjeant Musgrave's Dance* (1959) or *Armstrong* is the moral ambiguity, the uncertainty of viewpoint. Arden's description of the ballads as conveying their moral only by "the whole turn of the story" could equally be applied to Shakespeare's work. His best early plays tend, like Shakespeare's, strenuously to exercise the audience's judgement rather than to offer an explanation or a solution. Hence the ending to *Armstrong's Last Goodnight* in which Lindsay turns the responsibility for creating a better political morality than he has found possible on the audience: this is arguably similar to Prospero's appeal to the audience in his epilogue. Arden's dislike of openly judgemental drama is made clear in a number of statements of this period.[4]

Secondly, there is the characteristic fusion of personal and public issues. His success in this has sometimes been disputed as in the arguments about the relation of the accidental death of Sparky to the theme of colonial war in *Musgrave*,[5] but the fact remains that Arden's imagination does inhabit the territories of both Marx and Freud, as does Shakespeare's, though this is not to say that either Arden or Shakespeare shares the conceptual frameworks of Freud or Marx or that Arden is Shakespeare's equal. On the whole, despite his amazing grotesques, Jonson works on a more explicit level psychologically.

The Shakespearean comparisons to be made with Arden's belief that his work ought to be placed in the historical and legendary traditions of English culture, because social criticism not expressed within the framework of traditional poetic truths tended to be "dangerously ephemeral" ("True Tale" 129) hardly need elaborating. His rejection of what he regarded as his contemporaries' "documentary facility," so striking in retrospect at the outset of the 1960s in which documentary theatre flourished, is clearly relatable to Shakespeare's avoidance of much in the way of direct contem-

164 *Michael Cohen*

porary references. Jonson cannot be described as a documentary writer, but it was the contemporary scene at which he excelled in his city comedies, sometimes with dangerous consequences. Shakespeare, like many other Elizabethan playwrights, and Arden after them, is more inclined to migrate to other times, places, or both.

However, the enduring influence of Jonson and the centrality given to him must not be understated. In his longer tribute to Shakespeare's rival of 1972 we find the respective qualities of the two playwrights again being compared, and there is considerably more detail on Jonson's perceived usefulness as a model to those seeking a manual for play construction. The fact that this piece largely expands on the themes of the 1964 previously discussed, despite its place in what had become the second, much more embattled, phase of Arden and D'Arcy's careers as playwrights, illustrates the presence of continuities as well as changes in Arden's outlook.

He later summed up the factors underlying the change of direction which he and D'Arcy made in the sixties, a change which D'Arcy herself has also commented on.[6] What would seem to be his deepest feelings about the artistic crisis which this reorientation produced are expressed in his radio play *The Bagman* (1970), a Dantesque mid-life questioning of purpose, with its haunting lines, "You did not find what you expected / What you found you did not use / What you saw you did not look at / When you looked . . . you would not choose" (87). But the new phase cannot be tidily located in a new decade. Arden and D'Arcy's changed agenda as playwrights, including centrally the demand for control of their work, was already clearly worked out at the time of their clash with the Institute of Contemporary Arts over *The Hero Rises Up* (1968): "our right as co-author-directors to compose our own publicity material, our right to manage the production the way we wanted it managed, and our right to determine the type of audience we thought would be best served by the show we were putting on" (*To Present* 84).

This is a succinct summary of the proper functions of the playwright as Arden and D'Arcy now perceived them, however deeply opposed it was to the reality of the social relations of theatre with which they were actually confronted. The impact of this new programme on Arden's feelings about his sixteenth- and seventeenth-century forebears will now be considered. In 1972 he published the essay "What's Theatre For?" This, as the title suggests, seeks a functionalist explanation of the theatre's role. At first he appears to make an unsatisfactory assumption that there can be a single answer to the question, unsatisfactory because any one answer must be explanatorily inadequate in the case of so historically varied a phenomenon. But before long he begins to contrast his situation as a playwright with Jonson's. Had he lived in Jonson's time, he could have agreed with him that theatre was for "inculcating virtue and lashing vice" so that the audience saw their "own wisdom and follies recognizably portrayed" (10). Moreover, this would be an audience who lived in a small city and went regularly to the theatre. Interestingly, Arden rejects next what was until quite recently a common perception of the Elizabethan audience as one which constituted a cross-section of society, (though Backhouse in *Pearl* (1978) six years later opines that the drama of this period *had* spoken to "a whole people"). *Here* the case is that the audience *did not include* the emergent forces of Puritanism. Jonson and Shakespeare had mocked an apparently absurd minority, but within a few decades "the broad-based community to which the Elizabethan/Jacobean playwrights had so confidently addressed themselves was not the all-inclusive cross-section of the country that it had seemed. Malvolio and Zeal-of-the-Land-Busy were suddenly the government, accepted by consensus. And the theatres were closed." Jonson had done his duty as a dramatist up to a point in distinguishing vice from virtue but "he had failed to relate the fictions of his plays to the reality outside the playhouse." Thus the public did not understand why the revolution had taken place or what sort of revolution it was and "the theatre had failed in part of its purpose," which was to recreate life in such a way that "the right lessons can be drawn and the correct decisions made" (10). This being the playwright's role, he was obliged to watch both the world around him *and* the make-up of his audience. As the use of the phrases "right thinking" and "correct decisions" suggests, Arden's ideal of theatre has for a moment seemingly moved towards propaganda, and, significantly, D'Arcy and he undertook an agitprop production with *The Ballygombeen Bequest* (1972) in the same year that "What's Theatre For?" appeared.

At this stage Jonson is at least credited with having met the responsibilities of the playwright to some extent. Shakespeare appears merely to rate as one of those Elizabethan/Jacobean dramatists who mistakenly took themselves to be addressing a whole community. However, Arden's thinking about Shakespeare in the seventies proves more complex and shifting than this. As before, it is Shakespeare whom he turns to for a model when the subject is historical. Any ideological doubts which were developing came seldom to the surface in this phase, and Shakespeare certainly was not rejected as a formal exemplar even when so apparently incongruous a subject as the life and times of James Connolly was being considered. Again, just as the ostensibly agitprop *Ballygombeen Bequest*, far removed from the agitprop style of the twenties as it proved, was claimed for drama-proper in 1972,[7] so *The Non-Stop Connolly Show* (1975), despite its stylistic eclecticism, is closer to drama than the documentary theatre tradition which had been naturalized in Britain by Theatre Workshop. When Arden discusses the problems of dramatizing the lengthy arguments of socialist leaders in Part Four, he compares the difficulty with what Shakespeare was confronted with in Act Two of *Antony and Cleopatra* because the historical source material was undramatic (*To Present* 98) There is an echo too of Richard III, V, iii in the *Connolly Show*'s fine encounter between the hero and the ghosts of his political past (6, 2, 17). Indeed, an interesting comparison is possible between the length of the Connolly cycle and that of the Shakespearean historical tetralogies (Leach 12). Above all, when Arden spoke of his feelings about the *audience* for the Connolly plays in the original production he compared that audience with the Elizabethan one: "we actually had an audience for six full-length political plays, which was interested in the politics and regarded them as important to their daily life. This is the Elizabethan audience in fact" (Interview with Kreisler 22). What counts here is the perception of an ideal audience as an Elizabethan one rather than the fact that some members of the audience were very critical of the production and others enthused over it.[8] For Arden and D'Arcy the Connolly plays seem to represent the production in which they came closest to acting out their ideal roles as playwrights. Significantly the event could hardly have been more removed from the norms of mainstream theatre.

Throughout the seventies, it would seem, Shakespeare was for Arden a very positive figure on the whole, not least because he had an exemplary relation to the production of his work, which Arden, in the essay "Playwrights and Play-writers," argues is wholly unattainable for the contemporary dramatist (*To Present* 178-84). He goes on, in a Shakespearean essay of the first order, to analyse the mode of production in an Elizabethan company as he surmises it to have been. Most important is the fact that there was no role for a director. Rather the production of the work had something in common with the model proposed by Jósef Szajna, a *"happening* . . . whose contours should be shaped by the cast, together with the author" (*To Present* 173), though there was no question of disposing of any prior script in Elizabethan productions. The Globe theatre had mounted its presentation with the combined efforts of the actors, the "Prompter or the Stage Manager and no doubt some advice from the Poet" (*To Present* 178) This was possible because of the availability to playwright and players of "a complete series of received craft conventions" which had been developed over several preceding generations as the "standard craftsman's response to standard situations." Hence the dramatist was "continually and closely in touch with the work in rehearsal" (*To Present* 183-4)

The interaction between the playwright's lines and the company's stagecraft with its stock conventions gave a dual structure to a play in performance which Arden goes on to analyse in the cases of *Hamlet* and *Henry V*. *Hamlet* had conveyed *both* the story of a young man's revenge for the murder of his father and that of an heir to the throne's revenge in a nation on a war footing and this was signified more "by the stagecraft . . . than the speeches" (*To Present* 194). However, whereas in *Hamlet* speeches and stagecraft worked together, in *Henry V* there was deliberate disparity between what was said and what was done, and this was so for *ideological* reasons. Shakespeare, as a "true

168 Michael Cohen

poet," could not have brought himself to offer a Machiavellian tract about the advantage to monarchs in a difficult political situation of conducting a victorious military campaign abroad. True poets had detested conquest and bloodshed since the time of Homer. So Shakespeare, conscious of the danger of debunking openly a central part of Tudor ideology, had contrived a combination of an orthodox "overt text" and a "secret play" which was conveyed by things seen rather than said (*To Present* 199).

Here Shakespeare has been enlisted in Arden's tradition of "true poets" who are above all anti-militaristic, which recalls with equal force the themes of *The Island of the Mighty* (1972) and the anarchistic-pacifistic ideology of the younger Arden who was strongly influenced by Robert Graves and his cult of the "White Goddess."

No role remotely resembling Shakespeare's conjectured one was now available to Arden and D'Arcy or to anyone else who wished to become a play*wright* in the full sense of a craftsperson, rather than a mere playwriter who was usually excluded from the production process after the play script had been accepted. This was similar, even, it seems, in the "alternative theatre" with the unique exception of *The Non-Stop Connolly Show*. Hence, after working for a time with the leading British left-wing theatre group 7:84, Arden and D'Arcy ceased to write for the stage. In a long conversation with the two playwrights in 1983,[9] it was evident that they had found the parts allocated to them as dramatists by 7:84 little more satisfactory than those accorded to them by conventional theatre. The constitution of 7:84 had prevented them from having any more influence on the production of *Vandaleur's Folly* (1978) after the first stage of the play's tour even though the authors were nominally the directors. The actors then took over decisions about what should be modified in the production and were in a position to veto the foyer display which the playwrights had devised for it. Moreover, the desired audience seemed to them as remote as ever. In the conversation they expressed doubts about whether 7:84 was playing to anything like a *representative* working-class audience.

The issue of audience and the dramatist's control over his work are, of course, central to Arden's radio play of the same year, *Pearl*, which is as much a parable about the failure of political theatre as the relations between Britain and Ireland, occurring in a century when, Arden retrodictively imagines, history might have taken a different and better course. A political play aimed at the Puritans is the means by which this happier outcome may be brought about: momentarily it seems that the theatre, unlike poetry in Auden's line, *can* make something happen, but in ways which clearly reflect to some extent Arden and D'Arcy's feelings about their conflict with the Royal Shakespeare Company over *The Island of the Mighty*, in so far as Backhouse and Pearl's play is sabotaged almost as much by antagonistic interpretation on the part of the company as by the sinister Captain Catso and Lady Belladonna, the revolutionary moment is lost. A prerequisite for the kind of play which will succeed with the Puritans is that it should have an anti-tragic structure and climate of feeling which will permit the message to be taken in, but the production becomes a vehicle for the story of a tragic hero, which, ironically, Backhouse's patron Lord Grimscar actually admires whilst the playwright seethes with rage, as Arden and D'Arcy had done over the cutting of their last act coda to *The Island of the Mighty*, though the general implications of the parable may be equally relevant to other episodes in the history of political drama, such as Brecht's concern about early responses to *Mother Courage*.

In keeping with the parable's twin themes, Pearl's final speech when blind and mutilated dwells on both the tragic future history of Britain's treatment of Ireland and on a perceived parting of the ways between the drama and the ordinary people in Britain, for which the now-unbridgeable gulf between the Puritans and the theatre stands. Certain things are worth noting about the perspective here. Firstly, the play takes a very positive view of the Elizabethan/Jacobean period. Even the somewhat creaking performance of *Julius Caesar* at the beginning suggests a drama which, if dated in its execution, is a thoroughly worthy one. It is, after all, this which inspires Pearl to dedicate herself to the art, fragmentary as the performance is as a result of the response of the restive tradesmen. Again, as Backhouse

surveys his career from middle age, what he wishes to revive is
an era of drama which spoke to a "whole people." Finally, in
Pearl's lament for a lost theatre which united the popular with
the good there is strong suggestion of a *spiritual* loss for the
ordinary people as a result:

> From that day to this the word of the Common People
> of England, most powerful in the strength of the Lord,
> had little or nothing to do with the word of their
> tragic poets or the high genius of their actors. You
> may say this did small hurt to the body and bones,
> but deeper, within the soul . . . Let them live with it.
> (76)

We are a long way here from the standpoint of some of
Arden's contemporaries in the alternative theatre, to whom the
suggestion that the common people had suffered damage to the
soul because of their indifference to this particular cultural form
would have seemed condescending in the extreme.[10] Should we
conclude that his apparently implicit historical and cultural
assumptions here are, at best, quixotic, and that this is
increasingly realised in his most recent phase? The question is
complicated by the status of *Pearl* as a parable which deals in
analogies. *Historically*, it would be unconvincing to connect the
alienation of the Puritans from the Elizabethan/Jacobean theatre
with that of the modern working class from the contemporary
one. Following such a claim through, we should be compelled to
consider the fact that some descendants of the seventeenth-
century Puritans became lower-middle-class eighteenth-century
tradespeople who *were* to be found amongst the audiences for
the sentimental comedies of Steele and Cibber and, perhaps
more significantly in this context, for the *tragedies* of George
Lillo.[11] However irredeemably minor much of this drama may
now seem, the fact is that there proved to be no uncrossable
divide between a *possible* great-grandchild of Arden's Gideon
Grip and the eighteenth-century theatre. Again, the gulf between
the nineteenth-century industrial working class and the
Victorian *dramatic* stage—in the sense of a stage concerned with
"serious" or "classic" plays rather than melodrama or
pantomime[12]—can readily be hypothesised as the result of

inevitable class cultural differentiation, one of the components of which was a distinctly decadent school of Shakespearean interpretation on which Arden himself has commented (*To Present* 185) As for the twentieth century, with the diffusion of drama into several different media and its reception in so many different contexts, the questions become almost imponderable. *Is* the contemporary working class, however defined, indifferent to the "high genius" of British actors whom it may see in television drama, the most convincing claimant of the title "national theatre"? It seems unlikely.

It may be that these are unimportant questions for two main reasons. Firstly, *Pearl* is more appropriately responded to as a parable about Arden's own situation, that of one of the century's most gifted British dramatists who has withdrawn from the field because of the problematic social situation for theatre and that, had the parable been, like *Serjeant Musgrave,* less "historical," it would have presented no referential problem. Secondly, in any case, his perspective was to shift again, as will be seen, and *Pearl* no longer represents a declaration of faith, either historical or artistic.

In the most recent phase of Arden's development as a writer, we find that, though he and D'Arcy may no longer work in the theatre, the theatre understandably works on in his thoughts. It appears as a central theme in his two novels, *Silence Among the Weapons* (1982) and *Books of Bale* (1988), as well as in a story in *Cogs Tyrannic* (1991). Again, whilst his imagination has ranged ever more widely over history, either in his individual work or in his collaboration with D'Arcy on *Whose Is the Kingdom?* (1987), he has made some significant returns to the sixteenth- and seventeenth-century dramatic eras and authors under particular consideration here. There has been the radio play about John Skelton, *Garland for a Hoar Head* (1982), and *Books of Bale,* and some revealing passages in his sections of the joint collection with D'Arcy, *Awkward Corners* (1988).

Arden's historical imagination has often been esteemed. But not until the publication of his autobiographical essay in *Awkward Corners* did it become apparent how richly this imagination had been fed in his Yorkshire childhood. Here, amongst many fascinating details, one finds several which are

particularly relevant to this discussion. When he went to
Christmas dinners at the house of the Beverley branch of the
family there were portraits, some of Ardens, going back to the
seventeenth century. Before that the Ardens had lived in
Warwickshire and one of them, Mary Arden, had been
Shakespeare's mother! A knight's helmet hanging in Beverley
Minster had supposedly been Harry Hotspur's. St. Mary's
Church in Beverley had the most elaborately figured panelled
ceiling, including, "the legendary Brutus, great-grandson of
Aeneas the Trojan refugee, and running through Lear,
Cymbeline, William the Conqueror, Edwards and Henrys, up to
Henry VI" (*Corners* 64-5).

The information that Arden *could* be distantly related to
Shakespeare, if available at the time, say, of the quatercentenary
celebrations, would have been much relished by enthusiasts for
his work, and, if the playwright himself had been remotely the
sort of person who would exploit such a connection—and he
could hardly be less so—no doubt his marketability would have
been enhanced. *Now* one's response to the revelation is more
wary. Academically, it will not necessarily be an advantage for
his links with Shakespeare to be stressed, either at this very
distant hypothetical family level or through the sort of affinities
in his work discussed earlier. In some schools of thought
Shakespeare cannot be regarded as "our contemporary": rather
he was for an age and *not* for all time[13] and the age is hardly
Arden's one. Personally, he would in any case be likely to reject
any characterization of his work which subsumed it under
another playwright's. He has, as he has made clear, learnt a great
deal from Shakespeare and other Elizabethans, but he is very
much his own playwright, or, in collaboration with D'Arcy, part
of a team which is formidably independent in its artistic
judgements. Finally, he has become more ambiguous about
Shakespeare's age and has apparently moved closer in sympathy
with the age of Bale. Thus in *Awkward Corners*, we find in the
essay whose title inspired the title of this one—"Shift of
Perspective"—the seeming elevation of Bale to the status of a
pivotal figure in sixteenth-century drama: "the crucial protestant
link between the medieval catholic morality-drama and the new
secular theatre of Marlowe and Shakespeare," and the author, in

*King John,* of a play without which "the entire cycle of Elizabethan chronicle-plays might never have come to fruition." Bale is now an exemplar, practising as he did a theatre of *combat*: "He wrote . . . in combat: catholic playwrights were also putting their ideas at the same time onto the stage, and English theatre between 1530 and 1558 was a battlefield of opposed philosophies." This becomes exemplary enough to be considered, "exactly the sort of theatre that we at the Royal Court in the 1960s thought we might possibly be inaugurating" (*Corners* 17). The endorsement of, above all, a theatre of combat is linked presumably with Arden and D'Arcy's own long-standing estrangement from establishment theatre in Britain and their increasing commitment over twenty years to a battle against its modus operandi, especially in relation to the position of the playwright. But it also has more directly political implications. The age which was long perceived as one of England's greatest, the "age of Shakespeare," had still been apparently endorsed ten years before in *Pearl*, at least so far as the theatre was concerned. But a historical perspective increasingly determined by Irish left-nationalism had led to a progressive political disenchantment with the Elizabethan age. After all, Spenser and Ralegh had spent time in Ireland, "neither of them at all interested in the Irish readership," only to share "the signal distinction of having both taken part in a famous military atrocity, the massacre of the garrison at Dún-an-óir, the 'golden fort,' at Smerwick, Co. Kerry, 1580" (*Corners* 14). Thus "the sixteenth century—that glorious time, for the English, of poetry, pageant, and romantic buccaneering seafarers, which has fixed itself into our educational and literary tradition . . . as the generative seedbed of all the excellence that is said to have followed" (*Corners* 14), seems to be displaced now by the pre-Elizabethan age of Bale—even as the "generative seedbed" of drama.

In Arden's novel Bale is a far from heroic character in many respects, being almost comically ineffectual in much of his personal life, especially in his relations with his wife, Dorothy. Nevertheless, he personifies the political commitment which Arden now regards as the playwright's most important virtue. He is also linked with other key figures in the pre-Elizabethan dramatic tradition to whom Arden has paid tribute over the

years: Skelton and Lindsay. Like Arden, he seeks exemplary
dramatists among his predecessors, and when discussing his
plans for *King John* he declares, "Skelton Laureate my exemplar,
*Magnificence*" (*Bale* 153). As in Shakespeare's theatre, according
to Arden, conventions are ready-made for the sort of play Bale
has in mind: "Every stage-player well-knoweth how such a play
should be done" (*Bale* 153), and part of Williams's more complex
idea of convention is also given: there is "agreement to meet"
(44) insofar as "every audience can tell the shape of it from its
very commencement" (*Bale* 153). Bale, like Backhouse and Pearl,
writes drama which *could* have a political effect but fails to,
partly because the actors are not really committed (*Bale* 316).

Shakespeare features, though not a great deal, in those
sections of the novel in which Bale's daughter and granddaughter are caught up in the world of the Elizabethan theatre.
At least from the point of view of Shakespeare's opponents like
Anthony Munday, the dramatist's complexity and ambiguity
only serve to cloud his political judgement which ought to be
clarified by the play. Munday accuses him of "clever tricks" for
"he divides his plays this way and that till no-one knows what
they mean" (*Bale* 396). Interestingly, here Munday has been
outlining precisely the dual structure, and consequent dual
meaning, of *Henry V*, which Arden appeared to have admired in
the seventies. Admittedly Munday is presented as a distinctly
untrustworthy character.

Bale's daughter Lydia is a more formidable critic, both as
a member of a family representing unequivocal Protestant
morality values in drama and as the mother of Lucretia whom
Shakespeare has, figuratively, raped. In the final chapter she
confronts Shakespeare who is semi-masked in the make-up for
old Marcius Andronicus in the day's performance of *Titus* and
half-drunk. Lydia wears "puritan black" (526). She demands to
know the *point* of the play being acted: "To what purpose the
'maniac shambles'? . . . severed hands, severed tongues, violation
of rape, and devouring of man-flesh . . ." (527). Shakespeare at
first evades the issue. This is not the sort of play he would write
now but it has to be done as part of their contract with
Henslowe. But he also has a serious counter-thrust, telling her
about a discharged soldier from the Irish wars who had bawled

out in the taproom about deaths and mutilations in Enniskillen
and Fermagnagh and "how many in London had heard of it?"
Similarly in Roman Italy, how many had an inkling of the
gallons of blood which Andronicus's scullions had "to swab
away down their masters' drain-channels?" (*Bale* 528) She tells
him then about her knowledge of Topcliffe's house of inquisition
and torture of Catholics and of her bitter shame that this should
be done in the name of *her* religion, also warning him of the
danger to himself. He is at first astonished but then mocks her.
Her father had devoted his life to writing which was meant to
inspire England to Protestant rectitude without asking himself
whether this was what England wanted. He, however, is not a
Catholic though his father had been. He has forced himself to
witness the death of Southwell but his own policy is to glide
away from the plotting of people like Munday like "a damned
slippery gliding lizard-shape that runs into the running stream
and can neither be seen nor touched" (529). To cap this he
produces a copy of the manuscript of Bale's *King John* which has
now become a mere theatre commodity after Henslowe had
acquired it. She eventually hits him across the face, to which he
responds, "Hit me and hit me again . . . plays that would prove
history to be more than a maniac shambles are plumed untruth
cocking and crowing on a dry-rot scaffold, every line of 'em
brings a new murder" (*531*). He rushes out, giving her an
opportunity to take her father's manuscript. As she walks away,
Munday's complaint that Shakespeare "divides his plays this
way and that" so that no-one can know what they mean runs
through her head. This had not been the case with Bale,
whatever the faults of his doctrine. But how could one explain
anything in a "season of gliding lizards" (532)?

The episode has been recounted in some detail because it
illustrates the greater complexity with which the Bale versus
Shakespeare battle is handled here, as compared to the more
polemical essay in *Awkward Corners*. The choice between the two
doctrines about the purpose of theatre is here not such a clear
one. Shakespeare is allowed a palpable hit when he argues that
every line of righteous, crusading religious drama may bring a
new murder. What appears in the essay to be a perhaps naive
trans-historical identification with Bale and political relations of

drama including many features which the twentieth-century playwright would hardly wish to return to, would seem to be a passing polemical thrust. The dialectics of Arden's art produce a much more intricate situation.

Nevertheless, the embattled Bale, rather than the "gliding lizard" Shakespeare, is closer to the spirit of Arden and D'Arcy as it has been for many years now. "Awkward" they have often proved themselves to be in relations with the theatre, with academia, or with their own publishers at the "Methuen 500" conference in 1985, when D'Arcy led a group upstairs out of the main conference in the Royal Court Theatre whilst Arden, though remaining on the stage with the other playwrights, refused to sit and stood to one side for the rest of the proceedings. This is emblematic of an increasing isolation but also of an unbreakable courage and integrity: if the theatre will not serve what are perceived as the highest artistic and political goals, then there will be no compromise. They will not, in a remark used by D'Arcy in conversation be "bought,"[14] and feel themselves to be much less in danger of that in radio drama.

The loss is great, but it is, in a sense, *not* a loss to the theatre since the mainstream theatre would not "agree to meet" their major works of the seventies, two of the most innovative dramas of the century, *The Island of the Mighty* and *The Non-Stop Connolly Show*. The latter work, in particular, can be regarded as little short of an heroic enterprise, involving, unlike Arden's early dramas not a return to past conventions in the narrower sense to make renewed use of them in a theatre too habituated to realism, but the creation by D'Arcy and Arden of conventions and *a* convention: a unique theatrical *assembly*.

This discussion has sketched a long line of development in Arden's thought and work, and the indications are that he will go on developing: not for him a return to déjà vu, the title of his contemporary Osborne's latest play. At the Methuen 500 conference he described the performance of *The Workhouse Donkey* which was part of the weekend as "an archaeological experience." Whatever new direction he takes, however, it seems likely that, from time to time, the dialogue with his sixteenth- and seventeenth-century peers will be resumed.

# Notes

1. See my article, "The Politics of the Earlier Arden," *Modern Drama* 28 (1985): 198–210.

2. Michael Billington colorfully described the form as "a cross between Stratfordian Shakespeare . . . (and) Midland music hall." *The Guardian*, 20 May 1975.

3. This is not to deny *some* influence from Brecht, which Arden has acknowledged often enough.

4. For example: "I am not normally an enthusiast for didactic drama." Author's Notes to *Left-Handed Liberty* (London: Methuen, 1965), xii.

5. See for example: Ronald Hayman, *John Arden*, London: Heinemann, 1969, 25.

6. See D'Arcy, *Tell Them Everything*, London: Pluto Press, 1981, 125 and Arden, *To Present the Pretence*, 83–4.

7. "A stunning political drama." Michael Anderson, "Edinburgh 72" in *Plays and Players*, Nov. 1972, 7.

8. See the clash of view between Paddy Marsh in *Theatre Quarterly* 20 (1975–6):133–41 and Eamonn Smullen, *Theatre Quarterly* 11 (1977): 94.

9. At their London house in Muswell Hill, 3 January 1983.

10. See John McGrath, *A Good Night Out*, London: Eyre Methuen, 1981, 3.

11. Fielding's prologue to Lillo's *The Fatal Curiosity* (1736) urged the audience not to let its *equals* "move its pity less."

12. Clearly some of these distinctions are sometimes hard to draw.

13. See John Drakakis, *Alternative Shakespeares*, London: Eyre Methuen, 1985, 24.

14. Our conversation, 3 January 1981.

# Works Cited

Arden, John, and Margaretta D'Arcy. *Awkward Corners*. London: Methuen, 1988.

Arden, John. "The Bagman, or The Impromptu of Muswell Hill." *Two Autobiographical Plays*. London: Methuen, 1971. 35–88.

———. *Books of Bale*. London: Methuen, 1988.

———. Interview. By Maria Kreisler. *Elizabethan Trust News* 17 (1975): 21–3.

———. *Pearl*. London: Eyre Methuen, 1979.

———. "Telling a True Tale." *The Encore Reader*. Ed. Charles Marowitz et al. London: Methuen, 1965. 125–9.

———. "A Thoroughly Romantic View." *London Magazine* 7.7 (1960): 11–15.

———. "To a Young Dramatist." *The Guardian* 23 April 1964: 11.

———. *To Present the Pretence*. London: Eyre-Methuen, 1977.

———. "What's Theatre For?" Performance 4 (Sept.–Oct. 1972): 9–18.

Cohen, Michael. "The Politics of the Earlier Arden." *Modern Drama* 28 (1985): 198–210.

Leach, Robert. "Connolly Reclaimed." *Platform* 5 (1983): 12.

McGrath, John. *A Good Night Out*. London: Eyre Methuen, 1981.

Williams, Raymond. *Drama from Ibsen to Brecht*. London: Penguin, 1976.

# DEFINING ORTHODOXY: POWER AND PERSPECTIVE IN *WHOSE IS THE KINGDOM?*

## Donald Sandley

> The Council [of Nicea] gave the orthodox church the Nicene creed, to the Arians it gave little mercy, and to the state it gave both a challenge and dangerous precedent. It is a legacy which will last as long as the Christian churches hold that the beliefs of individual teachers, however gifted, are only valid if they conform to the truth that outshines brilliance. And whose is the authority to decide that truth? That kingdom is still in dispute (Gumley xiii).

Frances Gumley's prefatory essay effectively enunciates the issue and debate in John Arden and Margaretta D'Arcy's nine-part radio series *Whose Is the Kingdom?* (1988) As Gumley suggests, Arden and D'Arcy are investigating the creation and enforcement of orthodoxy. Around this issue is woven a tapestry of related issues that support the narrow structure of orthodoxy. This is to say that definitions of the relationship of the Trinity (Father, Son, Spirit) and related doctrines such as sin, justification, and the sacraments were established with little scope for variance by the fourth-century church fathers. Prior to *Whose Is the Kingdom?* Arden and D'Arcy's collaborations viewed outlook and authority as a given element in the Christian tradition. *The Island of the Mighty* (1972), for example, explores military enforcement of a Christian banner on an ancient and pagan populace. Other Arden and D'Arcy plays are more specifically concerned with political dogma, specifically *The Little Gray Home in the West* (1978) and *Vandaleur's Folly* (1978). The political orthodoxy they describe is one based in class warfare and misogynist deception. *Whose Is the Kingdom?*, however, is precisely about religious orthodoxy, the defining of faith for millions of people over two millennia. They start with a

historical milieu characterized by a power vacuum in the wake
of the collapse of Rome as it existed under the Caesars. The nine-
part radio drama's action begins in 305 A.D. prior to
Constantine's conversion, a period that follows the great persec-
utions of Diocletian and Maximin Daza. The work is a synthesis
of historical detail and fictive recreation intended, apparently, to
explore historical process and religious development (as much as
to comment on resulting injustices).

As is the case with most Arden and D'Arcy collaborations, the resulting product is an intriguing blend of dissimilar
voices—one thoughtful, reasoned, even timidly poetic; the other
shrill, assaultive, and polemical. *Whose Is the Kingdom?* is a
watershed in the collaborative careers of Arden and D'Arcy in
that it blends the styles more effectively and presents a more
unified voice than previous co-authored works, and yet, a
marked difference exists between the tone of *Whose Is the
Kingdom?* and that of Arden's individual products. The subject of
Christian doctrinal development and its resultant political and
social effects make for an ideal vehicle to combine D'Arcy's
political discourse and Arden's moral introspection.

Arden's literary domain is often concerned with why
evil or injustice exists, not its eradication. His introductory essay,
"The Pious Founders," reveals his approach as one similar to
that he assumed in *The Business of Good Government* (1960). Arden
declares that in writing *The Business of Good Government,* he and
D'Arcy hoped to "look at the evil in the world, find out how evil
it is, and who was mixed up in it" (Interview). He seems to
believe that the human condition dictates self-interested
behavior. Individuals, for Arden, are paradoxes capable of acts
equally civilized and base. Arden cites an example:

> Politically-speaking, it seemed that Diocletian, who
> was emperor at the end of the third century just
> before Constantine, had been "good." He was not
> debauched, he put his army and civil servants under
> very proper control, and his reforms in general made
> it possible for Constantine to exert a "moderate and
> humane" rule. Diocletian had also been the most
> deadly determined persecutor of Christianity ("Pious
> Founders" xvii).

Arden then is fascinated with the dual nature of the human, which is to say that each individual, whether emperor of Rome or servant to the emperor, is capable of acts of generosity, justice, and good will but equally capable of acts of dire cruelty. The wavering process of reasoning by which individuals choose good will or cruelty is for Arden the subject of good theatre.

The paradoxes of the human condition and its history make for Arden very interesting theatre. Christianity as an institution offers one of the most intriguing histories. The diversity of opinion regarding the person of Jesus of Nazareth is virtually infinite and has engendered an endless variety of applications. Importantly, Arden views Constantine's situation and response as the seminal, shaping moment in the history of the faith. Arden notes the significance of this time in the following:

> When he tried to handle this strange phenomenon called Christianity he was even more at a loss than are modern Western governments trying to stop communism: just as the word "communism" can be used to cover all varieties of dissidence from liberal American film scriptwriters to black nationalists in South Africa ... so the Christian community at the beginning of the fourth century contained so many different schools of thought that to talk of "the Church" and "the heresies" totally begs the question ("Pious Founders" xx).

The "heresies" Arden here refers to become embodied as characters in *Whose Is the Kingdom?* Arden imagines that each "heresy" was a school of political thought as well as theological (with potential economic and social ramifications). The Council of Nicea was convened in an effort to resolve the disparate positions in Christendom on the person of Christ, but the resultant Nicene Creed produced a political agenda that adversely affected women and non-Caucasian male groups. In fact, the Council of Nicea was, as Gumley describes it, "arguably not only the first ecumenical council but the first democratic international forum the world had known" (xiii). While the forum was convened on an initially democratic basis, the result clearly narrowed the field of voices when finally concluding in a set creed used to define who would be Christian. Arden explains that two general camps emerged in the days just prior to the Council of Nicea, with the various theological and political factions joining themselves to one camp or the other. Led by Eusebius, the camp that prevailed in the Council of Nicea was Pauline in orientation. In other words, the theology of this group espoused a doctrine that differentiated between the governance of earthly things from that of things earthly and heavenly. Eusebius' interpretation of St. Paul thus ascribed to the Empire absolute authority over earthly conduct and affairs while the Church was given dominion over matters eternal and spiritual. Arden claims that this Pauline strand, which was responsible for "the hierarchy of Bishops and Clergy, the subordination of Women, the deprecation of individual prophetic voices, and so forth," prevailed over a competing doctrine supposing that "the kingdom of God meant social revolution here-and-now, casting the mighty from their seats, exalting the humble and meek" ("Pious Founders" xxiii). This opposing camp is best exemplified for Arden by the Gnostics, whose writings were banned from canon literature as prescribed by the Council of Nicea. The Gnostics, in fact, rejected the entire premise of orthodoxy, and argued instead for autonomy and independent investigation. For the Gnostics, salvation was attainable through the private pursuit of knowledge. Clearly, the political consequence of such a doctrine was the absolute rejection of hierarchical authority. The Gnostics, who called themselves Christian, and the Pauline followers of Eusebius, who insisted that theirs was the divine revelation, could therefore not both thrive in this emerging empire without conflict. For Arden, *Whose Is the Kingdom?* examines the struggle between these two opposing doctrines. Their battle for power converges in the emergence of one eminent historical figure: Constantine.

Arden takes a cause-and-effect approach to history, one that lends itself well to the writing of theatre, if not to the fair appraisal of historical realities. C. Behan McCullagh notes the problems involved in this sort of historiography:

> It has been argued that causes are events or states of
> affairs which are at least contingently necessary for
> their effects. If this is so, then for any given event
> there is a very large number of causes, indeed a truly
> infinite number if indirect as well as direct causes are
> considered. (194)

Arden agrees that "cause and effect history" is imprecise, even specious. He seems to believe all history is little more than fiction based loosely on actual figures from time. Arden defends his effort as an act that counterbalances the mixture of myth, legend, and doctrine that makes up Western orthodoxy. Arden writes, "If heretics were censored and repressed, so, too, was official history. It is remarkable how hard it is to discover what really went on in the years covered by *Whose Is the Kingdom?*" (xxiv). With causes infinite in number, effects nebulous, and the equation oblique to the modern historian or author, the use of history as a tool for political fiction would seem a valid pursuit; at least this appears to be Arden's final judgment:

> For dramatists living and working some 1,650 years
> later, there is only one course: to invent. By and large,
> we have invented the areas of dissidence which
> church-and-state "magic" endeavored to "wish away"
> (xxiv).

Margaretta D'Arcy agrees that invention played a significant part in the process for the two writers. D'Arcy, however, regarded the task of fictionalization, not as a last resort in the absence of substantiated fact but as a preferable alternative to conventional interpretation. For D'Arcy, invention is inevitable in the writing of historical fiction. It is part of the process of interpretation and political in nature. D'Arcy subscribes to the notion that orthodox history is rendered by winners and that the losers' story lies in the "unexplained gaps," the awkward "eddies and backwaters" of the accepted narrative. D'Arcy is polemic in her approach to the radio drama and unabashed in her advocacy of women's issues. Women are for D'Arcy the most obvious occupants of the "eddies and backwaters" that compose the losers' history. Until the lacunae are explored and the losers' versions told, succeeding generations will cope with the conflict—uninformed and ill-equipped. *Whose Is the Kingdom?* is thus a vehicle for exploring the history of women in an emerging orthodoxy. D'Arcy hopes to show the audience what is missed as a result of Pauline supremacy. Two primary characters further carry the "feminine" revelation in *Whose Is the Kingdom?*: Fausta, the child bride of Constantine, and Oenothea, the priestess of the Babylonian Mother Goddess cult. These characters underscore life and birth, not death and after-life, a view in contrast to that of Constantine, the king whose life is centered around creating a legacy to succeed him in death, and Eumolpus, the secretary to the Bishop of Cordova (who finds the female sex evil by definition). Eumolpus' overriding suspicion of female kind precludes any chance of his accepting a feminine presence in the divine:

> EUMOLPUS
> Did not Tertullian tell us that the secret parts of
> women are in truth the Gates of Hell? (179).

Oenothea and Fausta are clear representations of divine work in the flesh, in contrast to Eumolpus' utter rejection of flesh in favor of spirit. This is a fundamental, polar conflict under the broad heading of Christianity. A doctrine that emphasizes the biological function of creation cannot be accepted into the rigid framework of an orthodoxy that claims as a basic tenet that biological processes are, on their face and by their nature, evil.

The writings of Joseph Campbell seem to support D'Arcy's argument that Western society proceeded in an altered course, a course that rewards military strength and justifies imperialist motivations, out of rejection of the female deity. In *The Power of Myth*, Campbell explains how the prevailing goddess-creator belief was uprooted in the fourth century B.C. by the Semite invaders, the people depicted in the Genesis account. The tribe of Jacob and his racially similar tribes were "animal-oriented" peoples, hunters and herders, with a predom-inant death-orientation. The god of the Semites was one of sword and death, a warrior-god, not a deity of phallus and womb. The Mother Goddess gave way to the father/hunter/warrior. Campbell points out that the virgin birth appears in the gospels by way of the Greek tradition. Only Luke describes the virgin birth, and, of the canon gospel authors, only Luke was Greek. Greek mythology, by contrast, is replete with images of virgins, or chaste, pure vessels, bearing the divinities—Leda and the Swan, Persephone and the Serpent, and so on. (Campbell 173). For D'Arcy the orthodoxy of the Council of Nicea united two distinct, mythic traditions—the Hebrew which, according to Campbell, could never have conceived of a man/god or a virgin birth, and the Greek, which deployed the pure woman as vessel for the male god. This synthesis displaced the tradition of the Mother Goddess in favor of the warrior-god. In D'Arcy's estimation this coupling of traditions authored our own reformed history.

   If history and its telling are agenda driven, the author must be unashamedly agenda-oriented as well. Objectivity for D'Arcy, the critic/author, must be likewise agenda oriented, and may, in fact, be illusory. D'Arcy writes:

> I feel strongly that the totality of Christian and post-Christian culture belongs to everyone—that the whole world, for good or ill has been affected by it—and that in principle everyone should have an equal right and opportunity to voice opinions and to raise and develop issues implicit in our interpretation of the Story ("Moon of the Dispossessed" xxxii).

*Whose Is the Kingdom?* thus renounces "objectivity." Instead, the work is a partnership that "come[s] to grips with our own experience, our own [Arden's and D'Arcy's] individual views and allows the gaps in narrative to be filled in by other voices" ("Moon of the Dispossessed" xxxii).

   It is evident that the authors approached the writing of this series in agreement as to the necessity and value of the series; however, each was motivated by somewhat different objectives. Arden appears to "fabricate" for the sake of reconstruction in hopes of redefining the past: "When Acts of State are presented as a religious revelation to be accepted by an act of faith, the world is given one big lie and must learn to make the best of it" ("Pious Founders" xiv). D'Arcy invents for the direct, radical purpose of changing the present: "It was said to me, in

joke, that I was 'writing a play, not making a revolution.'"
D'Arcy clarifies her position:

> I asserted it was impossible to understand the history
> of Nicea without first experiencing the various shifts
> and debates in modern feminism: and also the
> liberation theology in the Third World, which has
> revitalized so much of what Nicea had declared
> "heretical"—Christ—as human being involved with
> the struggles of subject-peoples of empire (xxvii).

D'Arcy paints a picture of a militant Christ, a revolutionary who
subverts imperial rule, while Arden sees Him as a rather
shadowy figure (defined only by subsequent generations). This
approach has been the subject of discussion for Arden and
D'Arcy's bilateral critics. Martin Esslin has said that their writing
partnership has harmed Arden's career: "By letting his wife
insert a very strong propaganda line which is very partisan, he
takes away his essence as a dramatist, which is to give each
character his proper weight" (Interview). Yet, unlike *Island of the
Mighty* or *The Ballygombeen Bequest*, *Whose Is the Kingdom?* does
not foray into extended political tirades. Instead, the piece
methodically develops characters and ideas and emerges as the
crowning achievement of the writing partnership, allowing for a
near complete synthesis of the two differing purposes.

The scope of the work is such that perhaps only the
medium of radio, with its emphasis on language and image,
could accommodate the effort. The sheer breadth of geography,
politics, theology, and other cerebral considerations, not to
mention the plethora of plots and subplots that make up this
narrative, would make the work untenable for film or stage. The
play's action covers thirty-two years, from Constantine's
consolidation of the Empire under one throne in 303 A.D. to his
death in 335 A.D. The events are narrated by an Epicurean
philosopher named Kybele, a figure forced to flee the Empire to
escape persecution *by* the Christians. Kybele recounts the events
of her travels and the life of Constantine from Hibernia, a site
outside the Empire, where she is being tried by the Druids for
*practicing* Christianity. If she cannot convince the Druids that she
is, in fact, a philosopher, she will die. As well as carrying the

narrative line, Kybele further introduces the key figures and voices the revolutionary sentiments of D'Arcy herself.

In the first episode Constantine attempts to consolidate power. His design is on the parcel of Empire controlled by Maxentius. The Emperor Constantine is accompanied on his military maneuvers by his child-wife, Fausta, who has begun to dabble in the reading of the sacred Christian texts. Fausta is introduced by her hairdresser, Semiramis, to a sub-sect of Christianity called the House of the True Way. Fausta has a mysterious scroll interpreted by a woman described as Mary the Companion. The interpretation reveals that the House of the True Way practices a type of Mother Goddess theology, worshipping Mary the Virgin as the Mother of God the Father. Mary the Companion translates the Empress's text in exchange for her jewelry. Mary implies that the act is holy and will provide for the survival of a child. Constantine meanwhile is confronted with a potentially critical dilemma; his army is in chaos as the Christians, now numerous among the ranks, refuse to fight the army of Maxentius, also peopled with a great many Christians. Fausta becomes the pivotal character in the episode connecting the political story line with the subtext line. Having insured the survival of Mary the Companion and her disciple, the African camp follower Melantho (who gives birth to a magic child), Fausta then, on the advice of Semiramis, attends to her frightened husband. She rubs him with oil and listens to his dilemma concerning the mutinous Christian soldiers and then provides him with a plausible solution:

> FAUSTA
> The cross of light against the sky
> Shall burn his head and dazzle out his eye
> Let him but follow where it shall travel,
> And there is an end to all his peril . . . (19)

With this verse prophecy Fausta implants the idea of following the lead of the Christians in the mind of Constantine. Constantine, who ironically has rejected Fausta to this point in their relationship, is skeptical of her mystic prophecy. In the sunrise light he is dazzled by the sight of bright, white crosses painted across the helmets and shields of the Christian soldiers.

Seeing a political opportunity, Constantine demands the entire army paint the crosses on their weaponry. The followers of Mithra willingly agree, accepting the cross as a symbol of the unconquered sun. The army of Maxentius is routed when the Christians refuse to stand against the sign of the cross, and Constantine is deluded, unable to distinguish trickery from mystic vision:

> CONSTANTINE
> Find out his power and use it. Make war in the name
> of Christ: Maximin Daza must go down. My life is his
> death: it was given me by this Christ. I alone received
> the vision of the Cross. (23)

Constantine has put his success in the hands of his Christian advisor, Hosius, Bishop of Cordova. Hosius has already begun to plant the idea of an "official church" in the mind of Constantine.

The second episode illustrates the demise of the Eastern emperor, Maximin Daza, whose center of government is located in Antioch. Maximin Daza has been loyal to the policy of Diocletian, specifically a methodical eradication of Christianity. Maximin Daza is introduced by way of the subplot concerning the followers of the House of the True Way. Melantho and her mysterious child, now called Helen-Fausta, arrive in Antioch, accompanied by the priestess Mary. Melantho is in search of her mother Oenothea, the leader of a Babylonian Mother Earth cult. Oenothea has ingratiated herself with Maximin Daza and convinced him that by following her cult's rituals, he can end the famine plaguing the Eastern empire. Also implied is a universal authority for Maximin Daza. The city of Antioch is near riot, mired in poverty and moral decay, when Maximin Daza follows Oenothea into the subterranean sewers for a period of fasting and prayer. Amid the raw sewage the ministers of Maximin Daza's cabinet await word from the high priestess Oenothea of Mother Earth's appeasement. Theotecnus, the priest of the cult of Zeus, fears he is losing his authority with the Emperor and discredits Oenothea by connecting her to the Christian House of the True Way. Theotecnus, sensing the collapse of Maximin Daza's government, encourages the Emperor to strike against the

Emperor Licinius and force a confrontation with Constantine for unified authority. While the streets of Antioch are looted by rioters, Maximin Daza orders the death or imprisonment of all Christians and declares war on Licinius. Maximin Daza, seeing himself as the demi-god heir to Diocletian, attempts to force marriage on Diocletian's daughter, Valeria (now a Christian), but is refused. Licinius, following the lead of Constantine, unites his army around the sign of the cross and defeats Maximin Daza. Maximin Daza, realizing his defeat, gives two final imperial orders.

> MAXIMIN DAZA
> First: Theotecnus and every other priest and sooth-sayer who urged me to this disastrous war shall immediately follow me, companions for my journey, my safe conduct through the miasmas of the River Styx. Second: As I drink ... in two minutes, I am a god, with new wide understanding of the errors of humanity: therefore all prisoners from minority cults are to be released, including the cult of Christ. For it is possible the Galilean is himself an Immortal: he may wish to thank me when he meets me. (46)

As if to confirm the declaration of Maximin Daza, the episode ends with revolutionaries declaring an end to earthly government:

> REVOLUTIONISTS
> The Meek shall inherit the Earth! Ours is the Kingdom! Neither Constantine nor Rome shall rule! No Rome, Christ alone! (47)

Episodes three and four serve to distinguish the religious and political tensions involved in Constantine's consolidation of power. Constantine makes a temporary peace with the elderly Licinius and marries his sister to Licinius as a sign of good faith. Constantine has, however, begun the maneuvers to dislocate Licinius and secure his power, the last conquered portion of the Empire, for Constantian rule. Episodes three and four also introduce the dowager Queen Helen, the mother of Constantine and first wife of Constantius. Helen is drawn to Christianity by the persuasive prophecy of Mary the

Companion and the mysterious precociousness of the angel child, Helen-Fausta. Helen is called to the court of Constantine to serve as a spiritual and political advisor to her son. On the long river journey, accompanied by Mary, Melantho, and the child, Helen is persuaded by Eumolpus, the ambitious and sycophantic secretary to Hosius of Cordova, that the women of the True Way cult are, in fact, witches. Helen banishes Melantho and Helen-Fausta from court but retains the services of Mary the Companion at the urging of Hosius. As his political rivals are eliminated, Constantine begins to suspect the Christian of wishing to usurp his power. Constantine employs a secret service agent, who is loyal to Mithra and was formerly in the employ of Licinius, to investigate any plots against his authority. This Jaxartes is suspicious of Constantine's eldest son Crispus, a successful and popular general, philosopher, and statesman. Jaxartes intercepts the mail of Crispus, particularly correspondence with his Christian mentor and later intercepts the mail of the philosopher Kybele. Jaxartes interprets Crispus' independence of thought as disloyalty to the throne. He also suspects the Pauline Christians led by Hosius of encroaching on the imperial authority. The clergy has begun plans for the Council of Nicea in order to clarify the outstanding differences of opinion and unofficially to identify the orthodox and the heretical. Hosius is forceful in convincing Constantine that, once established, orthodoxy will solidify the Emperor's authority, particularly if the orthodoxy follows Pauline teaching. Hosius identifies for Constantine those sects that, based on Christology, could be subversive.

Fausta and her servant, Semiramis, are confronted with a conflict regarding the male supremacy doctrine of both the Pauline and the Arian bishops. A former slave, freed and ascended to bourgeois authority, has appealed to the Bishop of Nicomedia for the return of Semiramis as his rightful wife. Fausta defends Semiramis' right to choose her own mate in the face of increasing political pressure. With the Council approaching and fearing a popular ground swell of support for Arian doctrine, Hosius avoids the issue, thereby forcing Fausta to aid Semiramis in an escape.

Jaxartes locates writings that will secure the theological position of the Arians. Jaxartes is forced to decide on a Christology. Arius' Christology suggests that Jesus was human; Pauline as interpreted by Hosius suggests divine. Jaxartes, fearing that Arius could parlay his doctrine and popular support into emperorship uses the documents to turn the Emperor to fear Hosius and force a doctrine securing the place of the Emperor.

Episode six narrates the circumstances of the Council of Nicea. Hosius and Eumolpus manage to regain a measure of imperial confidence and to wrestle doctrinal authority away from Arius and his followers, including the friend of the dowager Queen Helen and the Bishop of Nicomedia. While the theological destiny of the Empire is being decided, Nicea takes on a carnival-like atmosphere. Representatives of even the most extreme sects of Christianity find their way there. When the orthodoxy is announced and Arius is condemned as an anathema, a melee ensues. Street performers and peasants are driven by force from the city; some are killed. The sects, including the House of the True Way, are branded as heretical and their members face execution. Constantine is appointed thirteenth apostle by the Council, thus solidifying his political and religious authority in spite of the fact that he has yet to consent to baptism.

In the seventh episode Constantine's agent, Jaxartes, witnesses a bizarre mystic ritual and orgy amid the fleeing peasants driven out of Nicea. The angel child, Helen-Fausta, flies while her mother chants her audience into a mass hypnosis and apparently resurrects the slave, Semiramis, from the dead. Jaxartes recognizes a veiled participant as the Empress Fausta. Jaxartes is more convinced that Crispus and the Empress are in league with Persia for the overthrow of Constantine. Helen, too, is convinced of Fausta's designs on the throne and extracts a confession by torture from Mary the Companion.

In episode eight Semiramis and Melantho have escaped to the neutral province of the Arabian desert. Semiramis is reunited with her true husband, Joachim, and Melantho locates her mother, Oenothea. Melantho is horrified to discover her mother has sold Helen-Fausta to an Indian caravan. Eumolpus exerts his authority to establish an increasingly misogynist

hierarchy. The feminine leaders of the Christian churches are
driven underground or subjugated by the official orthodoxy.

In the final episode the physically ill Constantine is
visited by a specter which he believes to be Paul of Tarsus. With
the spectral Paul, Constantine debates the person of Christ and
the movement called Christianity. The specter proposes a
hypothesis. Paul suggests that Christ was no more than a man
who found a niche among a House of David cult. His
martyrdom opened a wide arena for his followers to create a
much more inclusive cult. This Paul suggests that even the
apostles fought among themselves for control. In a strange twist
Paul reminds Constantine that he (Paul) was the thirteenth
apostle:

> CONSTANTINE
> You the thirteenth? *Me!*
> "Paul of Tarsus"
> In that case we are one and the same, we are part of
> each other? I told you I was a hypothesis. (208)

Constantine is left with the realization that logic cannot prove
what only faith can avow. While the Emperor on his deathbed
struggles to find a faith in the Christ, Helen and Eutropa,
Fausta's mother, tour the Empire's endangered eastern provinces
in an effort to confirm the imperial authority. In a climactic last-
moment vision of Christ, Constantine realizes that only faith—
not doctrine, logic, or political methodology—can be the
criterion for his alliance. Constantine calls for baptism just before
death. The Empire is left divided again, this time in three parts,
and the Nicene orthodoxy is under attack.

D'Arcy and Arden create a literary artifact that
demonstrates how orthodoxy is born out of the marriage of
sincere commitment and political expediency. The effort is not
factual, but its images abound in truth. Both Arden's moderating
voice and D'Arcy's more militant voice are both apparent. Arden
describes his portrait of Constantine:

> It had, for instance, become apparent that Constantine
> was by no means the great decision-maker: nearly
> everything he did came upon him out of the blue, he
> spent his whole life trying desperately to keep up

with forces that were swaying his empire and he died
without having secured any form of equilibrium
("Pious Founders" xix).

Their portrait of Constantine does not reveal a man of belief. His
initial alliance with Christianity is tentative and based more on a
pseudo-mystical experience than on genuine conviction. Fausta
is able to manipulate him with sexuality, maternal concern, and
mystic imagery. Constantine attempts to balance the diverse
opinion presented to him (by bishops and political advisors) but
is never wholly convinced. Consequently, the emperor declares
his empire Christian, but never himself embraces the deity he
extols. Constantine's conversation with the mysterious St. Paul
in the final episode epitomizes Arden and D'Arcy's handling of
Constantine. The character Constantine is unable to decide for
himself what he believes and so conjures up the hallucination of
Paul of Tarsus (only to discover again that he confronts only
himself). The narrative of Paul's confrontation with the man
called Jesus is left open ended:

> PAUL
> The coincidence of the name: the empty tomb: could it
> be the same man, he had come out of it alive? (206)

Constantine, like Paul, had to decide who Jesus really
was. Was he divine? What was his purpose? As Paul had found,
only a personal leap of faith would be the deciding factor.
Constantine is confronted with the timeless dilemma of
accepting as proven the unprovable. Constantine's acceptance
stems as much from a fear of the unknown afterlife as from the
known applications of Christ in life. The teachings of Christ
("love thy neighbor," etc.) have immediate, tangible implications
but are open to individual application. The idea of eternal life
versus eternal death poses a more concrete choice. In the
characterization of Constantine, Arden and D'Arcy make the
point that the Christ is used for political expedience throughout
history and throughout individual life, but the true worth of the
Christ is evident only at the point of death. At death
Constantine, unable to decide about life, decides about death,
declaring himself a believer.

Arden and D'Arcy contrast the equivocal Constantine with Eumolpus, the secretary and advisor to the Bishop of Cordova. Eumolpus is single minded and follows a clear agenda. On the surface Eumolpus appears ludicrously misogynistic:

> EUMOLPUS (to CYPRIOT BISHOP)
> If your wife is a true Christian, she will rejoice in her deliverance from the eternal curse of fallen womanhood. (134)

In fact, Eumolpus is a composite of the prevailing theology that emerged from the Council of Nicea and which has been perpetuated for sixteen centuries. The great church father Tertullian evinced a fundamental distrust of women even to the point of defining them as spiritual others: "Even natural beauty [referring to women] ought to be obliterated by concealment and neglect, since it is dangerous to those who look upon it" (Tannahill 148). Tertullian was supported by the teachings of Jerome and St. Augustine who in turn influenced modern doctrine. The nineteenth-century American Baptist theologian James M. Pendleton states that

> Eve, though acting under a mistake and a delusion, was by no means excusable, but Adam was far more inexcusable than she, for he acted intelligently as well as voluntarily. It is to be remembered too that the sin of Adam had a far more important connection with the human race than the sin of Eve. The man, not the woman, was to be head and representative of the race. (165)

Pendleton's idea that woman is less guilty of wrong-doing supports the Tertullian myth that woman is simply woman, unable to control her actions and thus spiritually inferior. Pendleton is representative of modern conservative Christian doctrine. D'Arcy and Arden have not created an unnatural stereotype in the theocrat, Eumolpus. Eumolpus is indeed both a figure out of history and a present-day type.

Interestingly, however, they were willing to present a culpable female character, a virtual antithesis to Eumolpus— Oenothea, the priestess of the Mother Goddess. Oenothea is a misamasculent whose wrath for the male gender spills over into contempt for Christianity, a religion that just happens to center around a male messiah. Oenothea is as destructive to and distrusting of males as Eumolpus is of females:

> OENOTHEA
> The banner of a hanged man, an empty tale, an empty tomb, the empty hope of a eunuch carpenter who told his mother to get lost because the Son of Man alone— he said—is the one who will prevail against the abominable Woman of Babylon. (29)

Arden and D'Arcy seem to imply that females are capable of the same imperialist motives and gendercentric doctrine as men and, given an alternative set of circumstances, an orthodoxy based on an exclusively feminine divinity could have emerged.

Aside from the major gender opposition, the conflict that seems most to concern Arden involves freedom of thought. Jaxartes, acting as a devoted Roman and a non-Christian, influences Constantine to accept thought control and to limit spiritual investigation for the sake of central power. Jaxartes explains that the bishops who hold the Pauline doctrinal view represent the sect most likely to support a strong earthly authority and so encourages Constantine to suppress the Gnostics and the followers of Arius. The suppression of thought ultimately fuels the actions of Constantine, driving him to, as D'Arcy says, "murder" Fausta, his wife, and his son Crispus. The entire drama emerges as a working model of how thought control and political suppression emerge, detached from personal grief and consequences. Woven into the work, however, are the resulting suffering and human aspects, not contemplated by the power brokers. The dual vision of history provides their audience with a look at both why decisions are made and how they affect the disenfranchised.

Arden and D'Arcy create minor figures, fictional creations that represent the consequences of an unrelenting orthodoxy. The Druid pilgrim who arrives in Nicea to entertain and offer the beautiful wolfhounds as presents is caught up in the conflict (between the prevailing theological parties and those that lost their representative voices) and slaughtered. The Druid stands in for those whose lives are not centered in Christian belief or Western politics (the disenfranchised) but are nonetheless victimized by the ravages of violent enforcement or resistance (whether they be Kurdish refugees in Iraq or construction workers in a Northern Irish neighborhood).

Finally, Arden and D'Arcy give special emphasis to Kybele, the poet, philosopher, idealist. Kybele attempts to assimilate what she believes she has seen. Kybele is sometimes unsure as to whether her memory contains the events of actuality or the dream of hallucination. In essence, she is the playwrights' collective persona, who at times passes judgment within the drama:

> KYBELE
> Kybele says: boo to the Emperor. Kybele says boo to the bishops. And boo to the freedom for the new religion! Kybele beats her drum and says: let us have freedom from religion! (124)

At times Kybele narrates; other times she participates in the play's action. Finally, Kybele gives the balanced voice of sympathy. She comes to love the Hibernian Christian women who take her in; she grieves over their loss and recognizes *in* them the value of Christianity. She understands the hate in the Druid who hopes to have her killed. Kybele even looks beyond the present to comment on the future:

> KYBELE
> [T]he Council of Nicea has settled nothing. . . . The end of the story: but not the end of Empire, nor of Christianity. (212)

Kybele unites the protesting voice of D'Arcy with the introspective poet voice of Arden. At times the function of Kybele is unclear: why, in fact, is she involved? Ultimately, however, her function becomes clear: the history must be told by someone, even if the facts are insufficient and invention is inescapably partisan. She is the wandering spirit like the chorus of old women in *The Medea* of Euripides. By telling her tale, she exposes some truths and some lies of Christianity, Western politics, and personal motivation. Finally, through her, D'Arcy and Arden leave their audience personally engaged in the process of thinking about history and the accompanying drama of individual lives that are affected by the prevailing orthodoxies— religious, political, and artistic.

## Works Cited

Arden, John, and Margaretta D'Arcy. *Whose Is the Kingdom?* London: Methuen, 1988.
Arden, John. "Pious Founders." *Whose Is the Kingdom?*: xvii–xxiv.
———. Interview. August 1990.
Campbell, Joseph. *The Power of Myth*. New York: Doubleday, 1988.
D'Arcy, Margaretta. "Moon of the Dispossessed." *Whose is the Kingdom?*: xxv–xxxii.
Esslin, Martin. Interview. July 1990.
Gumley, Frances. "The Road to Nicea." *Whose Is the Kingdom?*: By John Arden and Margaretta D'Arcy. London: Methuen, 1988. xii–xiii.
McCullagh, C. Behan. *Justifying Historical Descriptions*. Cambridge: Cambridge University Press, 1984.
Pendleton, James M. *Christian Doctrines*. Valley Forge, PA: Judson Press, 1971.
Tannahill, Reay. *Sex in History*. New York: Stein and Day, 1980.

# WHO WROTE "JOHN ARDEN'S" PLAYS?

## Tish Dace

Ordinarily, critics respect the authorship designated on a play's title page or production program. Although occasionally authors who also direct their own plays may employ a pseudonym to avoid the suggestion of a vanity production, usually we take our playwrights at their word. Yet an extraordinary anomaly has persisted in the case of the 34-year collaboration of John Arden and Margaretta D'Arcy: most scholars discuss their plays as though Arden alone had written them.

The books, of course, all bear the title, with or without subtitle, *John Arden* or merely *Arden*. Ronald Hayman, who wrote the first such volume, may be forgiven for mentioning D'Arcy only twice in his 1968 *John Arden* (vii, 73) for three reasons. The two had collaborated for less than a decade at that point. Arden alone had written his better known plays. And they seem to have only belatedly agreed to acknowledge their work as jointly created.

That's right: Some of the pair's plays originally appeared as solely Arden's. When William Gaskill directed the premiere of *The Happy Haven* in Bristol in April 1960, the program credited only Arden. Yet when Gaskill again mounted the play in September of the same year at London's Royal Court, the program termed it "by John Arden in collaboration with Margaretta D'Arcy." It was published with the same joint attribution (*New English Dramatists, 4; Three Plays by John Arden*). Because Arden wrote *The Happy Haven* while a Visiting Fellow in the Bristol University Drama Department, we might speculate that he initially felt reluctant to acknowledge—in 1960, mind you—that his wife had co-authored a script which Bristol University had commissioned solely from the author of *Serjeant Musgrave's Dance*.

On the other hand, since Arden persisted in receiving sole credit for plays which later they attributed to their joint efforts, he, or they, may merely have been slow to evolve a contemporary consciousness that the labor of a man and a woman should not transmute into the man's property alone.

When the first edition of *The Business of Good Government* appeared from Methuen on May 23, 1963, Arden received the credit. When Grove Press finally put out an American edition on February 24, 1967, Arden's name still graced the title page. Yet two months later Arden asked his English publisher to add his wife's name as co-author to the reprint issued later that year. (I am indebted here and elsewhere to Nick Hern, who, while still an editor at Methuen, opened the editorial files to my perusal.)

To add to the confusion, *Ars Longa, Vita Brevis* appeared in *Encore* in March 1964 as Arden's work but was published by Cassell in February 1965 as the work of both Arden and D'Arcy. Evidently working out their own ground rules took the two playwrights a few years. Or perhaps publishers and producers tended to ignore their wishes. In any event, by the time the world learned (in 1967) of D'Arcy's part in writing *The Business of Good Government*, the pair had published four other plays with both names on the title page. Many others have followed.

The two playwrights' bibliographies of plays look like this:

| Arden: | Arden/D'Arcy: |
|---|---|
| *All Fall Down*, 1955 | *The Happy Haven*, 1960 (written 1959) |
| *The Life of Man* 1956, radio | *The Business of Good Government*, 1960 |
| *The Waters of Babylon*, 1957 | *Ars Longa, Vita Brevis*, 1964 (D/A) |
| *When Is a Door Not a Door*, 1958 | *Friday's Hiding*, 1966 (D/A) |
| *Live Like Pigs*, 1958 | *The Royal Pardon*, 1966 |
| *Serjeant Musgrave's Dance*, 1959 | *Vietnam Carnival*, 1967 (D/A) New York University |
| *Soldier, Soldier*, 1960, TV | *Harold Muggins Is a Martyr*, 1968 (D/A) |
| *Wet Fish*, 1961, TV | *The Hero Rises Up*, 1968 |

*Top Deck*, 1961, film

*The Dying Cowboy*, 1961, radio
*The Workhouse Donkey*, 1963

*Ironhand*, 1963

*Armstrong's Last Goodnight*,
    1964
*Left-Handed Liberty*, 1965

*The True History of Squire
    Jonathan and His Unfortunate
    Treasure*, 1968 (written 1963)
*The Bagman*, 1970, radio

*Pearl*, 1978, radio
*To Put It Frankly*, 1979, radio
*The Adventures of the Ingenious
    Gentleman, Don Quixote*,
    1980, radio
*Garland for a Hoar Head*, 1982,
    radio
*The Old Man Sleeps Alone*, 1982,
    radio

*The Ballygombeen Bequest*, 1972
    (a.k.a. *The Little Gray Home
    in the West*, 1978) (D/A)
*The Island of the Mighty*, 1972
*Keep Those People Moving!*,
    1972, radio
*The Devil & the Parish Pump*,
    1974 (D/A)
*The Non-Stop Connolly Show*,
    1975 (D/A)
*Sean O'Scrudu*, March 1976
    (D/A)
*The Hunting of the Mongrel Fox*,
    Oct. 1976 (D/A)

*No Room at the Inn*, Dec. 1976
    (D/A)
*Mary's Name*, 1977 (D/A)
*Vandaleur's Folly*, 1978 (D/A)
*The Manchester Enthusiasts*,
    1984, radio

*Whose Is the Kingdom?*, 1988,
    nine-part radio series
*A Suburban Suicide*, submitted
    to BBC radio, December
    1992.

You will note from this list that the last time Arden wrote a stage play alone was in 1965.

Although these are the plays which the more comprehensive survey of their work might include, additional dramatic work which ought to be taken into account includes these two titles by Arden:

> 1) Beethoven's *Fidelio*, adaptation for the 16 September 1965 performance at Saddler's Wells.

> 2) Stravinsky's *The Soldier's Tale*, adaptation for the Bath Festival, 1968.

Some of the less well-known collaborations between
D'Arcy and Arden include

1) The *Kirkbymoorside*[1] *Entertainment*, a month-long
festival in their home in 1963, which grew out of a 16-
millimeter film which D'Arcy made there.

2) *The Unfulfilled Dream*, Super-8 film, 1969, which
concerns a village land dispute; made for the Land
League, a political organization of small farmers.

3) Film: *The Galway Rent and Rate Strike*, Super-8, 1971.

4) Twenty-minute play based on *The Emperor's New
Clothes* as part of Roger Smith's *Two Hundred Years of
Labor History* during the winter of 1971 for a rally of
about 3,000 people sponsored by the Socialist Labor
League at Alexandra Palace.

5) Two agit-prop plays presented in Muswell Hill in
early spring 1971. These attacks on Heath's Tory
government, based upon *Little Red Riding Hood*, were
performed by a cast of Albert Hunt's students from
Bradford College of Art in Theatre of Cardboard style
with masks and placards.

6) *Oughterard 1972*, a Super 8 film, 1972, adapted from
*The Unfulfilled Dream*.

7) *Portrait of a Rebel*, a television documentary about
Sean O'Casey, spring 1973, RTE.

8) An eight-hour stage show which employs the
character of Henry Dub to consider the History of the
American labor movement, presented at the University of California, Davis, in 1973. Not to be confused
with the *Non-Stop Connolly Show* although the two
works are related.

9) A film about the AFSCME union on that campus,
1973.

10) *The Corrandulla Film* surveys life in a small village,
Super-8, 1974.

11) *The Crown Strike Play*, with University College,
Galway, presented in Fall 1975 in the city square. This
agit-prop piece should not be confused with *Sean
O'Scrudu*, which was inspired by the same on-going
union/management struggle.

12) *The Menace of Ireland?*, a 1979 compilation of
previous D'Arcy/Arden scenes plus debate stimu-
lated by them; designed and played for British
audiences.

13) Since 1987 they jointly have offered the theatre
workshop now termed *Duchas na Saoirse*, usually in
Belfast.

In addition, D'Arcy alone devised the play *A Pinprick of
History* (1977). In 1973 in a supermarket in California she shot a
film in which she employs the Henry Dub character to advocate
boycotting lettuce, and, while sitting outside the Arts Council
Offices in 1986, she filmed "Circus Expose of the New Cultural
Church," which was shown at the 1987 Celtic Film Festival in
Inverness and at the Derry Film Festival in 1988. She has also
filmed dozens of hours of videos with Galway Women in Media
and Entertainment. She founded Women's Sceal Radio, and she
is completing an opera, *Opera ag Obair*, to form part of *Utopia* for
presentation in Algeria in late summer 1993. Sections of *Opera ag
Obair* already have been performed at the London Irish Women's
Festival, 1987; the Huddersfield Women's Festival, 1987; and in
Galway, 1988.) Of course, like Arden, D'Arcy also publishes
reviews, essays, non-fiction (e.g., *Tell Them Everything*. London:
Pluto Press, 1981) and fiction ("The Budgeen," published in two
collections of feminist fairy tales, *Sweeping Beauties* (1989) and
*Ride on Rapunzel* (1992), both Dublin, Attic Press). (I am indebted
to D'Arcy and Arden for most of these additions to their usual
canon.)

Given the increasing quantity of joint authorship (to
date, during thirty-four years of collaboration, at least thirty-four
co-authored works), one would think that the studies which
followed Hayman's 1968 book would consider the two writers as
a team. Not so. The books, scholarly articles, and production
reviews alike tend to pay little, if any, attention to Margaretta
D'Arcy's credits on playbills and title pages. It is as though
English-speaking spectators and critics had forgotten how to
read whenever their eyes fell on her name.

The content of Simon Trussler's 1973 study, *John Arden*,
reflects its title. Trussler accurately attributes the third of the
plays in the bibliography of published primary works which

resulted from collaboration, yet he titles this list "Works of John Arden." In his text, he likewise correctly notes the joint author- ship of the unpublished *Harold Muggins Is a Martyr*, yet he dis- cusses this play and *The Business of Good Government* as though Arden alone had written them. Where he refers to D'Arcy, he does so as part of his disparagement of the collaborative work. Trussler thus justifies his pattern of ignoring D'Arcy: "the extent and nature of the Ardens' collaboration remains conjectural" (33).

Trussler has a short memory. In his 1966 interview with John Arden in *Tulane Drama Review*, Trussler learned first-hand about D'Arcy's part in the plays. As he has in other interviews, Arden persistently discusses D'Arcy's contributions even though Trussler never asks Arden about this or refers to her at all. The result is a series of exchanges in which Trussler single-mindedly inquires about Arden and Arden frequently couches his replies in terms of D'Arcy's creative input. Of *Left-Handed Liberty* (not one of the jointly attributed plays), for example, Arden recalls, "I did get a bit tangled in a confusion of baronial and episcopal minutiae, until Margaretta D'Arcy [Arden's wife] suggested that I use the Papal Legate—until then a very minor character—to pull the whole play together and set it in a framework of medieval theology and cosmology" (50).

Then Trussler asks how Arden came to write *Ars Longa, Vita Brevis* and receives this response (which he appears to have forgotten before asserting in 1973 that we have no way of knowing who contributed what to the collaboratively created plays):

> Having accepted, rather casually, a commission to write a piece for schoolchildren, I was at a complete loss until Margaretta D'Arcy reminded me of a curious inquest, reported in *The Times*, held on an art master shot in a wood while taking part in a Territorial Army exercise. Peter Brook then asked me for a little piece for his *Theatre of Cruelty* program, and we thought we would kill two birds with one stone. Miss D'Arcy had been doing some improvised plays with children in Kirbymoorside and also in Dublin, and she suggested that the peculiar directness and the

spontaneous development of "classical" conventions which we saw in their work would be a useful starting-off point. *Ars Longa* is really more her play than mine—she decided what was to happen in each scene, and I then wrote down a sort of stream-of-consciousness dialogue to illustrate it. In order not to make the play too rigid for its potential juvenile cast—we weren't so worried about Peter Brook's adults—I did not attempt to polish or even revise this dialogue. When we later directed the play ourselves with the Kirbymoorside Girl Guides we threw out all the dialogue, except two bits of verse, and let them improvise their own words throughout. The result was, we thought, much more successful than any of the productions we have seen where my dialogue was used. (50-1)

Arden continues by describing D'Arcy's part in *The Business of Good Government*, *Friday's Hiding*, *The Royal Pardon*, and what became *The Hero Rises Up* and concludes, "Oddly enough, *The Business of Good Government* and *Ars Longa* are the two most popular plays I have written . . . or rather, partly written" (51).

Trussler paid so little mind to this and other acknowledgement of D'Arcy's importance to the plays that he published with his interview a chronology of "John Arden's" plays which never mentions that Arden and D'Arcy wrote several of them.

The next book on "Arden," Glenda Leeming's 1974 *John Arden*, likewise mentions D'Arcy infrequently (4-5, 6-7, 26, 31, 32). Albert Hunt in 1974 refers to her somewhat more extensively—but note his title: *Arden: A Study of His Plays* ([11]-12, 32, 34, 63, 65-70, [108], 109, 110-142, 152-164, 171-2). Frances Gray in the 1982 *John Arden* devotes more attention to D'Arcy than her title suggests. Early on she notes "D'Arcy rather than Arden was the moving force behind the Carnival" (24), and throughout she proves more alert to the collaboration and quicker to acknowledge it and its importance than the authors of other books on "Arden." Surprisingly, however, Gray's insistence on considering the playwriting partnership has produced little impact on the ensuing ten years of scholarship.

By the time Malcolm Page's *John Arden* appeared in 1984, the stage had been set for appropriate credit to what should be a famous partnership. Yet the index to his 175-page book refers to D'Arcy only sporadically (4, 10-12, 22, 59, 66, 94, 95-6, 100, 109-10, 118, 130, 138, 144), and most of those citations involve convoluted excuses for avoiding discussing her. Although his bibliography acknowledges (unlike that in his more error-prone compilation *Arden on File*, issued by Methuen the following year) all the major collaborations through 1978, his text does not correctly attribute them. Beginning with the first two pages of his introduction, he refers to Arden as sole author of *The Happy Haven, The Hero Rises Up, The Island of the Mighty,* and the *Non-Stop Connolly Show* (xi-xii).

In his effort "to account for the decline of interest in John Arden's work" (xii), Page blames (1) fashion. (2) "Arden's" rejection of "careerism," for which he cites *The Royal Pardon, War Carnival, Muggins,* and *Connolly.* He neglects to mention that all four were collaborations. (3) quarrels over *The Hero Rises Up* and *The Island of the Mighty,* "giving him a reputation for being 'difficult.'" Again, no mention of his collaboration on these. Only in his fifth and sixth explanations does Page begin to refer to D'Arcy. Here and for much of the rest of his brief introduction, Page seems intent upon remedying what is wrong with the body of his volume: He actually considers the pair's creative partnership. Yet he concludes with a lame justification for ignoring her and/or dismissing her thereafter: "This book is called *John Arden.* More correctly, it might be entitled 'John Arden and Margaretta D'Arcy,' as so many of the plays are collaborative. As it is not possible to isolate D'Arcy's contribution, in general I have merely stated when a work is jointly written, then commented in terms of Arden's styles and themes. Also, D'Arcy is proudly Irish and would object to appearing in an English Authors Series" (xiii). Yet how can we conclude that the plays' themes and styles typify Arden rather than Arden and D'Arcy when both wrote them? Would we make such an absurd supposition about the works of Beaumont and Fletcher? Kaufman and Hart? Lawrence and Lee? Or other male collaborations?

Unwary readers thereafter, should they skip the preface, can easily conclude from the rest of the book that D'Arcy is merely Arden's wife, her sole issue her children. Page mentions that Arden reviews in the *New Statesman* but neglects to add that D'Arcy does, too. When, sporadically, he does remember playwright D'Arcy, it is as part of something called "the Ardens," an appellation which neither partner would approve. Towards the end, Page defends his methodology by reiterating "the reader can only speculate about her role" (138), but then, without proof, blames her for "broad effects and unsubtle characterizations" and immediately returns to referring to the scripts as Arden's alone. He tries to have it both ways, declining to credit her for the scripts' strengths because he presumes we can't tell what she wrote, but then blaming her for those features he doesn't care for.

Through the years, the doctoral dissertations have repeated the books' patterns of generally ignoring D'Arcy, the reference books have discussed only Arden, and nearly all the interviewers have spoken solely to him. Force of habit—along, we must infer, with sexism—has perpetuated the mistaken notion that Arden alone creates "his" plays. Throughout 34 years of this creative partnership, critics and journalists publishing essays, articles, and reviews also, almost to a "man," just haven't gotten it.

In an early instance of this blindness or bias, John Russell Taylor's introduction to *Three Plays* ignores the joint attribution on the play's title page and never mentions her name. Yet he deems this "one of his [sic] richest and most satisfying plays: a lot of it is very funny, and some of it is very beautiful. . . . Technically it is probably Arden's boldest play yet. . . . Of that sort of writing, with that sort of hardwon strength and sinew, only John Arden has the secret in the modern English theatre . . ." (14-15). Carol Rosen in *Plays of Impasse: Contemporary Drama Set in Confining Institutions* also analyzes "John Arden's *The Happy Haven*" without mentioning D'Arcy's name (54-72).

A survey of other scholars' contributions to books and journals turns up similar treatment—or often lack of treatment—of one half of this playwriting team. Although Katharine J. Worth in *Revolutions in Modern English Drama* considers *The*

*Happy Haven* and *The Royal Pardon* (108, 132-3), she fails to discuss the collaboration and barely acknowledges D'Arcy's existence, not even when she praises "the best English writing" as the product of authors (Arden, among others, but not D'Arcy) who also direct and act (descriptions which fit D'Arcy better than Arden).

Craig Clinton begins his "John Arden: The Promise Unfulfilled" by discussing *The Island of the Mighty* as though D'Arcy had nothing to do with it, referring to "the author and his wife" (48). But he switches gears in a few pages and blasts D'Arcy (especially 53-6) as an "outspoken proselyte of the leftist ideals both she and her husband hold in common" (55). Although the article appeared in 1978, Clinton's footnotes all cite sources no more recent than 1971, and he bases his attack on the 1968 *The Hero Rises Up*.

When Ronald Hayman returns to "Arden" in his 1979 *British Theatre Since 1955: A Reassessment,* he mentions D'Arcy five times, each time in a derogatory context, linking the collaboration to work which Hayman judges inferior to the product of Arden's pen (16, 82-5, 108, 126). The index also refers us to 92, where Hayman mentions "the Ardens," even though D'Arcy has always used her maiden name. Many critics have chosen to ignore her wishes in this matter. Hayman praises "his early plays, which are unquestionably works of art, whereas the priority in his later work is propagandistic." Hayman gets his facts wrong, however, dating the onset of Arden's "working partnership with his wife" to 1967 and claiming that Arden had always previously started "with a story that appealed to him" instead of a message he wishes to communicate (82). For refutation of this viewpoint, we need only turn to 13, where Hayman concludes about *Musgrave* "it is obvious that message preceded character," a view which he reiterates on 23.

Redmond O'Hanlon's "The Theatrical Values of John Arden" takes as his point of departure the 1977 publication of *To Present the Pretense*. Because Arden wrote most of those essays, we may appreciate why O'Hanlon's discussion of the plays refers to Arden's work, yet he engages in a sort of double-think in which Arden and D'Arcy (or, lamentably, the Ardens) picket their production at the Royal Shakespeare company, but Arden writes the plays. Javed Malick also practices an inconsistent approach: his "The Polarized Universe of *The Island of the Mighty*: Arden and D'Arcy's Dramaturgy," as the title suggests, tends to speak of playwrights, plural, although sometimes departing from that approach even though discussing collaborative work. Yet his "Society and History in Arden's Dramaturgy," although it occasionally refers to D'Arcy in passing, discusses the collaboratively created plays *The Royal Pardon, The Island of the Mighty*, and *The Non-Stop Connolly Show* as Arden's. He demonstrates enrichment in that author's plays from their increasingly political content, yet he ignores what many people would regard as her influence (and contribution) in that regard. Could the different editors for these two journals account for the shift in Malick's approach? Or did Malick write the second article first? Whatever the cause, the second approach represents a regression.

Journalists likewise frequently ignore D'Arcy's part in creating "Arden's" plays. Mel Gussow writes in this tradition in a *New York Times* review of *The Happy Haven*. Although he acknowledges the collaboration at the outset, thereafter he refers to the "author" as male, as in "One of the problems with 'The Happy Haven' is that the author is not quite clear about his own allegiances." We may find particularly puzzling Robert Brustein's "Picketing His Own Play," also in the *New York Times*, because whatever writers say, or fail to say, about the plays' authorship, most are quick to blame D'Arcy for condemning the Royal Shakespeare Company production of *The Island of the Mighty*. But Brustein, after telling us that the pair wrote this play, falls into using the third person singular male pronoun which his headline reflects. In all fairness, these reviewers shouldn't be singled out for special rebuke; reviews which ignore D'Arcy are ubiquitous.

A good index of the lack of interest in D'Arcy can be found in the clippings files of the Billy Rose research collection at the Lincoln Center division of the New York Public Library. The files marked "Arden" bulge with reviews and other journalism; the files on their jointly-written plays contain clippings which generally focus on him. The "D'Arcy" folder, however, contains a mere nine items—five of them carrying my own byline.

Of course, not everyone ignores or belittles or denounces D'Arcy's role in writing the plays. In addition to Frances Gray, Catherine Itzin's *Stages in the Revolution* maintains that Arden and D'Arcy both regard themselves as Irish and therefore feel they should not have been included in a book on British playwrights. (Arden does not, in fact, regard himself as Irish, but they do want their plays about Ireland to be seen as Irish.) Although she does not honor their wishes, Itzin at least considers them together, both in her discussion of *Harold Muggins Is a Martyr* (20-23) and her general discussion of the pair ([24]-38).

Similarly, Arthur Sainer discusses both writers in the *Village Voice* during the run of *The Ballygombeen Bequest*. James Leverett likewise departs from the established critical practice in his *Soho News* review of *The Non-Stop Connolly Show*. Robert Leach also appreciates their collaboration on that play. Though not the only examples, these number among the few publications which do not deny or castigate the partnership.

Why this prejudice against D'Arcy?

1) Ignorance. Lazy critics who know primarily *Serjeant Musgrave's Dance* and perhaps a few other of the early plays simply don't realize that most of "Arden's" work for the stage for the past 34 years has been co-authored with D'Arcy. Sloppy scholarship, however, should be no excuse for critical neglect of any writer.

2) Personal dislike. Such people reason she's a bitch, so it's her fault if critics ignore her. D'Arcy is not, as it happens, the harridan her detractors make her out. But even if she were, that's no excuse for punitive inaccuracies. I have never, incidentally, heard a woman denounce D'Arcy based on personal animosity—perhaps because so often she selects patriarchy as her primary antagonist. For the record, in my experience D'Arcy has proven joyous, spirited, assertive but not in the least self-pitying or abrasive—in short, a thoroughly easy person with whom to interact. Her reputation as a troublemaker stems from the passion of her convictions and not the genial manner in which she usually delivers them. What irritates some folks must be her persistence in trying to persuade them to march, demonstrate, write letters, and otherwise commit themselves visibly to the causes which they claim to espouse. For

this sin, she arouses a startling venom, as in the case of the well-known English writer who recently snarled in my presence, "That woman is a monster."

3) The fact D'Arcy used her maiden name years before that became common probably has contributed to the antipathy towards her of those who prefer patriarchy to partnership. (Note how many of those who notice her at all refer to her as part of something called "the Ardens.")

4) The equally sexist assumption that a female collaborator contributes only secretarial services. As it happens, I've watched the two at work on a script. In that instance, she dictated, while he typed. A variation on this involves believing that a woman in a romantic relationship with her partner could not truly collaborate with him professionally. (Hillary Rodham Clinton receives similar challenges.)

5) Fury because she's ruined his career—a dubious assumption considering the critical and financial failure of the first production of *Serjeant Musgrave's Dance* (which played a mere 28 performances to 20% capacity) and the popularity of such jointly written community dramas as *Ars Longa, Vita Brevis*. And their collaborations of the last twenty years will surely be appreciated by future writers not burdened by the political biases against Irish republicanism and feminism harbored by some late twentieth-century appraisers. *Whose Is the Kingdom?*, for example, will prove an extraordinary accomplishment once anger over its indictment of Christian misogyny has abated. In any event, Arden's own wishes about his career must count for something, and he has willingly chosen to link his personal and professional destinies to hers in what a close observer (as I was when I rented a room at the top of their Muswell Hill home in the winter of 1978) must judge an unusually happy partnership. Moreover, Arden and D'Arcy have chosen to try to change the world, and if commercial managements decide not to produce their plays, we can hardly blame the victims for that. Personally, I am elated that people of such good will make the attempt to improve life for us all.

6) Censorship of their subject matter—which critics often regard as really her subject matter—for its indictment of what Britain has done to the Irish. When censors target sexual mater-

ial, critics usually jump to the artists' defense. Do they not likewise champion these playwrights' freedom of speech because they object to the message?

7) Some folks find it hard to like—or even acknowledge the contributions of—a female hero. They find it hard to warm to the woman who, while she was incarcerated in Armagh, smuggled out to me, written in tiny letters on *one* square of toilet paper, the following letter concerning her plight and that of others in her wing of the prison:

> Dear Tish: . . . Thanks for your articles. Everyone here is in fighting form, but the conditions are horrifying. Some of the girls look like Auschwitz victims, old women—the doctor won't allow any outside medicos in. Death and decay like medieval gargoyles lurk in the open sewers which run past our cell doors. Flies, fleas and filth, darkness and excrement; we are the strange animals in the midden. Male guards dressed in green helmets with visors and female guards with gauze round their faces hang outside to jeer and sneer. Cold greasy food black with flies. We are locked up twenty-three hours a day: only two of us allowed out at a time, so we never see each other. I think when all this is over people are going to find it as difficult to believe as Hitler's concentration camps. Girls tortured before coming in and now being tortured with this cruel lying neglect all because they want justice, the right to some human dignity until the war is over. The women are amazing. I have never seen so much courage and self discipline. No self-pitying, always cheerful and keeping up the morale. How long they can go on, God knows. The Brits must be forced to have some humanity towards their prisoners. Otherwise hunger strike on a mass scale will be the next move. How many more must die until reason prevails? Love to you, Margaretta. (For a more detailed account, see her *Tell Them Everything*.)

Clearly D'Arcy possesses the qualities of character which, if evinced by a man of her generation, might have won her high political office, a position as a general in the armed forces, or eventually the sort of holiday which we've awarded to the equally persevering Martin Luther King, Jr.

Arden and D'Arcy themselves have reacted implicitly and explicitly to D'Arcy's negative reception—or the absence of any reception. We needn't read far between the lines to find pertinent this exchange from *Vandaleur's Folly*:

> THOMPSON. You are about to say I am a hypocrite. We shared our bed, we shared our book-writing, page between page, we shared everything all these years—
>
> ANNA. With men, it is a common condition.
>
> THOMPSON. As we have abundantly proven within the argument of our joint works. Our joint works with *my* name on them. (64)

In the preface to *John Arden Plays: One*, Arden laments "I am continually informed in all manner of print by all manner of critics that my later work (. . . since I started regularly working as the older half of the Arden/D'Arcy writing-production partnership) shows a distinct falling-off in dramatic tension and inspiration: I am accused of having turned my back upon the professional theatre—whereas the professional theatre, at least in certain large and influential areas, has let it be known that Arden's work is only acceptable if D'Arcy is not impertinently attached to it" (7). Yet, Arden explains, he rates his work with her as more important than his work alone because their collaborations involve the audience (7-8). As D'Arcy recently remarked to me, they have become less interested in performing in front of an audience than in participatory theatre in which the audience plays an integral role.

Arden also has commented on his work with D'Arcy in interviews (for instance with Raymond Gardner in 1972) and essays. In his introduction to the section titled "The Matter of Vietnam" in *To Present the Pretence*, Arden discusses the Vietnam Carnival at NYU: "The overall concept of the show was due largely to Margaretta D'Arcy. . . . [When asked by New York University] to conduct a group of students in whatever project suggested itself, I agreed, on condition that D'Arcy would be formally associated with me on all *practical* work, this being rather outside my own professional experience, whereas she was

already well-seasoned as a performer and experimental director"
(47). Later in the same volume (for those who still claim to have
no notion of what part D'Arcy plays in creating the plays) Arden
writes of their *Connolly* play that "D'Arcy divined a basic image
for his character on which we could build the play" (106) and "it
had been D'Arcy who originally conceived the Connolly idea"
(110).

On the distaste of theatres for staging the collaborative
work, he complains of this as censorship: "The great difficulty is
that dramatists will rarely be told: 'Your play is *subversive*: we
are imposing a political restriction upon its performance.' . . . In
my case it has been incontrovertibly passed on to me (though
never put down on paper in so many words) that any work of
mine done in collaboration with D'Arcy (which in effect means
all my Irish material) is altogether out of line with the
requirements of more than one subsidised theatre" (157). He
offers this plausible explanation of the genesis of the Royal
Shakespeare Company's mythology vis-a-vis D'Arcy as
termagant:

> She had, they hinted, come over for rehearsals only to
> sabotage the dignity of the RSC. Of course they were
> in a dilemma; it was necessary to attack the authors,
> for the authors were attacking them. But if they
> accused Arden of being a low-class troublemaker they
> would make people wonder why they chose to
> present the play in the first place. But the fact that
> there were two authors made it possible for the RSC
> handouts to attack one at the expense of the other,
> and they naturally chose the more vulnerable of the
> pair. D'Arcy was: (a) female, and (b) Irish. (166)

In his 1986 statement for the *Contemporary Authors
Autobiography Series*, Arden describes the importance of his
meeting D'Arcy in 1955:

> She was the first professional theatre-person I ever got
> to know: and through her I met many people without
> whom my career as a playwright could never have
> got off the ground. Two years later we were married.
> She was closely involved with the most progressive

aspects of the theatre of that time, aspects which I knew nothing of, with my limited Shakespearean provincial orientation and my academic (and indeed pompous) attitude towards the stage. She gave me a copy of Brecht—a writer I had only heard of: she introduced me to the works of Beckett, Strindberg, Toller, Behan. . . . Her name now appears sometimes first, sometimes second, together with mine, upon a great deal of published work which nonetheless the male critics, managements, publishers, and broadcasters, will insist upon referring to as "Arden's." Or, worse, as "the Ardens.'" . . . It would have been different if I had collaborated with a man called Hiram Hinks, or even with a woman called Evadne Pershore (assuming that she was known already as a professional author and *not* known to be married to, or living with, me). (29)

In addition to sexism, Arden identifies censorship as a cause of their troubles:

What did matter was the nature of the collaborative work, after 1968 anyway. Before then the problem had been but slight: because our plays were fairly conventional in form and content. After 1968 their political dimensions became less and less acceptable to the British cultural establishment, which has its own very decided notions of what liberties may be taken with the Imperial traditions. (30)

In a sense all D'Arcy's portion of *Awkward Corners* suggests her response to the discrimination she encounters or to the reasons why the patriarchy repudiates or ignores her or why she perseveres anyhow. Her remarks reflect her uncompromising and principled moral fibre. (See, for example, her descriptions of her imprisonment after her arrest at Greenham, 226-8). She communicates a powerful image of the bond between her and Arden in "To John Who Complains I Never Write Nice Poems to Him": "If you died / I / Would have / No / Past / Or / Future / Only / Now: / No dreams / No time. / Conscious for only each second that passes / As the earth spins / With / Me / On it / With out / You" (217). She likewise describes

jocularly their working relationship: "When I want a clear
story / Arden always complicates it / By putting in too much.
Like yesterday— / A simple joke in a short scene: /One
philosopher has taken five years to / Develop an argument, /
The other has / Five hours / Before they are both eaten by
lions. / But Arden / Has to put in how / Long they've lived, /
Who they are. / I say I say / Old boy, / A shouting match—
/All to show that / Arden can write" (215-6).

Her opening essay endeavors to reply to the query from
Nick Hern "Why do certain people find you so obnoxious,
Margaretta?" ([121]). She considers the ways her candid dissent
threatens and frightens people who label her a terrorist (of all
things). In Communist countries, she reasons, we call such
people dissidents "and praise them: but here in the West . . . ?"
(123). Here, her experience demonstrates, it lands them in prison.
In the essay "Breaking Chains" she traces their collaboration and
the cost on their careers of the censorship of their work on
English stages, which she dates from her outspoken writing
beginning in the 60's when the British army occupied the Six
Counties in Northern Ireland. The repression included coercion
of the theatres which wished to stage their plays, loss of grants to
such theatres, and the libel suit which prevented for several
years further staging of *The Ballygombeen Bequest* and eventually
forced its revision (133-4). "Theatre in an Age of Reform"
contains similar analysis of government and press efforts to
equate their exercise of freedom of expression (with respect to
*Vandaleur's Folly*) with terrorism ([176]-191). And "Statement for
the National Council of Civil Liberties Concerning the
Prevention of Terrorism Act" recounts several further instances
of government pressure in the form of withdrawal of funding
which have prevented the production of their work on grounds
of her "terrorism," a code word for her impertinence in
presuming to criticize British policies ([204]-9).

Lest anyone continue to refuse to credit the collaboration, *Arden/D'Arcy: D'Arcy/Arden*'s title page carries their
notation as to which author took the leading part in writing each
play (two for Arden, ten for D'Arcy). D'Arcy details in her
introduction her contributions to some of their work([ix]-xiii).

Biases must not be allowed to disqualify D'Arcy's contributions from critical consideration. Critics and scholars can, of course, dislike her kind of dramaturgy and analyze what they perceive as its faults. But the ad hominem attacks on her and the pretense that only John Arden writes the Arden/D'Arcy and D'Arcy/Arden plays must no longer be tolerated. Any less will perpetuate an injustice.

Moreover, benefits will accrue from considering these two as a team. They have proven quite cooperative and forthcoming with scholars who do so, whereas those who try to deal with Arden alone have been known to meet with a less cordial reception. Entree to research assistance, interviews, and so on should prove easier to anyone who corresponds with—and respects—them both.

Those concerned with a handful of Arden-only plays will find attention to D'Arcy provides them with insights into some of the most significant influences on his drama. D'Arcy worked as a professional actor from the age of fifteen (after she left school in 1949); she, not Arden, had acquired considerable professional theatre experience by the time they met. D'Arcy had found her first acting work after her arrival in England with director Stuart Burge in a company at Hornchurch. In 1958 George Devine asked D'Arcy to join the new Royal Court Theatre company. By then D'Arcy had already met, through mutual Irish friends, the young architect Arden, unknown as a playwright. As a professional actor with a wide acquaintance-ship among theatre people, D'Arcy was able to offer him introductions.

Thereafter, she originated the roles of Rosie in *Live Like Pigs*, Teresa in *The Waters of Babylon*, the King of France (disguised by a male stage name) in *The Royal Pardon*, and numerous parts in subsequent plays. She has directed or co-directed many of the plays, beginning with *The Business of Good Government*, and she discussed plays with Arden as he was conceiving and writing them. Her father Joseph D'Arcy's personality even "inspired much of" *The Workhouse Donkey* (5). Arden dedicated *Musgrave* to her and acknowledged her help in his preface to *The Workhouse Donkey* (*John Arden Plays: One* 112). And would Arden have written *Pearl* had he not known D'Arcy?

Certainly the Irish actor/playwright/social activist Pearl, betrayed and cast out to die, could serve as a metaphor for D'Arcy's treatment. As Jon Wike has observed, the root of Margaretta (<Latin *margarita,* <Greek *margaron* ) means "pearl." And we cannot ignore the obvious autobiographical stimulus for Arden's short story "The Fork in the Head," in which the artist husband's political activist, artist wife urges him "You ought to be in there, Jackson, doing your utmost" (107), while he prefers to watch lewd films or enjoy pleasant weather (*Corners* [103]-15). Of course, he has deliberately trivialized the "Arden" character to emphasize a self-preoccupation and avoidance of political responsibility not really typical of him.

Only the short-sighted critic would assume all the Arden plays would have been written had D'Arcy not played such a crucial role in his life. Whether we like it or not, D'Arcy has profoundly affected Arden's sense of theatre, his choices of material—especially the Irish subjects—and his socialist stands. Ignoring her diminishes our understanding of the genesis and details of all that we regard as quintessentially "Arden": his view of theatre as a vehicle for social change; his celebration of Celtic, curvilinear qualities; the conflict between the forces of order and disorder (which develop into the opposition of oppression and rebellion); and the very vigor and theatricality of "his" style. Arden told me in 1976 that his plays focus more on the psycho-pathology of society than on individual aberrance; Musgrave's disturbance, he said, reflects society's. Perhaps his work does not differ so profoundly from hers and theirs; if so, analysis of his plays would benefit from that insight.

And what riches await critics who turn their attention to the collaborative plays. D'Arcy has imbued these plays with a contemporary relevance and power which those who have not read or seen them should anticipate experiencing with pleasure. The kind of indomitable spirit which animates this woman who does not shrink from repeated imprisonment (while still objecting to repeated strip searches), the sort of integrity which commits her to the cause of humanity no matter what the cost to herself animates their courageous characters. My own students prefer *The Little Gray Home in the West* to other twentieth-century plays which they read in my English and Irish drama course. A full-scale, multi-evening mounting of *The Island of the Mighty* which does not reverse its sympathies (as did the truncated RSC version) would doubtless prompt further professional production of this, *The Little Gray Home,* and *Vandaleur's Folly,* but in the meantime the latter two and the radio plays should keep analysts occupied for some months. *Whose Is the Kingdom?,* for instance, will repay critical attention to its intense, theatrical, and original dramatization of the suppression of differences and dissent, as patriarchy evolves into a Christian principle, displacing the several women among Christian and pagan leaders, and the Church imposes both conformity and acceptance of its approved versions of truth and history. This nine-part series for BBC radio speaks clearly to Americans reeling from the revelations of Irangate, Iraqgate, and GOP campaigns against departure from certain sanctioned norms. For those not familiar with this and other recent collaborative plays, what riches await your critical appraisal!

# Notes

1. This, not "Kirbymoorside," is the correct spelling.

# Works Cited

Arden, John. Interview with Raymond Gardner. "Exit, Stage Left." *Guardian* November 28, 1972: 10.
———. Interview with Simon Trussler. "Who's for a Revolution?" *Tulane Drama Review* 11.2 (Winter 1966): [49]–53.
———. "John Arden." *Contemporary Authors Autobiography Series.* Vol. 4. Detroit: Gale Research, 1986. 29–47.
———. *John Arden Plays: One.* London: Eyre Methuen Ltd., 1977.
———. *The Workhouse Donkey.* New York: Grove Press, 1964.
Arden, John, and Margaretta D'Arcy. *Arden/D'Arcy: D'Arcy/Arden Plays: One.* London: Methuen Drama, 1991.

————. "Ars Longa, Vita Brevis." *Encore* 11.2 (March–April 1964): 13–20.

————. *Ars Longa, Vita Brevis. Eight Plays.* Ed. Malcolm Stuart Fellows. London: Cassell, 1965.

————. *Awkward Corners.* London: Methuen London Ltd., 1988.

————. *The Business of Good Government.* London: Methuen, 1967 reprint.

————. "The Happy Haven." *New English Dramatists*, 4. Ed. Tom Maschler. Harmondsworth: Penguin , 1962. [85]–[167].

————. "The Happy Haven." *Three Plays by John Arden.* Harmondsworth: Penguin, 1964. [191]–[272].

Brustein, Robert. "Picketing His Own Play." *New York Times* 7 January 1973: [D1], D5.

Clinton, Craig. "John Arden: The Promise Unfulfilled." *Modern Drama* 21 (1978): 47–57.

Dace, Tish. "Stung." *Soho Weekly News* 22 November 1979: 47–8.

————. "A Small Number." *Other Stages* 20 March 1980: 3.

————. "Outrages in Ireland." *Other Stages* 12 June 1980: 2.

————. "The Cells of Armagh." *Soho Weekly News* 2 July 1980: 8.

————. "Incredible Chaos." *Other Stages* 25 September 1980: 2.

D'Arcy, Margaretta. *Tell Them Everything: A Sojourn in the Prison of Her Majesty Queen Elizabeth II at Ard Macha (Armagh).* London: Pluto Press, 1981.

D'Arcy, Margaretta, and John Arden. *Vandaleur's Folly.* London: Eyre Methuen, 1981.

Gray, Frances. *John Arden.* New York: Grove Press, 1982.

Gussow, Mel. "Theater: 'Happy Haven,' Spoof of Welfare State." *New York Times*, April 5, 1977: 38.

Hayman, Ronald. *British Theatre Since 1955: A Reassessment.* Oxford: Oxford University Press, 1979.

————. *John Arden.* London: Heinemann Educational Books, 1968.

Hunt, Albert. *Arden: A Study of His Plays.* London: Eyre Methuen, 1974.

Itzin, Catherine. *Stages in the Revolution: Political Theatre in Britain Since 1968.* London: Eyre Methuen, 1980.

Leach, Robert. "*The Non-Stop Connolly Show*: Into the Future." *Theatre Ireland* 28 (Summer 1992): 39–42.

Leeming, Glenda. *John Arden.* Harlow: For the British Council by Longman Group, 1974.

Leverett, James. "Present Past." *Soho Weekly News,* April 9, 1980: 29, 56, 59.

O'Hanlon, Redmond. "The Theatrical Values of John Arden." *Theatre Research International* 5 (Autumn 1980): 218–36.

Malick, Javed. "The Polarized Universe of *The Island of the Mighty*: Arden and D'Arcy's Dramaturgy." *New Theatre Quarterly* 2 (February 1986): 38–53.

———. "Society and History in Arden's Dramaturgy." *Theatre Journal* 42 (May 1990): 208–24.

Page, Malcolm. *Arden on File.* London: Methuen, 1985.

———. *John Arden.* Boston: Twayne, 1984.

Rosen, Carol. *Plays of Impasse: Contemporary Drama Set in Confining Institutions.* Princeton: Princeton University Press, 1983.

Sainer, Arthur. "Agitprop Strikes Back." *Village Voice* 6 December 1976: 99, 101.

Taylor, John Russell. "Introduction." *Three Plays by John Arden.* Harmondsworth: Penguin, 1964. 7–[15].

Trussler, Simon. *John Arden.* New York: Columbia University Press, 1973.

Worth, Katharine J. *Revolutions in Modern English Drama.* London: G. Bell & Sons, 1972.

# EMPIRE AND THE GODDESS: THE FICTION OF JOHN ARDEN

## Jonathan Wike

Although the pursuit of fiction has now taken up about a third of John Arden's career as a writer, it has received very little in the way of critical attention. For the most part critics have merely satisfied themselves that Arden has withdrawn from the theatre,[1] and little notice has been taken of his reemergence in a new medium. But he has written three substantial and engaging works of fiction, the novels *Silence Among the Weapons* (published in the U.S. as *Vox Pop*) and *Books of Bale*, and *Cogs Tyrannic*, a set of four short novels: "Slow Journey, Swift Writing," "The Little Old Woman and Her Two Big Books," "Uses of Iron," and "'Like a *Dream* of a Gun . . .'" These are very accomplished, ingenious works in their own right, but whatever their merits as novels, they should also be of great interest to those who study Arden the playwright, for two obvious reasons. First, theatre people, ideas, and innovations figure prominently in much of the work, making it a continuation of the dialogue or debate on dramatic issues Arden has carried on with his public and his critics in other forums. Second, it offers much more of the same Arden material, very recognizable situations, types, and attitudes but here refined and expanded, allowing the reader to see the broad range and remarkable consistency of all of his writing.

Two earlier pieces, reprinted in *Awkward Corners*, offer a good introduction to Arden's fiction. Both involve, though in significantly different ways, his collaboration with Margaretta D'Arcy. In the short story "The Fork in the Head," an English "layout designer" named Jackson and an Irish "children's book illustrator" named Fionnuala are partners in sex and in art: they "produce freelance 'visual motifs'" (104):

> Their relationship, already under stress from his Britishness and her Irishness, had lately become exceedingly unstable—or at least it might have seemed to their intimates. But then intimates are

> rarely as intimate as all that: and in fact the pair of
> them held together remarkably well. Probably the real
> reason they still held together was that he loved her
> drawings; and she loved the way he could adapt and
> develop her drawings within the context of the
> industries they served. At all events, they had not
> seriously quarrelled over anything for very long.
> Despite her political obsessions—as he regarded it—
> she was a decent, tolerant, and courageous person;
> and despite his laziness and egocentricity—as she
> regarded it—he had never questioned the correctness
> of the left-republican line on the national issue—and
> he was a very good cook. (105)

While "freelance 'visual motifs'" may seem a far cry from
something like *The Non-Stop Connolly Show*, it is difficult not to
read Arden and D'Arcy themselves into these roles, and we
could take as an answer her own non-fictional account of their
marriage: "His language and sense of history excited me in his
work: his provincial conservatism did not attract me" (*Corners*
132). In the "Fork" story, Arden is making light of their
collaboration—he is even having fun with those who fail to
appreciate it, who are "rarely as intimate as all that"—but the
story is also filled with anguish. The art they produce is
superficial, but politics can be dangerous.

Jackson, returning from England to Ireland, retires to his
vacation hut on a lake island for a "thoroughly self-indulgent
afternoon" with a copy of the *Satyricon*, crossing paths with
Fionnuala, on her way to take part in an anti-nuclear protest.
Reading in his rowboat, he drops a fork into the lake. Fionnuala
appears to him that night in a frightening vision, the fork stuck
into her head. He learns the next day that Fionnuala has been
killed during the demonstration. To the policemen who come to
inform and harass him he attempts through his fear and remorse
to assert his affinity with Ireland.

This story has obvious autobiographical, even cathartic
purposes. Arden confesses a great deal in his writing. This may
seem a strange thing to say, given all that is usually written
about the detachment with which he supposedly creates his
characters, but his writings after a while take on an almost

embarrassingly personal aspect. This is especially true, of course, when stories like this one, his autobiographical plays, and other prose pieces are taken into consideration. It is as if every anxiety, every possible cause for guilt, about his own situation in the world—political, social, religious, regional—must be worked out with great pains for all to see. His characters may themselves lack an inner life, as many critics have complained, but in large and small ways, in details and in the very choice of subjects, they combine to give a picture of something like the inner life of the author. We must know, for example, by this time, that he is one who worries about the efficacy of art, its power to affect the thinking and habits of people, and the worth of the artist who should be found in some way ineffectual.[2]

At the same time, it is important to point out that Arden is creating himself and probably D'Arcy as characters and not just for the purpose of this particular fiction. Many other characters range between the two poles established in Jackson and Fionnuala, that is, between effete, intellectualized detachment, hiding in art, and vigorous, social-minded engagement, working through art. Jackson is already a recognizable Arden character, the prurient, or priapic, man of the theatre, whom we find in the character Ivory in *Silence*, Bale in *Books of Bale*, and Arden himself in his account of the New York University Anti-War Carnival, collected in *To Present the Pretence*. Arden's need for self-revelation is balanced by an instinct for seeing the type in the individual. We find even in his straightforward autobiographical writing that his family members fall into familiar patterns, to be defined not so much by intrinsic qualities as again by their historically peculiar and no less historically determined combinations of social class, education, gender, and, where appropriate, temperament.

In "Shift of Discipline," Arden gives a very self-effacing, amused account of the writing of his first novel, *Silence Among the Weapons*, and its nomination for the Booker Prize. It begins,

> At the beginning of 1981 I had reached the age of fifty and had hardly any money: I did not just need an income, I needed a large chunk of it all in one go. I had lost interest in writing stage-plays. The inability

of the playwright to control his or her material in the
face of financially-pressed, hence timid and intransi-
gent, managements . . . had finally worn me out.

The turn to novel writing is presented, then, as the last act in
Arden's long dispute with the theatrical establishment over the
issue of the playwright's status as a craftsman.[3] It also marks an
important phase in his collaboration with D'Arcy, who at the
time was writing *Tell Them Everything,* her "narrative account of
three months she spent in Armagh Gaol" (44). The team split up:

> She went into a private room, sat down with pen and
> notebook, and actually began to write—at a steady
> rate of so many words per day. This obsessive pro-
> cess, going on in my own home, infuriated me. I went
> into another room: opened the typewriter . . . and
> began likewise.

The gesture is significant: these works of fiction are
specifically not produced by the Arden/D'Arcy collaboration,
though, as in "The Fork in the Head," her presence is distinctly
noticeable. In fact, the polemic of Arden's fiction is bound up
with that of D'Arcy's non-fiction, particularly in the types of
intrigues his characters are mixed up in and the questions raised
in or even forced into the narrative about changes in dramatic
technique and the ways in which these are related to patterns of
political, religious, and sexual authority. His *Bale* and "The Little
Old Woman," for example, are shot through with the kind of
anti-clerical attitude to be found in her preface to *The Island of the
Mighty* and, of course, in *Whose Is the Kingdom?* To the extent that
they seek a coherent exposition of these patterns, Arden's novels
follow the thinking we find in an essay of D'Arcy's called
"Breaking Chains," a kind of "Male Cultural Domination and Its
Discontents." There she decries the ideal of perfection that has
pervaded Western ideas of art and religion:

> The predominant religion of the West is, of course,
> Christianity. The perfect God, controller of us all—
> imperfect man, fallen because of Eve, in constant
> pursuit of that perfection. Only through art could the
> male challenge the female, the source of his imper-
> fection. An art that aspires to perfection must also

aspire to permanence. Therefore all those ephemeral aspects of art—deriving from the senses of smell, touch, taste—are seen as uncontrollable, therefore not perfect, and only the static art-disciplines involving the senses of sight and hearing are recognized as constituting "high art": literature, music, painting, sculpture. (*Corners* 136)

D'Arcy goes on to say that a perfectionist art based on male anxiety tends to monopolize power and prestige through art establishments in just the same spirit that it invests itself with political and military power, creating a monolithic structure characterized by rigidity and paranoia:

[N]uclear weapons have now reached such a pitch of perfection that the most powerful ruler in the west, the American president, can execute the world's destruction without consulting anybody else by touching a button: because the scientific and military experts have told us that he alone is fit to do it. We can see and hear: but we mustn't touch. Mr Reagan only is allowed to touch. Just so, Adam and Eve were allowed to see the apple but not touch it. When Eve touched it and ate it, the order was broken. (*Corners* 136)

Without speculating about what more tactile or gustatory forms of art might be, one can point out that this is in line with much of what we hear from both Arden and D'Arcy about theatre, especially their preference for "rough theatre," with its potential for spontaneity and for political impact, over more traditional forms with their bourgeois complacency. This essay also elaborates on the kind of historical ideas we get from Arden and D'Arcy in the preface to *The Hero Rises Up*, for example, where they outline "rectilinear" and "curvilinear"[4] history and begin to present this historical and political apparatus as an approach to art. Arden says elsewhere that what he benefited from most in his collaboration with D'Arcy was her ability to elucidate the historical dimensions of the dramatic situation. In their articulation of the relations between art and power, his novels look for examples of the situation of which D'Arcy presents the archetype in "Breaking Chains," the moment at which male-determined and dominated cultural forms supersede, violently and irrevocably, ones that remain open to female influence.

In Arden's first novel, *Silence Among the Weapons*, a Greek theatrical manager, whose nickname is Ivory, is caught up in the sexual intrigues of his troupe and the political intrigues of the Roman republic of the time of Sulla. Ivory is a grotesque, crippled satyr-like figure. His women, who bear the scars of male force, are associated in various ways with the goddesses whose cults threaten male authority. One of them, Irene, outlives Ivory by aligning herself with the chief rival to Roman authority in the East, King Mithridates. A similar atmosphere is to be found in *Books of Bale*, Arden's second novel and probably the most ambitious of all his works, which centers on the English playwright John Bale but deals with the whole sweep of sixteenth-century English politics and drama. Bale, characterized by his hapless concupiscence, is a transition figure. As a playwright, he connects medieval religious drama to later English Renaissance forms. As a clergyman, he makes an uneasy switch from "Old Guise" to "New Guise" as Henry VIII's marriage difficulties move England away from Rome. Bale marries the actress Dorothy who is buffeted about by male politics and lust; their granddaughter is involved in later intrigues in the time of Shakespeare and Marlowe.

Arden's latest work of fiction, *Cogs Tyrannic*, continues in the trend established by these two novels. Though they do not all deal with actors or playwrights, these four short novels show a similarly broad historical scope and a similar interest in patterns of authority, and they display fully the clashes of historical forces one finds in *Silence* and *Bale*. In this regard they also recall the methods of Robert Graves. The chronological designations in *Cogs Tyrannic* ("Twelfth Century Before Christ," "Fifteenth Century After Christ") remind one of the list furnished by Graves in the opening page of *Homer's Daughter*, which presents his novels as a single chronicle extending from the thirteenth century B.C. (*Hercules, My Shipmate*) to "Post-Historical" times (*Watch the North Wind Rise*) and ranging through ten different periods in between. A similar and even more impressive list could be compiled from John Arden's plays and novels.

The importance of Graves's example can be seen at other points in Arden's career, most notably in *The Island of the Mighty*, but the connections are particularly striking in the fiction, where Arden is working on Graves's home territory, the historical novel. Readings of Arden after *The Island* should look to Graves, not only because its material owes a great deal to *The White Goddess* but because from this point on it is apparent that Arden's socialist pronouncements make up only a part of his overall concerns. Class conflicts, important though they may be in a work like the *Connolly Show*, are not always what determine Arden's conception of the historical moment he places his plots in, clearly a very important issue for him and for us.

Various details remind one of Graves's novels. For example, the first section of *Cogs Tyrannic* offers a Gravesian reversal of perspective, with the delightful surprise of seeing Odysseus as of a kind with the gypsies of *Live Like Pigs* or the Picts of *Island of the Mighty*. It also rehabilitates the Homeric material by presenting it as part of a greater historical context. Arden's somewhat undignified Odysseus may even owe something to the pseudo-Odysseus, Aethon, in *Homer's Daughter*. And the handling of the death of Ivory in *Silence* is like that of Claudius, who is also survived by a more politically astute woman, in *Claudius the God*. But beyond this it is apparent that Arden's whole project in historical fiction, or drama, for that matter, is similar to Graves's. It is not simply that each is retelling a familiar historical sequence from another, almost subversive point of view or even that there are striking similarities in their choices of historical sequences. Rather it is that in those broad historical series each has constructed we can see developing a critique of particular authority centers as they have grown and changed over the centuries, a kind of genealogy of power. This may seem obvious in Graves, the nostalgic quality of whose work is probably its most characteristic feature, but it is important to point it out in Arden. If we treat Arden simply as a typical late fifties playwright, his interest in earlier periods appears merely a way of making the depressing point that repression has always existed in ways that can be shown to correspond to current configurations with some adjustments for changes in speech and dress. The only function of the work is as a parable, and the model play is the pseudo-historical *Serjeant Musgrave's Dance*.[5] If we see Arden as a historical novelist, somewhat in the manner of Robert Graves, however, we can see him engaged in a rather more ambitious project, connecting contemporary patterns of Western authority and art to their actual sources by tracing them through various historical metamorphoses. It is significant that the major dramatic effort Arden and D'Arcy were involved in during the time Arden was writing these works of fiction was *Whose Is the Kingdom?*, a radio series entirely involved in the same project and from which a great deal of the historical model for all of these works emerges: the source of authority is Rome and its successor Britain, and history's victims have been all those peoples and traditions the empire has pushed aside.

Arden associates a female tradition or technique with the moment before a male-dominated tradition is imposed, again with works like Graves's *White Goddess* and *Homer's Daughter* as possible models. Later only the masculine tradition is apparent, and the feminine one is pushed to the edges, where it is likely doomed to stay, as not having continued and not being available in a lasting medium and, of course, not being sanctioned by male authority. In *Bale*, for example, we find the character Dorothy performing a kind of private theatre in which, among other things, she addresses the audience directly. This breaking of the familiar distance between performer and audience clearly recalls Arden's own long practice, in plays like *Left-Handed Liberty*, and many of his pronouncements about staging. Here, however, the striking thing is how he has reconceived this attitude toward technique as a specifically female practice. Other women characters pursue similar forms of presentation, from various fictional characters in *Silence* to the nineteenth-century actress Fanny Kemble, fictionalized in "Uses of Iron." Arden has long admired and promoted practitioners of a particular popular theatrical tradition: Jonson, O'Casey, Lorca, Boucicault, even in a way John Bale. But D'Arcy insists on the recognition that alternative forms of presentation are not simply lost but are repressed:

> Before theatre and religion became functions of
> centralized government—which means even before
> the classical theatre of the Athenian city-state—they
> were acts of communal collective celebration or
> mourning. There was no dividing line between artistic
> activities and a passive recipient audience. To reclaim
> this position is the task I have set myself. (*Corners* 137)

In *Tell Them Everything*, D'Arcy describes the singing
that pervaded Armagh prison and lifted the spirits of the
prisoners: "A lot of the time was spent in singing pop songs. . . .
It was like a humming aviary, joined by the pigeons sitting on
the ledge outside" (71). Strikingly, Arden elaborates on this
image in *Books of Bale*, where the "aviary" is not a prison but the
strange lodgings called the "Birdcage" where Dorothy and other
female performers "entertain" men like Wentworth and Bale, a
place where women seek some refuge from male political and
sexual turbulence and ply independent, private, female forms of
theatre. As a character, at least, D'Arcy seems to have filled the
role of the woman of the theatre for Arden at least since *Pearl*; it
should be noted that "Pearl" is etymologically related to
"Margaretta" and is a nickname of the kind Arden is fond of, as
in the many characters' names in *Silence*. This character, which
also goes back to Nimue in *The Island*, takes a predictable form.
One of her most striking features is her capacity for physical
torture, even to the point of showing scars, which Arden
presents as an emblem of social, and therefore cultural, as well as
physical violence. Arden draws on himself and D'Arcy as
characters, not as a form of self-promotion surely, but as a way
to create a very large and fruitful space for dramatic language. In
this pairing of male and female artists, parodied in Jackson and
Fionnuala, apotheosized in John Bale and his wife Dorothy in
*Books of Bale*, Arden has constructed a very effective, imaginative,
and historically meaningful dialogue between center and
margin, the one patriarchal, "rectilinear," and English, or
ultimately Roman; the other matriarchal, "curvilinear," and,
ultimately, Irish—Empire and the Goddess.[6] These forces,
developed in Arden's plays, drive his novels, whose male
characters are fascinated with dangerous, witch-like women and
whose female characters seek moments of refuge from male

violence, only to disclose in their unconscious, as presented in their dreams, visions of Empire. Power and its victims exist for and reflect one another. A fine example of this entire schematic comes in the second story of *Cogs Tyrannic*, in which printing, a new process of cultural diffusion, is made exclusively a male domain at the cost of the mutilation of Hulda, the woman who attempts to adapt it to more progressive, "modern" thinking. Religion consistently demonizes women; conservative, power-serving science, or rather technology, replaces more curious, freedom-seeking science; and the pain of cultural domination is inscribed on the bodies of its female victims. It so happens that in this section, entitled "The Little Old Woman and Her Two Big Books," Arden is elaborating on the exploits of two fifteenth-century witch-hunters, Heinrich Kraemer and Jakob Sprenger, authors of the *Malleus Maleficarum*, whom D'Arcy credits with having fomented a virtual war against women:

> The extermination of perhaps as many as nine million women over the next two hundred years can be laid directly at Kraemer and Sprenger's door. This book could have served as an example for all future forms of witch-hunt, including, perhaps, the Nazi Holocaust ("Goddess" 71-2).

She discusses the Irish triple goddess as a historical and political force, the inspiration behind anti-British and anti-nuclear protests, in a 1990 essay called "The Voice of the Bitch Goddess," which appeared close to but before Arden's *Cogs Tyrannic*.

In many respects, Arden gains from the change to novel writing. For instance, the novel may be better suited to achieve the historical irony Arden aims for. In a piece like "Uses of Iron," for example, no explanatory preface or notes are necessary as in *Whose Is the Kingdom?* Readers should have time to recognize that this scene precedes the first Reform Bill and the demise of the Wellington government and so on. In addition, the moral "ambiguity" or "indifference" so often noticed in his early plays now appears not in the conflicts between the characters so much as in the descriptive or narrative passages and their painstaking qualifications. Sometimes these are tedious, but taken together they build an extraordinarily complex conception, a historically determined situation created by opposing forces. Arden allows peculiarity to these moments, but the conflicts are of certain consistent types, and this is one of the main arguments throughout all of his writing. We can expect the same determining factors, political, religious, cultural, economic. We also find, however, many of the same details. No matter the period, the same elements are there, a set of archetypal scenes and characters that run through all his works: the same overbearing martial types, conniving promoters of the police state, pressgangs, inquisitors, spies, noble or not-so-noble populist spokesmen and spokeswomen, hapless agit-prop people, prostitutes and other women, often mutilated, possibly symbolic of deeper and older repression. Arden's fiction deals with theatre people, but the theatricality of his plays now appears more in the way all of his characters are playing a complicated set of roles, in ways that connect his "objective," politically oriented plays to his "subjective," aesthetically oriented ones. They live in a paranoiac police-state atmosphere. Their adoption of masks is not a matter of psychological confusion but of survival.

A close look at his fiction, however, shows that Arden is not entirely restricted to a form of historical syncretism, the notion that all historical periods are in essence the same.[7] True, one does have the feeling that Arden and D'Arcy have devoted a large amount of energy to proving that Ireland, Nicaragua, and a good deal of the rest of the world, are doomed by precedent as well as by any number of other forces, but I believe that in the last fifteen years or so of their careers they have produced a richer view of history. In it past events are realized in their own particularity *and* made matters of true contemporary social concern; the latter is largely D'Arcy's contribution, often by personal example, but it is the dimension we find in her prefaces to the collaborative plays, such as *The Island of the Mighty*. There Arden's rather academic interest in the matter of Britain is tempered by her more direct sympathy for the downtrodden, whose continuation through historical change is one solid thing history offers: "I found I wasn't at all interested in the Arthur bit, but the Picts clicked with me" (17). D'Arcy gives the plays whatever relevance they will accept by forcing a connection with contemporary events, in the case of *Island*, those in India. She formulates a conflict between authority and tradition that serves as a blueprint for Arden's later work: "A continuous struggle was taking place within the new post-imperialist state: tribal, religious and familial loyalties were in constant conflict with the centralized secular administration at New Delhi" (19). By doing so, she prevents the presentation from lapsing into mere spectacle: "I felt particularly that what was lacking in the TV scripts was a sense of precise sociological realism—there was altogether too much importance given to picturesque historical detail and not enough consideration accorded to the fact that even during the most frenzied periods of economic and political disturbance people have to go on living" (20). Arden's own important contribution is to mythologize this entire pattern, especially in the role now assigned to women, who undergo a remarkable transformation from the often very minor presences in his plays to emblems of otherness, much as Fionnuala emerges in Jackson's vision as nature, Ireland, woman incarnate. In Arden's history, woman as victim has merged with Graves's goddess, and D'Arcy's; she can appear as the object of pagan worship or as the Virgin Mary. Again, Arden's and D'Arcy's major dramatic project in the eighties has been *Whose Is the Kingdom?*, which deals with the expulsion from Christianity of its chthonic, feminine aspect at the time of the Council of Nicaea. In the preface to this play, D'Arcy assembles all of the elements of Arden's fictional plots, the machinations of "the patriarchal Athenian drama-adjudicators," for example, and "the old conflict between the idea of a mother-goddess who is *all nature inclusive*, and a father-god who has *created* nature" (xxix).

The novels refine our understanding of the historical moments chosen in the plays. On the whole, I do not believe that this later conception of the historical moment or Arden's idea of historical process is the same as the one he expressed in relation to the Connolly cycle, exemplified by those plays and by the 7:84 company adaptation of *Serjeant Musgrave's Dance*, though the circumstances surrounding a "socialist hero" may necessarily be somewhat oversimplified, as in the conception of the hero himself:

> Our first solution [to the problem of the socialist hero's lack of tragic imperfection] was to write a series of plays about a number of historical characters, each of whom had been involved in *some sort of revolutionary process of change, or at any rate attempt at one*. (*To Present* 103; emphasis added)

Their impossibly ambitious list puts James Connolly alongside Jesus, Gandhi, and Rosa Luxemburg. John Bale is no such character. There is none to speak of in the novels.

It would be quite easy to attribute Arden's switch to fiction to the simple matter of his frustration with theatre and thus to relate it once again to the socialist debate over the artist's control of his own production, but that is not a sufficient explanation by itself. After all, we do not find him simply writing new works along the lines of *Musgrave*, or even *Connolly*, only this time as novels. The adoption of the novel form derives as much from the historical and political scene Arden is interested in showing as was his adoption of and experimentation with play-writing. Generally speaking, in the plays Arden is exploring the potentialities in popular dramatic forms for political awakening. The history of these forms is bound up in a corresponding history of class relations; complexities arise as the discourse of peasant petition to or protest against royal authority is adapted to later class relations under capitalism. This entire program, however, is reduced drastically in the novel, where it is made only a part of the narrative, and it is presented as part of a larger set of relations and with different patterns of authority. The novels do pick up a strain that is already present in Arden's plays, especially in *The Island of the Mighty*, but on the whole it is inadequate to assume that we are dealing with the same old Arden; clearly, at least, this is not the resolutely socialist Arden of the Connolly plays who is advancing so boldly into the traditionally bourgeois ground of the historical novel.

On the whole, Arden's view of history comes across as rather pessimistic. *Bale*, for example, shows us what are habitually seen as the advances of Elizabethan drama as a kind of decadence.[8] As a dramatist, Arden is naturally concerned with formulating a view of historical change that will correspond to changes in audience attitude effected by the presentation. Instead of a Brechtian conception of the dramatic moment, in which the audience is carried forward toward an understanding of emergent historical possibilities, Arden's view is primarily retrospective. History is seen as a process of suppression in which potentialities are closed off, not opened up. Instead of a dramatic conception involving a rational idea of progress winning out over conflicting impulses, Arden substitutes an anti-dialectic in which the status quo cunningly preserves itself, emerging in a new guise despite superficial movement. The very deliberate inclusion of theatre in the historical scheme merely reinforces this conclusion, for theatre consistently appears to have little practical impact.

The four stories in *Cogs Tyrannic*, whose unifying theme is technology, present just such a grim critique of the idea of progress. Arden's introduction sounds very much like D'Arcy's attack on the Western drive to perfection:

> These stories are set in very different periods of history, but are linked by one theme—the essential fallibility of the human being as a tool-making tool-using animal. We are . . . obsessed by technical progress of some sort, whether mechanical or theatrical. . . . But practical inventiveness always seems to have had the utmost difficulty in walking in step with moral and social responsibility. (xi)

The third story, "Uses of Iron," probably best illustrates how this critique works out. The nascent railroad provides a pure image of progress from the era of greatest faith in material improvement, and the era from which our most persuasive notions of it are derived, the nineteenth century. Here Arden's historical moment is the most compactly and dramatically conceived. It radiates from the death of William Huskisson, run over by a railway carriage being demonstrated by Robert Stephenson, just as he is trying to reach out to Wellington, the embodiment of power, in a scene that uses space, character, and symbol in fine Ardenesque fashion, reminiscent of *Armstrong's Last Goodnight*. Here technology is specifically seen as the force annihilating the possibilities for real historical change, of the kind Huskisson's move might have brought about. The whole moment is a negative one, of lost energy, as power solidifies itself and forestalls historical dynamism; it recalls similar instances of failed compromise or agreement in *The Workhouse Donkey*, *Connolly*, *Armstrong*, and *Left-Handed Liberty*. The theatre person in the story, Fanny Kemble, who is wooed ungracefully by Wellington, adds the familiar element of change in dramatic style, as she is called on to represent a subversive, alternative mode of performance. She also evinces a fascination with power, in the form of Wellington, a fascination which, it must be said, Arden himself has always shared.

But Mrs. Kemble is not the only player in this episode. When Stephenson's demonstration of his railroad meets with protest from a working men's group, we see another, very important element in Arden's general design, and I think it shows the place of comedy in his work as well as his ideas on another kind of theatre. The labor protest in "Uses of Iron" is a type of "rough" theatre, the kind of thing so long admired by Arden and D'Arcy. It fails miserably, ending in confusion and bathos, in a manner reminiscent of many other similar attempts in Arden's work, such as Bale's virulently Protestant plays for the Irish. In Arden, especially in his novels, the scene is one of general victimization and haplessness in the face of historical inevitability, but specific events against that background are often ridiculous, amounting to little; those who wish to influence the forces of historical change escape as Bale does from Ireland, having convinced no one, made to look absurd, but relatively unscathed. Such scenes, and others like Bale's ludicrous encounter with King Edward VI, are a great source of humor in Arden's works, but they also say a great deal about his view of the efficacy of the playwright or of ordinary folk engaged in anti-establishment theatre. Their efforts have little effect, and their stagings turn to slapstick, but, for that matter, so does much of what happens on the supposedly serious level of actual, unself-conscious political activity. D'Arcy, for example, has observed, "I don't know why: but all the events in the North of Ireland seem to have heavy elements of knockabout farce" (*Everything* 35). Arden captures this quality in *"Dream* of a Gun," from *Cogs Tyrannic*: there the story is built around an outrageous scene in

which an Irish woman is forced to hear poetry as part of British
harassment, but this takes place in a context of much more
serious and long-standing cultural violence, richly conceived
because of Arden's and D'Arcy's acquaintance with the present
situation and made all the more impressive by all the analogous
historical patterns in Arden's previous works. In many ways this
story returns to the atmosphere of *Silence Among the Weapons*,
bringing Arden's fiction full circle across the centuries: members
of the British counter-culture live in the same relation to power
as the members of Ivory's acting company.

Since attempts to change public consciousness through
theatre collapse in this way in Arden's novels, it is tempting to
see this as his own final view of the possibility in theatre for
social transformation, and it may be largely so. Elements of
Arden's and D'Arcy's own careers, their protest of *Island*, for
example, or even their staging of *Connolly*, support this view, in
the sense that Arden is again mocking himself; one gets a very
strong sense of his sympathy with a character like Bale,
grotesque, self-defeating, but all the time courageous and
creative. But this attitude has long been present in Arden's
works—

> "Bull-in-the-bush," yes; and also "Bale-zebub." It
> appeared he was obsessed with minstrel-shows and
> stage-plays. He travelled the east parts preaching,
> very hard contorted sermons: but always he took time
> off to insert himself in the crowd at all manner of
> popular entertainments. (*Bale* 75)

Bale is the apotheosis of a favorite Arden type, the Puritanical
showman, going back to *Serjeant Musgrave*. Musgrave himself is
just such a stager of failed spectacles, and like many others
Arden creates he fears the distractions of women, sneering at
"life and love." This is a common problem in Arden's plays,
including the autobiographical ones, and at least one thing that
can be said about it is that it has to do with the socially-
motivated playwright's concern that the need for spectacle will
distract from a didactic message, as may the need to present the
play in a form that will please the audience and not challenge
their expectations, though this may mean doing violence to the

complexities of the historical situation the play is about. As Arden presents his and D'Arcy's collaboration, this is one of the problems it solves through compromise, and it is Arden who seems to speak for formal coherence, D'Arcy for social truth. It is also a major obstacle in Arden/D'Arcy criticism generally, as critics have found it difficult to accept Arden's particular solutions to the problems of formal coherence and social impact.

Bale is probably Arden's most meaningful and most problematic character. He is also Arden's latest, and probably last, dismissal of an undesirable aspect in himself. Ultimately this very English playwright cannot even begin to bridge the gap between England and Ireland, and all that they stand for, as even poor Jackson does. Rather, he is like that type Arden rejects in various guises, in Squire Jonathan, for example, and in Merlin:

> The liberal intellectual who no longer knows what is liberality and what is tyranny, who is unable to draw a distinction between poetic ambiguity and political dishonesty, the religious sceptic who continually uses such adjectives as "profound" or "crucial" to describe his pointless agonizing over the existence of God, the sexual failure who masks his fear of women by spiteful little rudenesses and overdone criticism. (Preface to *Island* 14)

Whether this sense of the need for engagement carries over to the whole text, however, is more open to question. For one thing, it is possible to see the shift from play- to novel-writing as stemming not from Arden's becoming frustrated with one medium and taking refuge in another, however much that may fit his or his critics' views about contemporary English theatre, but from the ideas as they develop in his works, in other words in the necessity of adapting form to content. Hence his move to the historical novel, inherently not progressive, even utopian, like drama, but nostalgic, even reactionary. Similarly, as has been noted, there is Graves's example for a subversive version of history; Graves himself, in *Good-Bye to All That*, cultivates his own Irishness as a source of alternative ways of thinking. Like Bale, Arden works from artistic necessity or philosophical commitment, whichever suits. The specifics of the collaboration with D'Arcy, the dialectic of their "asymmetrical prefaces," may generate material for the novels, but the collaboration is also now contained by the novels. At the same time, an attack on the workings of authority is problematic when the desire for formal coherence itself can have a bad name, when it can seem just another aspect of the drive for perfection. This is yet another aspect of the rich dialogue Arden and D'Arcy have created, in which even form and content are fruitfully at odds.

# Notes

1. I do not mean to suggest that Arden has stopped writing plays, only that in the last decade or more he has devoted much of his energy to writing novels. He has written and collaborated on radio plays and has contributed, for example, with D'Arcy to the project *Duchas na Saoirse*. (See the special issue of *Theatre Ireland*, Summer 1992).

2. Michael Etherton says that Arden "is the truly radical British playwright of this century, whose poetic and political vision has negated his white, male, middle class upbringing. Furthermore, he has transformed this negation into a positive and accomplished art" (209).

3. Much of Arden's fiction can be read as his view of the controversies he and D'Arcy have been engaged in. Accounts of these controversies abound, including fairly sympathetic ones, such as Colin Chambers and Mike Prior's in *Playwrights' Progress: Patterns of Postwar British Drama* (Oxford: Amber Lane Press, 1987).

4. "Asymmetrical Preface." Cf. Brecht's distinction between dramatic and epic theater, the former having a "linear development," the latter moving "in curves" (*Brecht on Theatre* 37).

5. Arden's own treatment of *Serjeant Musgrave's Dance* is a good illustration of the problems he poses for critics and scholars. He avoids their pat, humanistic emphasis on the play's universality,

insisting instead on its applicability to specific political situations.

6. "Slow Journey, Swift Writing" seems to have been written specifically to outline this polarity and to establish its historical priority: imperial (pharaonic) authority, with established science and writing itself in its service, encounters the strange goddess Pa-lassa-'thnai (Pallas Athena).

7. Simon Trussler, who in one place labels Arden's approach a "Whig historical overview" (29), feels that Arden "is the one modern playwright apart from Brecht who has been able to dramatize history into more than hopefully intellectual costume dramas." He adds that history also lends "that degree of *distance* from an action that Arden, again like Brecht, prefers to maintain—though in Arden's case this distance serves not so much Brecht's purpose of making the familiar strange as of making the strange familiar, often by suggesting a parallel that tangentially illuminates the present" (45).

Brecht's attitude is developed in *A Short Organum for the Theatre* (§35–39). He finds this degree of historical alienation essential for allowing the audience to see their own society as historically determined and motivating them to change it. Such motivation is certainly D'Arcy and Arden's purpose in the Connolly plays, but to what extent is it part of Arden's novels?

8. In Ben Jonson, Arden finds a precursor of both the English popular and the Brechtian tradition, a playwright who could be a liberating example for the theater, no matter how long he takes to be rediscovered. Arden credits Bale, on the other hand, with having forged a particularly vicious connection between form and content. This point may be made more clearly in a 1979 article on Bale than in the 1988 novel:

> I suppose John Bale did more harm to Anglo-Irish relations than any one man in history in so brief a space of time: and yet he remains the father of modern British theatre: in the terms of the 16th century he was a man of the "left"; and he believed it his duty to impose upon the Irish not only English civil and ecclesiastical government, but also the

forms, manner and content of officially-received
English culture as expressed in his own theatrical
milieu. He, more than anyone, began the justification
of ideological imperialism abroad by social and
religious radicalism at home; and the later importa-
tion of "the King's Protestants" to dominate Ulster
did no more than reinforce the noxious collusion
("Irish Kerns" 57).

Arden's disgust with the political side of this "noxious
collusion" radically inflects his participation in it as an artist.

## Works Cited

Arden, John. *Books of Bale: A Fiction of History*. London: Methuen,
    1988.
———. Cogs Tyrannic: Four Stories. London: Methuen, 1991.
———. "Rug-Headed Irish Kerns and British Poets." *New States-
    man* 13 July 1979, 56–7.
———. *Silence Among the Weapons. Some Events at the Time of the
    Failure of a Republic*. London: Methuen, 1982.
———. *To Present the Pretence: Essays on the Theatre and Its Public*.
    London: Eyre Methuen, 1977.
Arden, John, and Margaretta D'Arcy. *Awkward Corners: Essays,
    Papers, Fragments*. London: Methuen, 1988.
———. *The Island of the Mighty: A Play on a Traditional British
    Theme in Three Parts*. London: Eyre Methuen, 1974.
———. *Whose Is the Kingdom?* London: Methuen, 1988.
Brecht, Bertolt. *Brecht on Theatre: The Development of an Aesthetic*.
    Trans. John Willett. London: Methuen, 1964.
D'Arcy, Margaretta. *Tell Them Everything: A Sojourn in the Prison
    of Her Majesty Queen Elizabeth II at Ard Macha (Armagh)*.
    London: Pluto Press, 1981.
———. "The Voice of the Bitch Goddess." *Voices of the Goddess: A
    Chorus of Sibyls*. Ed. Caitlín Matthews. Wellingborough,
    Northamptonshire: Aquarian Books, 1990. 67–83.

Etherton, Michael. "The Irish Plays of Margaretta D'Arcy and John Arden." *Contemporary Irish Dramatists.* New York: St. Martin's, 1989. 209–230.
Trussler, Simon. *John Arden.* New York: Columbia University Press, 1973.

# BIBLIOGRAPHY

## Major Criticism

Note: A useful list of secondary sources up to 1976 can be found in a bibliography published by the general editor of this volume (Kimball King, ed., *Twenty Modern British Playwrights: A Bibliography, 1956 to 1976*, New York: Garland, 1977, 1–26). The following is a selected bibliography, with descriptive notes, of important studies of Arden and D'Arcy written since 1976.

Anderson, Michael. "John Arden: from Detachment to Anger." In *Anger and Detachment: A Study of Arden, Osborne and Pinter*. London: Pitman, 1976. 50–87.
Arden's "'uncommitted' stance has moved closer and closer to the revolutionary viewpoint of the radical left," Anderson writes. Discussing several plays, including *The Island of the Mighty*, at length, Anderson shows how Arden explores "society as a fluid, reciprocal relationship between individuals and the community."

Chambers, Colin, and Mike Prior. "John Arden and Margaretta D'Arcy: Uneasy Lies the Head." *Playwrights' Progress: Patterns of Postwar British Drama*. Oxford: Amber Lane, 1987. 146–56.
Chambers and Prior set out to "challenge without going to the opposite extreme the artistic judgement that divides the [Arden] canon in two, with a supposed break in form, content and the deployment of traditional skills whenever D'Arcy appears to pull Arden into the yawning pit of propagandist agitprop." They recount Arden and D'Arcy's conflicts with the theatre establishment as part of an "attempt . . . to make theatre a live event which draws on and communicates directly with its audience outside of traditional constraints."

Clinton, Craig. "John Arden: The Promise Unfulfilled." *Modern Drama* 21 (1978),47–57.
Clinton sees Arden as a playwright of failed promise, sometimes indulged by critics but largely ignored by audiences. In the representative *Armstrong's Last Goodnight*, "one gets the impression that within the body of an Arden play there is no heart: the mind is doing the pumping." His collaboration with D'Arcy has "succeeded in channeling Arden's nonspecific liberal tendencies into drama rooted in radical dogma," but the results have not been favorable.

Cohen, Michael. "A Defence of D'Arcy and Arden's *Non-Stop Connolly Show.*" *Theatre Research International* 15.1 (1990), 78–88.
*The Non-Stop Connolly Show* is, according to Cohen, "probably the most ambitious attempt in English to dramatize working-class and socialist history." The cycle has been unfairly labeled as propagandistic, tedious, and undramatic by criticism bound by Aristotelian norms. In being true to their material, D'Arcy and Arden have made the kind of break with convention that has often driven the theatre forward and have produced a richer work than Arden's *Serjeant Musgrave's Dance*.

———. "The Politics of the Earlier Arden." *Modern Drama* 28 (1985): 198–210.
Cohen argues that anarchy, rather than liberalism, is the dominant political principle of plays by Arden (and D'Arcy) until their move toward socialism in the late sixties.

Dahl, Mary Karen. "*Serjeant Musgrave's Dance*: The Priest Adrift." In *Political Violence in Drama: Classical Models, Contemporary Variations*. Ann Arbor: UMI Research Press, 1987.
Musgrave's actions follow a traditional pattern of ritual sacrifice intended to purify a community. Because his purpose is flawed by his too-rigid logic and his detachment from the community, Musgrave's efforts

backfire, releasing "the uncontrollable contagion of violence."

Etherton, Michael. "The Irish Plays of Margaretta D'Arcy and John Arden." *Contemporary Irish Dramatists*. New York: St. Martin's, 1989. 209–30.
Etherton presents D'Arcy and Arden as innovative Irish playwrights who write on working-class issues in the context of alternative popular and socialist theatre worldwide as best shown in *The Non-Stop Connolly Show*. D'Arcy and Arden "have committed themselves and their art, both as writers and performers, to Ireland, to republican and socialist analysis and praxis, and to internationalism and the fight against Third World oppression in a one-world economy."

Gray, Frances. *John Arden*. London: Macmillan, 1982. New York: Grove Press, 1983.
In a reading of Arden's plays up to and including *Pearl*, Gray discusses Arden as an innovator who has worked to re-educate audiences and critics about the function of theatre and who has been under-valued for various reasons, such as his work outside the London mainstream or his and D'Arcy's focus on English-Irish relations.

Hilton, Julian. "The Court and Its Favours." In *Contemporary English Drama*. Ed. Christopher Bigsby. New York: Holmes and Meier, 1981. 138–55.
In an article on the association of Hampton, Storey, and Arden with the Royal Court Theatre, Hilton describes Arden's great versatility as a dramatist, his challenges to audiences and critics. A George Devine production of *Bartholomew Fair* enthralled a young Arden, and Devine later invited Arden to read and write plays. Hilton examines Arden's Royal Court projects as well as *The Island of the Mighty* and *The Non-Stop Connolly Show*.

Innes, Christopher. "John Arden (1930– ): The Popular Tradition and Epic Alternatives." In *Modern British Drama, 1890–1990*. Cambridge: Cambridge University Press, 1992. 137–56.
Arden borrows heavily from Brecht in early plays but transcends the Brechtian model in *The Hero Rises Up*; the same is true of *Serjeant Musgrave's Dance* and O'Casey. Innes also discusses Arden's "shift to Agitprop theatre" and difficulties for critical evaluation posed by Arden and D'Arcy's later plays.

Itzin, Catherine. "John Arden and Margaretta D'Arcy." In *Stages in the Revolution: Political Theatre in Britain Since 1968*. London: Methuen, 1980. 24–38.
Arden and D'Arcy provide early examples in Itzin's study as she follows them from pacifist to socialist to anti-British attitudes: "From their point of view, inclusion in a book such as *Stages in the Revolution* quite literally constituted a form of betrayal."

Malick, Javed. "Society and History in Arden's Dramaturgy." *Theatre Journal* 42 (1990): 208–24.
Malick describes Arden's creation of "dramatic agents" rather than conventional characters: "The exteriorization of agents, instead of divesting them of life and energy as the individualist aesthetics would have us believe, releases in them a kind of energy and vitality which is both theatrically exciting and cognitively enriching."

———. "The Polarized Universe of 'The Island of the Mighty': The Dramaturgy of Arden and D'Arcy." *New Theatre Quarterly* 5 (1986): 38–53.
Arguing that Arden presents "a universe polarized between the privileged and the un- or under-privileged, the powerful and the powerless, those who are 'included' and those who are left out of societal power," Malick details the contrary "dramaturgic categories" of "oppressor" and "oppressed" in a reading of *The Island of the Mighty*.

Marsh, Paddy. "Easter at Liberty Hall: the Ardens' *Non-Stop Connolly Show." Theatre Quarterly* 5 (Dec. 1975–Feb. 1976): 133–41.
Marsh outlines the Connolly cycle and recounts problems faced in the Dublin production, many caused by Arden and D'Arcy's insistence on a "cooperative effort," using many non-professional actors with little preparation.

O'Hanlon, Redmond. "John Arden: Theatre and Commitment." *Crane Bag* 6.1 (1983): 155–61.
"If we follow Arden's essays in chronological order," O'Hanlon writes, "we can discover a tense and fascinating interplay between the growing pressure of history and his valiant attempts to preserve the integrity and specificity of theatre in the face of such pressure." Looking at Arden and D'Arcy's writing on theatre, O'Hanlon shows the increasing importance of political commitment in their conception of theatre. An uneasy synthesis of idea and praxis breaks down in the *Connolly Show*, as the playwrights' work becomes more didactic and over-conceptualized.

————. "The Theatrical Values of John Arden." *Theatre Research International* 5 (1980): 218–36.
In an examination of *To Present the Pretence*, O'Hanlon finds that Arden's statements on theatrical production and interpretation contain inconsistencies related to "an increasing domination of specifically dramatic values by political values and truths," while his "dramatic analyses of individual plays, show far less obviously the pressure exerted by political commitment."

Page, Malcolm. *Arden on File*. London: Methuen, 1985.
Page provides publication and performance information for Arden's plays, with D'Arcy listed as co-writer, with plot summaries and supporting material from interviews and articles by the authors as well as a "select bibliography" of works by and about Arden and D'Arcy.

————. *John Arden*. Boston: Twayne, 1984.

Page discusses Arden's plays from "The Life of Man" (1956) to "Garland for a Hoar Head" (1982), with some mention of D'Arcy's contribution. Arden's plays are challenging, and they have unfortunately not reached a wider public. "[Their] difficulties fall into place, however," Page concludes, "after the recurring theme has been grasped—that of authority and the place of the rare, free, vital, spontaneous man in modern ordered societies."

Peacock, D. Keith. *Radical Stages: Alternative History in Modern British Drama*. Westport: Greenwood Press, 1991. 45–55, 71–7, 95–100.

In three early plays, *Ironhand, Armstrong's Last Goodnight*, and *Left-Handed Liberty*, Arden opposes "curvilinear" figures, Goetz, Armstrong, and, in a less clear way, King John, to "rectilinear" authority. The more politically radical Arden and D'Arcy then turn to caricaturing the "bourgeois hero" in *The Hero Rises Up* and to promoting the socialist hero in *The Non-Stop Connolly Show*.

Schvey, Henry I. "From Paradox to Propaganda: The Plays of John Arden." In *Essays on Contemporary British Drama*. Ed. Hedwig Bock and Albert Wertheim. Munich: Max Hueber, 1981. 47–70.

Arden's autobiographical play *The Bagman of Muswell Hill* presents a politically aloof craftsman, a stance which Arden came to abandon in favor of agitprop. The socialist plays after *The Island of the Mighty* must be judged on their own terms; Schvey finds *The Ballygombeen Bequest* successful on the order of Brecht's *Lehrstücke, The Non-Stop Connolly Show* less so for its long-windedness, and wonders if Arden has not sacrificed art for political commitment.

Winkler, Elizabeth Hale. "Folk Song Tradition and Theatrical Experimentation: The Drama of John Arden and Margaretta D'Arcy." In *The Function of Song in*

*Contemporary British Drama.* Newark: University of Delaware Press, 1990. 56–130.

"John Arden is an innovator in the field of poetic drama in the postwar period, and Arden and D'Arcy as collaborators are two of the most interesting epic playwrights active in contemporary theater," Winkler writes. She examines many of the ways in which Arden and D'Arcy have incorporated the popular song tradition into their plays from Arden's early work to their more recent "Anglo-Irish" joint efforts.

# CONTRIBUTORS

**SUSAN BENNETT** is an Assistant Professor in the Department of English at the University of Calgary. She is author of *Theatre Audiences: A Theory of Production and Reception* (Routledge, 1990) and is currently co-editing a book on feminist theatre and social change.

**DOUGLAS BRUSTER** is an Assistant Professor of English at the University of Chicago and author of *Drama and the Market in the Age of Shakespeare*.

Formerly Senior Lecturer in English, University of Salford, England, **MICHAEL COHEN** is now part-time Lecturer there. His essays on aspects of modern political drama have appeared in collections and leading journals and include previous articles on Arden and on D'Arcy and Arden.

**TISH DACE**, Professor of English at the University of Massachusetts, Dartmouth, has published books, essays, and articles about English, Irish, and American theatre for thirty years. A theatre critic in New York and London since 1975, she currently reviews for *Back Stage* and *Plays International*.

**MARY KAREN DAHL** is an Assistant Professor of Theatre and Drama at the University of Wisconsin-Madison, where she teaches Continental and British theatre. Her book *Political Violence in Drama* received a 1987 *Choice* award for academic excellence. Currently she is writing a book on drama and performance in the United Kingdom titled *Theatre, State Power, and the Individual*.

**CATHERINE GRAHAM** is a Ph.D. candidate at McGill University, where she is researching the dramaturgy of audience participation in English-Canadian and Québecois popular theatre.

**CLAUDIA W. HARRIS** teaches drama in the English Department at Brigham Young University. She fulfills some of her interests in drama by collaborating in writing musicals and then directing them—*Beowulf the Musical* (1990), *The Ascent of the Locks* ("The Rape of the Lock," 1991), and *Hester's Song: The Scarlet Letters* (1992). As a freelance journalist and theatre critic, she has developed over the years an abiding interest in Ireland, going there nearly every year since 1983 to continue her research on Irish theatre and politics.

**JEFFREY L. ROBERTS** is Professor of English at Worcester State College where he teaches modern and contemporary drama. His dissertation, *The Theatre of John Arden*, completed in 1971, was one of the earliest full-length studies of John Arden's works.

**DONALD SANDLEY** is Director of Theatre at Oklahoma Baptist University and is currently completing his doctoral dissertation on the subject of Christianity in selected works of John Arden. Sandley interviewed Arden in Galway City, Republic of Ireland, in August of 1990.

**MARIANNE A. STENBAEK** is professor of communications in the English Department at McGill University, Montreal. Her interest in theatre led her to a career in mass media. She is also the director of the Centre for Northern Studies and Research.

**TRAMBLE T. TURNER** is an Assistant Professor of English at The Pennsylvania State University, Ogontz Campus. He has published on Shaw and has forthcoming essays on William Kennedy and Thomas Wolfe. A specialist in modern drama and Irish literature, his dissertation examined Bernard Shaw's influence on Sean O'Casey's later plays. Current projects include a study of a theory of dramatic composition.

**KAYLA McKINNEY WIGGINS** is professor of literature, speech, and drama at Martin Methodist College in Pulaski, Tennessee. The author of a dissertation on modern verse drama, she is currently at work on a study of radio drama in verse.

**JONATHAN WIKE** received his Ph.D. in English from the University of North Carolina at Chapel Hill. He has been known to write about another architect turned writer, Thomas Hardy.

# INDEX